MW00576928

CREATIVITY
STEPPING INTO WHOLENESS
DR HELEN FERRARA

Although the author and publisher have made every effort to ensure that the information in this book was correct at press time, the author and publisher do not assume and hereby disclaim any liability to any party for any loss, damage, or disruption caused by errors or omissions, whether such errors or omissions result from negligence, accident, or any other cause.

This is a work of non-fiction, however, the prologue and epilogue have been fictionalised for the purpose of narrative.

Copyright © Dr Helen Ferrara 2020

All rights reserved. No part of this book may be reproduced in any form without permission in writing from the publisher, except by a reviewer who may quote brief pages in review.

1st Edition, December 2020

Inspiration for the cover from an original work by Elizabeth R. Stein (AKA Wendy Donellan)

Book Design by www.bodhi-design.co.uk

ISBN 978-1-913479-64-0 (paperback)

ISBN 978-1-913479-65-7 (ebook)

Published by That Guy's House

www.ThatGuysHouse.com

About Me

My first conscious encounter with creativity was when I was seven and my teacher had asked my class to write a short story. I don't remember what I wrote, but I will never forget what happened – it was as if I had entered another world, one that was full of light where the colours were much brighter. It was pure magic; from deep in reverie words seemed to suddenly appear and float before me so that I could weave them together in the shapes I wanted, to create meaning. From that experience I applied creativity to whatever I could, whenever I could, as holistically as children do.

Fast-forwarding from this, after finishing school, I was attracted to teaching because I found that through it I could elicit the same sort of authentic experience for others. This led me to varied work with both groups and individuals - mentoring, teaching, tutoring, facilitating, editing, and researching. I have worked in a number of schools and universities in diverse roles in Australia, as well as in private practice when I lived in Italy for some time.

Completing a PhD on creativity, some ten years ago, was for me not only an in-depth scholarly process but also a soul-searching experience. I emerged from it with the deep conviction that we all have an innate impulse to thrive rather than just survive, and that to do this we need to express ourselves creatively. This belief has held me steadily since then, while I 'walked my talk' and organically wove my insights into a book that I could share with everyone.

Preface

The idea of creativity invariably meets with general approval. This is not surprising, as together with innovation, creativity has become a common catchcry of our times and we constantly look to it for solutions and answers to almost everything. Yet ironically not many of us believe that we're creative. While it is one thing to like the idea of something, it is however quite another to be willing to find out all you can about it, interact with it, and share it with others. This is the difference between thinking and doing, and the difference between theory and reality. Theory could be described as the formalised version of someone's thoughts on something in particular (usually a scholar's), whereas reality is the whole where living unfolds, often unplanned; so while there's already considerable difference between thinking and doing, there's a chasm between theory and reality.

This book originates from a doctoral thesis that is an account of an actual occurrence – a personal transformation and a change in attitude. It tells the story of my journey, my quest of consciously opening to perceiving with an attitude of creativity, by attending to the nurturing of creativity. Although such a journey is obviously unique to the individual taking it, it is also as much about relationships and connections as it is about personal growth; in fact, the two are inextricably linked. Regardless of the paths we follow, we are all travellers of life, and as such our journeys can serve as inspiration for others. It is my hope that through the voices of the many that are interwoven in this book, you, the readers, will rekindle a deeper connection to your whole selves and rediscover your own journey of creativity.

Three individuals have been greatly influential in my quest to creativity; they are: Carl Jung for his validation on the importance of exploring the whole of the 'self',

David Bohm for his brilliant clarity in expressing a holistic view of reality, and Robert Nash for his encouragement on including lived experience in academic writing through the use of scholarly personal narrative. While this last author was instrumental to legitimising the approach I took in writing my thesis, for this book I have used this same approach to include academic research in ways that are more accessible to a wider audience. Besides these three, I have sought out, read and consulted the work of many others, both on creativity and its nurturing. In delving into creativity both within and outside the territory of the 'self', I have also explored how societal pressures affect our perception, since how we deal with these pressures is key to our ability to accept creativity. Of these, the principal one I look at is patriarchy, as it is the hierarchical order (or worldview) that still dominates our lives.

My search for creativity made me realise the need to nurture my own creativity in order to find it. This, in turn, led me to recognise wholeness as being essential for creativity to thrive and guided me to make connections, all sorts of connections. Undertaking this felt almost instinctive, and I found myself weaving webs of connections to bridge academic writing with lived experience and creative nurturing by using as holistic a perspective as I could. A web is built organically, from one point of connection to another with more being added as they are found, until they become almost innumerable. Similarly, in our diverse human community, ever-expanding clusters of creative interconnections are constantly emerging and growing.

Since writing my thesis I've been 'walking my talk' by putting into practice what I've researched and written about; this has blossomed into some brilliant new growth that continues to open up my reality and how I live in it. Now, close to ten years later, I strongly feel the time has come to share this ongoing journey and sow the seeds for a wider conversation on creativity to further open our perception to wholeness.

Nonna's Legacy

This book is dedicated to the memory of an extraordinary ordinary woman who was my mother and my daughters' nonna.

Through her love, passion and curiosity she taught me about nurturing, sowing seeds that, like the plants under the care of her 'green thumb', will endure and grow.

TABLE OF CONTENTS

Prologue:

NURTURING CREATIVITY – THE BEGINNING OF A STORY...

She smiles, letting her gaze sweep across the universe as stars of all sizes and brightness come into view, some clumped close together, some scattered thinly across vast and dark expanses of space and time. She reaches for the more brightly coloured ones that look to be just the right distance apart and unravels a strand of light from each, holding them yet leaving them attached to their stars. Singing to them, she fashions each beam's dimensions to suit her design, and with an intricate dance, she fastens them together to form a loom.

It looks just as it had in her dream – a sparkling living web of light waiting to be woven onto! Excitedly she claps her hands and laughs; then awed as the sound ricochets across the loom, she watches it spread until it catches and is held fast, glistening and humming as its vibrations are sent rippling throughout the universe...

Introduction

BEING AND BECOMING

All of the creativity and free-ranging mobility that we have come to associate with the human intellect is, in truth, an elaboration, or recapitulation, of a profound creativity already underway at the most immediate level of sensory perception.[1]

– David Abram

There is something deep within me that keeps me striving, keeps me going. It's what gets me out of bed in the morning and somehow infuses me with a willingness to return to the world all the times I've felt like stepping off or hiding in a corner forever. It is equally present whether I'm facing challenges or feeling fearful, or releasing myself to laughter and pleasure, as in all cases it lights up in me a profound awareness that I'm alive. Although this 'something' is obviously extremely important to me, I know I've spent much of my time not quite consciously aware of it. In becoming more aware of it, I've also become aware that throughout my life there has been constant pressure pushing me to ignore its subtle messages, so that in fact for some periods of time I was almost deaf to its quiet voice and lived disconnected from it.

Upon embarking on a PhD degree at the tender age of forty plus, I really felt as though I'd finally grown up. For a long time, I had the impression that I'd been preparing for something, and I had a strong sensation that this academic journey was 'it' – it was now that I would be fulfilling my life's purpose. Yet what started to become very obvious to me was the interior discord between this 'deep something' within me and the many other facets of my life, including my academic journey. In retrospect, I realised that much of this dissonance was due to the topic I'd chosen to focus on – the nurturing of creativity – which enhanced my awareness of my internal world to an extent I never considered possible.

Although it didn't at first start out that way, my PhD thesis was essentially a description of the transformation I experienced in choosing to consciously nurture creativity. Above all, this process led me to gain a greater understanding of both my inner and outer worlds, and I began to see how these meshed. On every level, my transformation felt holistic. In other words, I began to both feel and see myself as being more whole, rather than fragmented. The way I perceived things started to subtly change, and I could see how conflicts (both inner and outer, mine and others') seemed to be mostly caused by the maintaining of a tenacious focus on only specific parts; when I allowed my focus to shift and open I could see connections much more clearly, and with these in place, the reasons for conflict would often dissolve.

This new way of navigating the world opened me up to a way of doing things that, although spontaneous and tentative rather than guided by a plan, was more flowing and joyous than my previous way of being. I was purposely listening to myself, and I was doing this in a very open way – questioning everything, and taking time to understand what it all meant, or at least what it meant for me. It was during this time, just as I was approaching the final stages of my PhD and about to start writing my thesis, that one of my supervisors lent me the 'perfect' book at just the right time – Robert Nash's *Liberating Scholarly Writing – The Power of Personal Narrative*. Reading it gave me a great sense of freedom, and released me from pressures I had not even realised I'd been under, as it showed me how I could include what I'd been experiencing in my thesis.

Here was an ideal tool to help me weave my thesis together, something that would allow me to tell *my* research story. Nash explains that this way of writing 'begins from the inside out, rather than from the outside in.'[2] It allows a more holistic approach to academic writing by providing as full a revelation as possible. In Nash's words:

>   While it is personal, it is also social. While it is practical, it is also theoretical.

While it is reflective, it is also public. While it is local, it is also political. While it narrates, it also proposes. While it is self-revealing, it also evokes self-examination from readers. … a SPN's [scholarly personal narrative] central purpose is to make an impact on both writer and reader, on both the individual and the community. Its overall goal, in the words of David Bleich and Deborah H. Holdstein, is "to admit the full range of human experience into formal scholarly writing."[3]

It seems reasonable to want to allow the full range of human experience into writing that is about our discoveries, research and studies. I use the word 'reasonable', here and throughout the book, in the Socratic sense. Socrates, who many (starting with Plato) held to have been the ideal of reasonableness, endeavoured through investigation and reflection to reach acceptable ways of seeing things and to uncover the truth as much as possible. In other words, he would arrive at reasonableness through conscientious inquiry and deliberation that took into consideration what was apparent, as well as all that he could find out.

Inscribed on the temple of Apollo in Delphi, among many other inscriptions, is: 'Know thyself'. Attributed to one of the 'Seven Wise Men' (Greek sages of ancient times, before even Plato and Socrates), this might appear to be a common-sense instruction that we've heard repeated countless times by teachers, spiritual guides, writers, philosophers and so on. Yet, despite being at the heart of all major spiritual teachings, this saying – know thyself – is at the same time so deep and elusive that in practice it has mostly been overlooked by our Western civilization in its quest for knowledge. For me, the counsel given by this phrase goes hand in hand with Shakespeare's words: 'To thine own self be true' (taken from *Hamlet*, this is Polonius' advice to his son Laertes), though the original meaning might not necessarily have been intended to be profound. I see these two phrases as being linked, for it is only by being true to yourself that you can come to know yourself, and only through knowing yourself that you can be true to yourself. This isn't just a paradox, as it might at first appear, but rather shorthand for explaining a process that can be understood by going beyond basic linear thinking. Imagine these two recommendations – 'Know thyself' and 'To thine own self be true' – forming a spiral as over time they flow in and out of each other as if they were dancing together, each taking a turn in informing and being informed by the other, together gradually gaining fulfilment and depth.

I see being true to one's 'own self' essentially as being honest with oneself throughout the process of getting to know oneself; this is something that could take a lifetime and still remain unfinished. By being honest, I mean allowing the self to experience emotions, thoughts, attitudes and life openly as they occur, without using controls and filters from rationalising processes that may have agendas to fulfil according to specific ideologies or societal tendencies. Ordinarily, many layers of rationalising filters are used in the raising of a child, including all those brought in by the individual child in growing up. This is the reason we grow up believing that in life there are necessarily matters that are unquestionable, including what we've been taught is the 'right' way to do things and see things. These beliefs can be so intrinsic, so deeply embedded within us, that we might never even become aware that they are our beliefs.

At this point, we could argue that we are made up by everything we've been taught and have encountered, including those controls and filters. However, it is also plausible that we might not be a 'blank slate' when we're born. Being willing to consider the possibility that each of us is a unique being with a unique 'essence' or 'self', like a seed of sorts, ready to grow and fulfil its potential, makes it easier to see how any imposed controls and filters might at best hinder and stifle our growth, or at worst could even go as far as warping our inherent nature.

Carl Jung (1875-1961), founder of analytic psychology, calls a human being's essence: 'the "Self" and describes it as the totality of the whole psyche, in order to distinguish it from the "ego", which constitutes only a small part of the total psyche ... [or] inner center...'[4]. Jung also emphasises the importance of knowing and understanding oneself through the exploration of the 'self'. Biologically, it's a fact that we each start life as an invisible tiny core, which, despite differing beliefs, many of us would also agree contains a unique combination of genes. In *Social Intelligence*, psychologist Daniel Goleman tells us how through the relatively new science of epigenetics – the study of how our experiences bring change to the way our genes function – it has been discovered that:

> It is biologically impossible for a gene to operate independently of its
> environment: genes are designed to be regulated by signals from their

immediate surround, including hormones from the endocrine system and neurotransmitters in the brain – some of which are profoundly influenced by our social interactions.[5]

This genetic response starts to occur from the moment we're conceived and continues throughout our life. Acknowledging this, I see myself (who I am and who I might become) as being a unique result of a combination of nature and nurture. What's more, this nature (our human nature) shows itself to be essentially creative through its varied choices of responses to all that we experience. In remaining open to being deeply affected by these experiences, this nature is also clearly vulnerable, and so needs nurturing to be able to express itself and come to fulfilment.

I had a dream soon after I began writing the final draft of my PhD thesis: *I was in a maze-like labyrinth that was open to the sky, with walls made of sheets of blue cobalt steel welded together. The passages were the size of common corridors, neither wide nor narrow, but in some spots contained lots of people, so that it was crowded and difficult to get through. I could see that there were rooms in places attached to the corridors, where people lived. I kept walking and soon found that I encountered less and less people, I felt that I was getting to the edges. Eventually, when there were no more people, I turned a corner and came to what looked like a 'dead end'. The way seemed blocked ahead by two panels of steel joined side by side, but as I walked towards them the perspective changed and I realised that they were not in fact attached to each other, but that the panel on the right was further away from me. As I kept walking towards it, and past the panel on the left, I saw that there were no more panels beyond it but instead, there was an opening onto beautiful countryside which, from where I was standing inside the labyrinth, revealed a copse of trees on the right and a gentle grassy slope on the left, leading to what looked like a lush and inviting valley. I felt my heart start beating in my throat, excited at the thought that I would soon be running down to that valley, finally free from constraint. But then I was surprised by an unexpected thought: 'Now that I know this is here, I must remember it and not go too far from it so that I can come back and show it to others.' And with this I turned from the opening and started winding my way*

back through the labyrinth again... the dream ended there.

Dreams have, throughout the ages, been seen as both sources of mystery and revelation. While there remains much speculation on what dreams are primarily specifically for, and research on dreaming continues within the fields of psychology and neurology, they've also been explained as being an integral part of how we process our experiences and a way for our subconscious to communicate with our conscious minds. I use the term 'subconscious', in place of the term 'unconscious' as used by Jung, to highlight the possibility we have of becoming aware of what we are currently unconscious of. According to Jungian psychologist, Marie–Louise von Franz, 'Jung discovered that dreams can also give civilized man [sic] the guidance he needs in finding his way through the problems of both his inner and his outer life.'[6] She further specifies that:

> In our civilized world, most dreams have to do with the development (by our ego) of the 'right' inner attitude toward the Self, for this relationship is far more disturbed in us by modern ways of thinking and behaving than is the case with primitive [sic] people. They generally live directly from the inner center, but we, with our uprooted consciousness, are so entangled with external, completely foreign matters that it is very difficult for the messages of the Self to get through to us. Our conscious mind continually creates the illusion of a clearly shaped, "real" outer world that blocks off many perceptions. Yet through our unconscious nature we are inexplicably connected to our psychic and physical environment.[7]

In other words, by giving intellectual credence only to matters that can be scientifically or technologically 'proven' and defined, Western society effectively chooses to ignore all other matters, regardless of how pivotal a part they play in our lives and within our beings. Not surprisingly, many of our dreams hold messages that would correct this self-imposed myopia, and try to get through to us when we're not consciously in control. Despite some individuals claiming that they don't dream, or hardly ever remember dreaming, with almost a third of our lives spent sleeping, our joint experience undoubtedly includes a lot of dreaming; because of this it seems to me reasonable to assume that dreams are a significant part of our human experience.

Having grown up in Australia from the age of nine (when my family moved here from Italy), Jung's explanation of dreams feels especially relevant for me. This is because 'the Dreaming' is a term that's used by Indigenous Australians – Australia's First Nations People – for their complex relationship to the whole of life. This is the closest that an English word can get to their meaning, the sense of which can never actually be captured in a Western language. In the words of Aboriginal man Midnight Davies:

> The Dreaming completely surrounds us, we are shown proof of it every day. It's not some old book written thousands of years ago, it is the living world itself. The Dreaming belongs to every Aboriginal person – it isn't the sacred property of a few priests/rabbis/imams, it is the property of everyone – every ceremony, every right, every tradition, every bit of knowledge is destined to be known to an individual sometime within their lifetime.[8]

I extrapolate from Davies' explanation of the Dreaming to an understanding that our relationship with the 'self' is greatly limited by the constructed partial reality of dominant Western culture. Despite most of us being a long way from our ancestral home, and in many cases not even knowing where this is, we are in fact all descendants of First Nations people, even though they may no longer exist. It therefore follows, and makes sense to me, that our 'dreaming' (relegated to the times when we're not conscious) would try to reconnect us to the wholeness that Western culture has excised us from.

I have found that choosing to be consciously open to wholeness helps me to gain insights that clarify meaning. In relation to my academic research, this has meant that rather than deciding what would or would not be included (and where I would look for this) I chose to be impartially open so as to follow where the research led me. It was due to this that the focus of my research, which first started out as 'the nurturing of creativity in education', shifted and widened to become 'the nurturing of creativity within me, and in the world I saw and connected with'.

In the course of interviewing people from the educational community, including parents, principals, teachers and students, they relayed to me their disillusionment with high schools. They shared that they had found creativity to be hardly nurtured within the confines of formal education; according to them, it was more often the case that education stifled creativity. Indeed, what they said confirmed what I had found as a student teacher, when I had gained a Diploma of Education and then subsequently taught part-time. Though I had initially considered my teaching experience as highly personal, and not necessarily indicative of the way things were, my view on this gradually changed as others shared their stories with me, and I saw that indeed our experiences reflected each other.

As I was collecting material and data for my research, reading and interviewing participants, I began to feel very uncomfortable about the idea of setting myself up as an expert. Ultimately, that is what doing a PhD is all about – researching a specific topic of interest that hasn't been majorly focused on before, at least not in the particular way that is being pursued in the PhD, and filling a gap in humanity's shared knowledge by making a contribution of new and original knowledge. Though this might be considered ambitious, living as we do in a world that's so very abundant with distinct 'things' – more numerous than 'the ten thousand things' referred to throughout Lao Tzu's *Tao Te Ching* – it is safe to assume that something can always be found that hasn't been looked at before. What's more, we are each of us different, with uniquenesses that permeate all levels, deep ones as well as those that only show up in appearance. We are different in our physical details – we each have a specific combination of genes giving us a unique mix of characteristics. These include particularly individual ones, like an exclusive set of fingerprints, and irises with so many distinctive features that iris recognition has been hailed as one of the most secure ways of authenticating people's identities. We also each have a unique intelligence, as Sir Ken Robinson (one of creativity's most insistent proponents) pointed out at the 2005 Melbourne held conference 'Backing our Creativity':

> ... your intelligence is different from everybody else's intelligence on Earth. You have a hundred billion neurons, a unique biography, a unique set of experiences, capacities, wishes, longings, and values. There has been no person like you in history, and there won't be again. And we cannot afford to squander the resource. You're unique. Your brain, incidentally, I'm told – your personal brain – is as different from everyone else's brain, it's as different from my brain as your face is different from my face, or as alike as mine, similar, but unique to you.[9]

Given all this, we could assume that the inclusion of the 'self' within the process of research would be sufficient to ensure that the requirement of 'new and original contribution to knowledge' was suitably met. In other words, it would be reasonable to expect our unique intelligence and subjectivity to creatively transform anything we were studying into something equally unique. Regardless of the topic of research, allowing and even encouraging researchers to be guided by their inner subjective perspective, rather than demanding that they remain objective, would go a considerable way to guaranteeing this. This would then bring in new knowledge, new ways of looking at things, new applications and so on; in fact, the list is as endless as there are researchers… or people, as we are all researchers in one way or another.

Openly promoting academic subjectivity would foster scholarship that was both rigorous and holistic, with the learning and discovering not only grounded in academic methodologies, but also buttressed by the context of the bigger picture that the wisdom of self-knowledge and understanding would provide. However, rather than embracing our unique subjectivity as a bonus that can open up inimitable opportunities, the accepted academic convention is to insist on following tested ways of doing things. As a process this is quite contrary to the creative one of discovery and innovation, despite this not being openly acknowledged or made obvious.

During most of my PhD journey, I found myself pressured into constantly meeting specific requirements, many of which were nothing more than 'academic red tape' that would lead my attention away from my inner sense of being, that important deep something within me. As a result I experienced a feeling of being lost, which I later realised was due to a disconnection from my 'beingness'. At the time of writing my thesis, I couldn't find the term 'beingness' in any dictionary. My awareness of this profound sense of myself kept growing stronger with my research, and so I coined the term 'beingness' from 'awareness' and 'being' to more precisely mean *the experience of the continuity of oneself as a living being.* I see the 'self' as metaphorically akin to an iceberg (to use the well-known metaphor), where only the smaller visible part can be seen while the majority of it is submerged, so while I've been aware of my consciousness, my *beingness* has often been ignored and overlooked, yet it has always been present in me as an underlying foundation that is an integral part to my consciousness.

In following the research guidelines I had set for myself, versions of the overall established directives for postgraduates, I felt stifled and pressured for time. While I was fulfilling requirements that were meant to further me along the PhD path, ironically these were in fact stopping me from delving into a vast and enticing new territory to be researched that was opening up before me. I could see it, but because it wasn't in my plans I felt held back from delving into it. Having no map for it as such, I couldn't justify entering the 'fanciful unknown' – there were reports to complete, meetings to attend and books to read, and of course, a PhD has to be confined within clearly defined boundaries…

It was at this time that phrases like 'It's after your PhD that you get to write what you really want to write,' and 'After your PhD comes your really important work' began floating around. I had a sinking feeling in the pit of my stomach on hearing this – was the PhD just another hoop to jump through? Was it all for show? And how could I contribute something that was new and original if I couldn't explore all that I wanted, and needed to, as it unfolded? This maze of mind games was making me question the path of becoming an expert even more, because if becoming an 'expert' meant getting further away from where my *beingness* wanted me to go, then I definitely didn't want to be one.

In *Writing from the Heart,* Nancy Aronie shares:

> … when you're an expert there's no room for error. There's no chance for discovery. There's no "anything is possible" because the expert has explored all the possibilities and the expert knows exactly how it should be done. Gone is the magic. Gone is the spontaneity.[10]

Though of course it is impossible for anybody to explore *all* of the possibilities of any particular scenario, this still fittingly conveys the attitude of an expert - believing to be an expert is synonymous to locking your mind and heart away from any chance of wonder.

I began to consider the idea of dropping much of the educational focus (the external) from my PhD thesis and instead concentrate on the actual nurturing of creativity (the internal). But, as my supervisors were quick to point out, the 'nurturing of creativity' was a huge topic and this needed to be made more specific for a PhD thesis. This is where uncertainty took hold; on one hand, I yearned to be true to myself and explore the nurturing of creativity, however and wherever I was led to it, but on the other hand, I found it hard to give up what I'd planned – it was so neat, a perfect fit within the lines of requirements.

Though at the time I'd been so excited about it, I now see the PhD journey I had originally set up for myself in a very different light: conformist and therefore incongruous to the nurturing of creativity, to walk it I would have had to sacrifice creativity so as to pursue a rigid and methodical exposition of possible ways of achieving (at least in appearance) the nurturing of creativity in high schools. Continuing on this journey would've meant excluding the subjectivity of the self, and so the research would have remained theoretical and hollow regardless of how much action research was included in it. Claiming objectivity, it would've skirted around the topic, chasing knowledge without ever daring to get to the heart of it by refusing to give voice to the non-academic experiences of the 'self' – both myself and the 'selves' of those interviewed.

Regardless of how theoretically sound any amount of knowledge put into words is, or how objective it appears to be, the inescapable fact remains that it has had to be put into words by a 'self'. With this 'self' being first of all a corporeal reality, which, as philosopher David Abram points out, 'actually experiences things, this poised and animate power that initiates all our projects and suffers all our passions.'[11] In addition, as professor and author Liz Stanley states, 'At a certain point, surely we must accept that material reality exists, that it continually knocks up against us, that texts are not the only thing.'[12] From this, it doesn't take much reflection to see that it's both fitting and necessary to give recognition to the subjectivity of all the 'selves' involved in whatever research we conduct (or indeed whatever we're doing) for to exclude this would mean to ultimately distort the findings.

Honesty without compromise was at this point what I felt I had to commit to in order to come out of the stalemate I found myself in, and yet it was difficult to let go of years of training to do things the 'right way', and of 'paying my dues'. It was difficult to even rationalise doing things my way when I couldn't quite see myself as a rebel, as though 'colouring in outside the lines' were actually a rebellious act! Although I thought I knew the way I wanted to go, I found it challenging to bring myself to start heading in that direction. And then something unthinkable happened, shaking my life to such an extent that I was left reeling from the shock of it and on the verge of abandoning my PhD altogether: my sister died.

It has now been over ten years since then, but I still cannot find the words to adequately describe the pain I felt, the sadness, the endless guilt ... wondering if I could've done something of influence to prevent it from happening – maybe loving more, helping more, being more involved in advocating more strongly for a different medical approach ... it was as if I were searching for a way to go back in time and change the outcome. I found her death almost impossible to accept and it made me sharply aware of my own mortality. Many of the things that I thought mattered suddenly lost all importance, and I found I had little patience with anything I perceived to be even remotely autocratic. At the same time, some things gained in meaning and relevance, like working with nature's gifts of soil, sun and water to cultivate beautiful gardens. Still other things were revealed to me as being absolutely precious, so that I found myself cherishing times spent with my children and loved ones, and I learned to be more present for them.

Surprisingly, while the consciously busy side of my research – those things commonly associated with doing a PhD, like reading, writing, adding to a bibliography, and so on – slowed down considerably, my relationship to the nurturing of creativity somehow deepened. From being just a concept, one merely confined within my thoughts and research, creativity became something real that could hold me. I recall this as being an amazing and almost tactile experience – I simply let go (of so many previously held assumptions) and stepped into creativity. It was as if stepping into a flowing stream, and I felt myself being buoyed up despite all the burdens I was carrying – the pain, sadness, guilt, confusion, and fear – I didn't need to prove myself, I was accepted just as I was, or as the saying goes, 'warts and all'. As my focus turned inward, connecting to my beingness, I became aware of opportunities to undertake creative endeavours involving little known facets of myself, like exploring dancing and drawing.

This led to the development of a very different thesis from the one I had originally set myself to write, but it was now a thesis that I could wholly own with integrity, being as much a part of it, as it was a part of me – it was *my* research story. As author Robert Atkinson tells us in *The Gift of Stories*:

> Story is a tool for making us whole ... a tool for self-discovery; stories tell us

new things about ourselves that we wouldn't have been as aware of without having told the story ... Our stories illustrate our inherent connectedness with others. ... In the life story of each person is a reflection of another's life story.[13]

From my initial hunch that the nurturing of creativity was important, my PhD journey has confirmed this to me unequivocally, as not only did nurturing my creativity support me through this journey, but it also enabled me to uncover other times throughout my life where this had occurred and helped me greatly. Having been led to consciously and willingly nurture creativity, I have now experienced its worth on a personal level, so that in writing about what I've researched, my experiences serve as grounding and nourishment. Furthermore, these experiences have helped me 'walk the talk', making the nurturing of creativity become second nature to me. This has led me to recognise myself as being a mentor for creativity and its nurturing. As a title, or label (not usually something I endorse), 'mentor' is more acceptable to me than any other labels might be, especially that of 'expert'. Being a mentor is dynamic, and I see myself part of an ongoing process that allows me to foster creativity more and more, including the nurturing and developing of my own creativity. Ultimately, the main motivation for writing this book is to facilitate the nurturing of creativity for all who might wish it, for to do so is the natural outcome of nurturing my own creativity.

The order of the chapters in this book has been somewhat changed from the original thesis. Being of central significance, Chapter One explores creativity, including its need to be nurtured in order to gain expression. As such, it might prove helpful to refer to it as often as needed when reading the rest of the book, especially when reading Chapter Four, which focuses on time and trust as facets of everyday living that are essential to the nurturing of the self's creative nature. Chapters Two and Three are explanatory chapters, with Chapter Two establishing the starting point of all experience as the 'self', in this case, myself — a unique self holistically positioned within a number of contexts. From this, Chapter Three metaphorically builds supporting scaffolding (a loom) from many of the writings and theories of authors and scholars, each chosen to expand on and add depth to what I discuss.

Chapters Five to Seven develop from the core chapters (One and Four) by relating the 'inner' to the 'outer' through an unfolding of narratives (interspersed throughout) drawn from the nurturing of creativity. Some of these narratives are a personal sharing of my experiences, while others are insights from stories related to me. This sharing of others' stories demonstrates the generative nature of narratives and how they're interconnected – each begets another or many others, these being qualities that are also displayed in the process of nurturing creativity. Lastly, Chapter Eight weaves together all the threads of what has been discussed, and in doing so describes what the whole picture of creativity might look like. To do this, it includes a thorough reflection on the value of big picture (or holistic) perspectives. Additionally, it outlines possible future directions that could be taken by looking at ways in which the effects of nurturing creativity could be made lasting and transformative.

Throughout the book are also quotes from those I interviewed. Though my research shifted from its initial planned focus of 'creativity in education' to a more holistic approach to creativity, it still seemed relevant to include the voices of those I interviewed, as they were speaking about creativity nonetheless. In total, sixty-seven people, mostly from the educational communities of high schools around Perth (Australia), shared their view of creativity with me, and I have 'woven' their voices into this research story. These are presented in italics so that they might stand out and be more easily recognisable; to maintain the anonymity of each individual, I indicate only the group they belong to (in brackets after each quote) – student, parent or teacher/educator.

One of the obvious effects of using a holistic approach in the writing of this book is that it meanders here and there, briefly sketching different things as in a painting, then returning to them later to fill in more details and give emphasis. Because of this, so as to help the reader keep track of the journey undertaken (which by wandering covers much ground), at the end of each chapter I revisit the connections that have been made, highlighting those that could be considered landmarks on the journey. While these 'inter-chapters' can help provide a better sense of the story that's being woven, it's important to remember that they are just individual parts of the whole, and as such, they cannot stand for the whole story that's being told – the story of a journey of personal transformation through the nurturing of creativity.

Chapter One:

CREATIVITY

Creativity is the true expression of your self. If you've got a self, you've got creativity.[1]

– Nancy Aronie

We're hardwired for creativity; if we're not creative, we die.

– (High-school teacher)

Creativity is a way of expressing yourself, your feelings, in different kinds of ways.

– (High-school student)

Creativity is how you look at things – your own ideas about anything.

– (Parent of high-school student)

An eclectic and complex topic like creativity does not fit neatly within the boundaries of a specific definition; instead, it encompasses a wide scope of definitions that vary depending on the context and who is discussing it. In *Out of Our Minds: Learning to Be Creative*, Sir Ken Robinson (one of the world's most insistent voices for the vital importance of creativity in education) approaches creativity in a circuitous way. He takes five pages to build a 'definition', with phrases like: '*imaginative processes with outcomes that are original and of value*'[2], specifying that this is 'his' definition of creativity, and then further develops various meanings that he draws from it. Similarly, at the beginning of *On Creativity*, David Bohm (1917-1992), a physicist and theorist said to have been 'one of the most original thinkers of the second half of the twentieth century'[3], imparts his view that 'Creativity is ... something that it is impossible to define in words'[4], and from there he takes the whole chapter to convey to the reader what creativity means to him.

While both Robinson and Bohm make it very clear that creativity is close to impossible to define, they are nonetheless able to share how they see it and experience it. What becomes apparent to me from this is that an all-encompassing concept like creativity cannot itself be contained. It would not be coherent to try to do so; any attempt at containment through definition could only be reductive, and so would cause confusion rather than help understanding. Does this lack of a specific definition make 'creativity' a meaningless term? I don't believe so; a definition doesn't have the exclusive on imparting meaning but merely provides an explanation by communicating ideas of what that meaning might be. Although the meaning of creativity isn't easy to attain, a way to get closer to understanding it is to open up our own borders of perception. At the same time, it is important to remember that while creativity could therefore potentially be 'anything', that does not mean that it will be 'everything', but rather that its meaning will vary depending on the context. It is from within this contextuality, which allows us to see its specific connection to the 'whole picture', that each of us will infer a meaning for creativity, or even many connected meanings that may continue to change (as our understanding grows) each time they are re-visited.

Given my experience, with everyone I interviewed about creativity expressing their own particular idea about it, it seems reasonable to invite you (as readers) to start from your own views of what creativity means to you. Regardless of how disparate these initial views may be, in the course of reading I trust that they will in some way connect to the picture of creativity shown in this book. In fact, my aim in this chapter is to primarily encourage a holistic understanding of creativity, as well as to communicate as clearly as possible how this understanding began to develop during my research, and continues to develop even now.

In recognising that the whole is necessarily made up of interconnected multiple views, rather than one view chosen over another, it is important to acknowledge that this whole therefore contains views that are yet to be perceived, and also those that remain 'silent', or little known, by not having been widely shared through discussion or publishing. To uphold this recognition I have chosen to open a dialogue on the many meanings of creativity. This of course requires patience on behalf of all those involved in the dialogue, and the willingness to remain with the process as it unfolds, since it takes time for a picture to start becoming clear. As in a jigsaw puzzle, enough of the pieces need to be added for the whole to begin to become apparent, and even then there can be last minute surprises. Professor of psychology Arthur J. Cropley lists 'tolerance for ambiguity'[5] as one of the main conditions for creativity, meaning that to be able to make use of creativity and nurture it, one needs to be open-minded and accepting of uncertainty. This 'not knowing' and being comfortable with it is the biggest boon we could give creativity; it is like extending a warm, welcoming invitation.

As is acknowledged in countless books and articles written about it, creativity is a complex concept. In every which way one looks at it, creativity holds a special fascination, so much so in fact that it has become quite a 'buzzword', with the 21st century being heralded by many as the 'Creative Age'[6]. Complex concepts have a tendency to become very 'big' in our minds, since they literally take up a lot of mental space as we repeatedly attempt to contain them within ideas and explanations. As psychiatrist and psychoanalyst Norman Doidge explains, we use different areas of the brain to store words so as to include: their meanings, their visual appearance when written, and their sound. In order for us to be able to make use of hearing, seeing, and understanding at the same time, these different areas where the information is stored need to be networked together, so that the neurons can be 'activated' together.[7] In academic writing, given its characteristic propensity to be definitory and analytical, if a concept is particularly complex (and therefore big) the inclination is to 'cut' a portion of it from the whole, then having argued why that particular portion is the one most worthy of study, only that part will be looked at in depth, while the rest is ignored. An example of this approach, in regard to creativity, is the book *Changing the World: A Framework for the Study of Creativity*. At the very start of the book, the authors David Henry Feldman, Mihaly Csikszentmihalyi and Howard Gardner (the second author being the well-known proponent of 'flow', while the last one introduced to us 'the theory of multiple intelligences') state that:

> We are thus concerned with what is sometimes called "big" creativity, in contrast for example, to the more humble ... tendency to bring a fresh and lively interpretation to any endeavour, [which is termed "small" creativity] ... big creativity only occurs when something of enduring value is contributed to an existing body of knowledge, thereby transforming it.[8]

Although their book contains insightful discussions and much that is enlightening about creativity, the above quote shows that it begins with a reductive, though common, approach to research. Two meanings of creativity are defined, and then one of them is let go to make room for the other, which is chosen to become the focus of thorough examination. Even though dividing up a topic and focusing only on the part that is of main interest is a perfectly valid approach, it is important to remember that doing this means that from this point on 'small creativity' is no longer going to be considered relevant to anything that will be discussed. In fact, it won't be considered at all. This means that whatever is connected to 'small creativity' – all that supports 'small creativity', or any qualities that are engendered from it that could eventually even give rise to 'big creativity' – cannot be used to inform the understanding of creativity. That is because anything to do with 'small creativity' has been shuttered off; it is no longer allowed to come into the picture. Consequently, the whole complex concept of creativity has been reduced to only a part of it at the very start of the book.

Focusing only on a particular part of creativity, especially given that it is such a huge subject, is not what I'm advocating against. I agree that there is only so much that can be looked at in depth when discussing creativity or other complex concepts; however, this could be done without specifically excising the part that is not being focused on. Consciously setting up parameters that include parts of a topic while completely excluding other parts, almost to the point of 'obliterating' them, not only fragments what is being looked at but at the same time it fragments one's actual approach to research (and by extension to life); by preventing an attitude that is open to discovery and creativity it imposes limits on what can actually be found.

As David Bohm states in *Wholeness and the Implicate Order*, 'fragmentation is an attempt to extend the analysis of the world into separate parts beyond the domain in which to do this is appropriate, it is in effect an attempt to divide what is really indivisible.'[9] Similarly, the main issue concerning creativity being divided into 'small creativity' and 'big creativity' is that it is an arbitrary division. How could we possibly decide, in all instances, which specific creativity might be deemed to be either 'big creativity' or 'small creativity'? And why are they separate? Might it not be, at least in some cases, that a series of acts of 'small creativity' eventually establishes a change in someone's attitude, which then leads him or her to 'big creativity'?

The setting up of artificial, and mostly hierarchical, divisions between parts of the same whole (something that regularly occurs in academic research and writing, as well as in governmental policy writing, and also many industries and corporations) can lead us to adopt a habitual approach that sets up rigid boundaries as a matter of course, and this can therefore hold us back from working toward clearer understanding. Bohm very importantly reminds us that 'our theories are *not* [my emphasis] 'descriptions of reality as it is' but, rather, ever changing forms of insight, which can point to or indicate a reality that is implicit and not describable or specifiable in its totality.'[10] For me this quote draws attention to one of the most fundamental realities of our universe, and were this to be truly considered and integrated by researchers and scholars in their work, this would result in our society becoming more holistic. However, in most cases, this reality seems to be ignored.

So this is how it goes – we (particularly our scientists and researchers across the many disciplines we have) come up with theories in order to describe and explain why certain things in the world happen the way they do. Yet all too soon these theories, which are in fact basically stories that serve as explanations and so can only be as complete as our understanding is, become almost irreplaceable stand-ins for the actual processes that they were merely meant to help clarify. By focusing solely on these theories, since they are now all that we know and are taught, we end up forgetting that there is still much about the processes (those things that the theories were initially simply meant to help explain) that we don't yet understand and that we have not worked out. Similarly, it is important to remember that words, and especially written words, can only go so far in describing reality or any facet of life.

As author and journalist Arthur Koestler points out in *The Act of Creation*, although '[w]ords are essential tools for formulating and communicating thoughts, and also for putting them into the storage of memory ... words can also become snares, decoys, or strait-jackets.'[11] In fact, once something has been defined (and therefore labelled), even when the view and understanding of that something shifts, having the definition (label) in place can prevent us from clearly seeing the *thing*, as what we are used to seeing is just the label as the 'stand-in' for that *thing* This is why there appears to be such a resistance to change. Only a holistic approach – an approach that looks at a topic as a 'whole picture' – can ensure that we remain aware that reality is much bigger, and more complete than any theories and written explanations of any parts of it can ever describe. A holistic approach allows us to more easily flow with change as we learn and grow.

Rather than trying to formulate 'acceptable' definitions by excluding certain parts of the concepts in question in order to make them 'fit' the theories we want to postulate, a holistic approach would go about finding new and clearer ways of elucidating what we see, hear, feel, touch, smell, taste and so on. By being open to perceiving the new, a holistic approach is supportive of creativity. As Bohm explains:

> ... by becoming aware of preconceptions that have been conditioning us unconsciously we are able to *perceive* and to *understand* the world in a fresh way. One can then "feel out" and explore what is unknown, rather than go on ... with mere variations on old themes, leading to modifications ... within the framework of what has already been known ... Thus, one's work can begin to be really creative, not only in the sense that it will contain genuinely original features, but also in that these will cohere with what is being continued from the past to form one harmonious, living, evolving, totality.[12]

A willingness to being open to perceiving the 'new' brings understanding, which then invariably leads to further insights and new understanding. This can be seen as a cycle that is forever ongoing as it constantly renews itself; it could therefore be termed to be an 'awakening', through which we could discover and understand more and more of the whole (the world, ourselves, and everything) that we would then also be able to partake in more consciously. By imagining the possibility of this process being fostered in all people, and across all areas of life, we are led to a vision of a world where creativity is nurtured and celebrated – a thriving world. What would a world like this be like to live in? Such a vision warrants a pause so that we can internalise it, and consciously bring it about through our actions – imagine what a world like this would be like to live in. For me, the main feelings that arise from this vision are excitement, joy and beauty.

Research on creativity began in earnest in the 1950s, with the publishing of an article in *American Psychologist*. Titled 'Creativity', and written by psychologist Joy Paul Guildford, it highlighted the importance of 'divergent' thinking.[13] A common test for creativity at the time specified that creative thinking should lead to innovative outcome, that is to say to some kind of tangible product – from works of art, to scientific discoveries, to specific plans and ideas. Perhaps it was this focus on 'product' that promulgated the belief that creativity was a gift that only a few individuals possessed. Or perhaps it was from this already existing belief that the focus on product developed. Regardless of which way round it was, the idea that the output of people's creativity could be increased coexisted with the belief of specific giftedness. The passing of The National Defense Education Act in the USA, aiming to promote creativity in schools, bears witness to this. This Act was put forward as USA's response to Russia's engineers beating them in launching the first satellite in 1957.

Notably, at this time it was also commonly believed that our brains were 'hard-wired'; this is shorthand for saying that the neuron connections in the circuitry of the brain are fixed, or at least pre-set by a young age. Progress in neuroscience has since then helped to counter this idea, especially given the findings of the brain's innate plasticity, through the demonstration that new experiences and knowledge can result in the brain 'rewiring' itself into completely new circuits, regardless of one's age. More precisely termed 'neuroplasticity', this ability of the brain to restructure itself is the topic of Norman Doidge's *The Brain That Changes Itself*. In his book, Doidge most importantly dislodges the idea of the mechanistic brain, upheld since the 'universal' adoption of Descartes' division of mind and body. Doidge does this by giving evidence (through examples) of how by being able to 'change its own structure and function through thought and activity ... the brain differs from one person to the next and ... changes in the course of our individual lives.'[14] He also discusses how regardless whether one 'does' or 'imagines' an action, many of the same networks of neurons are fired, with this showing that action and imagination are intrinsically linked, and that '[e]ach thought alters the physical state of your brain synapses at a microscopic level.'[15]

Neuroplasticity is thus clearly connected to our innate potential for creativity, a fact that many neuroscientists eagerly and widely want us to know. Among them is Evian Gordon, author of *Integrative Neuroscience*, who states that '[t]he brain is the essence of creativity' and that 'we're all born creative'[16]. Gordon is holistic in his approach to neuroscience, highlighting the connectedness of the conscious to the unconscious (subconscious); he also advocates self-exploration and creativity through art as a means for brain development.[17] In *Out of Our Minds*, Ken Robinson looks at this same connectedness: 'there is an intimate relationship between knowing and feeling: how we feel is directly related to what we know and think ... There are times when we are immersed in something that completely engages our creative capabilities and draws equally from our knowledge, feelings and intuitive powers.'[18]

Creativity makes use of all of these – emotion, intuition, and information gained from both physical responses to the environment and intellectual reasoning – which when integrated together are synthesised to generate 'forms' that can be truly innovative. These may be ideas, objects, and discoveries, solutions to problems, or even simply 'ways of being' and new ways of perceiving the world. Another neuroscientist, Antonio Damasio, explains the workings of this very well, as he tells us that creativity can only be discussed in an interdisciplinary context:

> ...from the interactions between individuals and environment emerge the social and cultural artifacts that we talk about when we discuss creativity. These artifacts cannot be reduced simply to the neural circuitry of an adult brain and even less to the genes behind our brains. It follows that the sort of activity that leads to creative behaviour ... [includes] something that results from the interactions of the brain with physical, social and cultural environments. That is why extremely reductionist views cannot capture all the issues we wish to understand when we discuss creativity.[19]

Though creativity is more like a complex and dynamic process than it is like a 'thing' – an object that can be statically labelled and defined – we nonetheless often associate it with specific individuals. In other words, creativity is commonly thought of as something that certain people possess more than others. What Damasio challenges us to recognise, however, is that creativity is a dynamic and complex social interplay of both nature and nurture; this then clearly takes it beyond the confines of belonging solely to specific people.

Similarly, although we speak of the 'mind' – which, because it's a noun, we almost instinctively imagine to be something, some-thing, a 'thing' – what has been discussed about creativity can also be applied to the mind, thus it might in fact be more useful to see the 'mind' as an ever-changing process connected to the brain. To quote biologist Jack Cohen and mathematician Ian Stewart, from their book *The Collapse of Chaos*, 'Mind seems to be an emergent property of brains ... That is, mind is a process, not a thing (or a product), and it emerges from the collective interactions of appropriately organized bits of ordinary matter.'[20] It is important not to give the phrase 'appropriately organised' any excessive concrete meaning, for as we've seen in looking at the brain's neuroplasticity, although the mind might emerge from the brain, likewise the brain is forever emerging from the mind through the input of thoughts, beliefs, feelings, and so on. Furthermore, both the brain and the mind are inherent parts of the processes of life that are constantly in motion, which adds to their overall complexity.

Creativity could be said to somewhat parallel 'the mind', as they both involve dynamic processes rather than static concepts. Clearly creativity and the mind are connected, by extending beyond the mind (as Damasio suggests above) creativity is therefore what connects minds and brains to everything else that is part of life. In constantly observing creativity to be an intrinsic part of the dynamic process of life, I, and many others, see it as being indivisible from life. Wondering at what point 'mind' ends and 'life' (and creativity) start, is like asking the age-old Eastern philosophical question of at what point waves end and the ocean begins.

It was in the Age of Enlightenment that 'reason' was positioned as the acme of human development.[21] This belief in the supremacy of the 'rational mind', mirrored by the hierarchical values assigned to different things and roles in our society, was birthed 'to condemn darkness and superstition ... [and was proclaimed] as the new solution to man's [sic] problem.'[22] Despite these 'noble ideals' for what seemed like all the right reasons, Bohm explains how revolutions, which as history shows have been typically imposed through force and violence, inevitably merely replace one oppressive order with a different oppressive order:

> ... a preconceived idea of producing social harmony is in reality just as mechanical and arbitrary as is the chaotic state of conflicting orders which it aims to eliminate ... Indeed, no really creative transformation can possibly be effected by human beings, either in nature or in society, unless they are in the creative state of mind that is generally sensitive to the differences that always exist between the observed fact and any preconceived ideas ...[23]

In other words, systems that demand rigid adherence to specific ideals (whatever these may be) are in fact more closely connected to the systems that proclaim themselves to be diametrically opposed to them, than to the ideals they profess to hold. It is the quality of their outlook (in this case their rigidity) that makes these presumably opposed systems so alike, and they will therefore cause equivalent outcomes, among which is the oppression of anyone who sees things differently. An open mind can clearly see this; an open mind also understands how these systems (which I would add are representative of the majority of the current political systems in the world) hugely contrast a more flexible way of seeing, being, and governing.

To ensure the development of a holistic perspective that can come closer to perceiving wholeness, it might be wise and advisable to reposition 'reason' from its place of supremacy (since supremacy in anything is hardly a reasonable premise) to a more equal position of shared importance and value, together with other forms of 'knowing', like emotion, intuition, physical responses, and of course creativity. However, to be able to do this we need to relinquish the conformist ideals of the importance of the 'expert', and of wanting to prove things right. In society's current state of affairs, this might seem a lot to ask, but it is necessary if we want to allow creativity more space. Educator and author Bill Lucas points out that a creative state of mind 'requires the capacity to live with complexity and uncertainty. It will be difficult to nurture it in communities where only certainty is rewarded.'[24] With a reliance on certainty, or on even only an appearance of certainty, comes the belief that control needs to be maintained over people and things, and as long as that is what most, or many, believe, then that is what is most likely to eventuate, and so the status quo is firmly upheld.

Given that 'rationality' still appears to have a high standing in our society, it seems appropriate to ask ourselves – is it actually rational to continue establishing 'facts' that can only ever be a 'part' of reality, since when we stipulate them we are not consciously aware of the whole? It is, at this point, also important to consider that we may never become completely conscious of the whole reality; this is because wholeness cannot be contained, it is we (together with our whole world) who are contained within it. Bohm reminds us that this habit we have of establishing 'facts' is the very thing that 'prevents theoretical insights from going beyond existing limitations and changing to meet new facts ... [since] the belief that theories give true knowledge of reality ... implies ... that they need never change.'[25] From that, it's only a small step to establishing all the rigid and reductive dogmas that we allow to rule our lives, fragment the perception of the wholeness that holds us, and keep us from growing.

Despite the countering of creativity being so prevalent in our society, creativity nonetheless constantly grabs our attention; this is because creativity is such an integral part of ourselves, it is part of what makes us up. Though in many cases, it is still viewed as a somewhat magical way to achieve an outcome or product, it is also finally being looked at more holistically, as a process in its full complexity, and as a way of interacting with the environment, which is to say it's being looked at in a cultural and social sense, as well as in a personal and in a spiritual sense (though not necessarily all of these together, all of the time). While the complexity of creativity, together with its relevance and connectedness to all areas of life, has been 'spelt out' by neuroscientists such as Antonio Damasio (quoted above), there are others who have arrived at similar conclusions from totally different directions, and they too have highlighted the need to nurture creativity in their specific fields. From a choice of many there are three I want to introduce to you, as I've found their way of seeing creativity very relevant and useful to everyday life:

- John Paul Lederach (Professor of International Peacebuilding) believes, as a result of personal and professional experience, that creativity opens up a new vision of possibilities that make it an integral part of peace building and reconciliation. He writes in his book *The Moral Imagination: The Art and Soul of Building Peace:* 'The peacebuilder must have one foot in what is and one foot beyond what exists ... creativity moves beyond what exists toward something new and unexpected while rising from and speaking to the everyday.'[26]

- Professor Federico Mayor Zaragoza (Director-General of UNESCO from 1987 to 1999) on 3 November 1999 made an 'Appeal for the promotion of arts education and creativity at school as part of the construction of a culture of peace'[27]. In the full text of the Appeal (included in the appendix of this book) he links creativity with mediation and clearly points to its importance in helping humanity live in harmony and without violence.

- Mark Earls (formerly the director of one of the UK's largest communications groups, and also author of bestseller *Herd*) assures us that 'creativity is what we should employ at work, and value above all else.'[28] He stresses the importance of networking and of group creativity and gives numerous examples of how creativity is being seriously considered in more diverse fields than ever before.

Reflecting on all that has been looked at and discussed so far in this chapter, it is clear to see how this links back to my initial statement about creativity being a 'big-picture' concept. I therefore propose that creativity is in fact such a huge concept as to be able to encompass life, or in other words, that it is intrinsically interwoven within life as a perspective that underpins it. Because of its scope, creativity might be best understood as being one's attitude, or one's approach, to the process of living – one's way of being. *Having an attitude of creativity is a way of actually 'being' in the world, as well as a way of perceiving the world.* The nurturing of creativity is a natural extension of this attitude of creativity, for it is the very nature of this 'attitude' that, once accepted, leads one to become an advocate for creativity, and to foster it in others as well as in the self.

I did not arrive at the concept of creativity being an attitude from just theoretical insight, but also from the very tangible experience of creativity and my personal transformation through it. From deep within me has been awakened an underlying attitude of creativity which provides a meaningful way for me to recognise and understand the patterns in the threads of how I'm weaving my life. It is this attitude of creativity that has made it possible for me to reclaim the whole of myself. And even though I cannot know what the completeness of this might be (as it's part of the ongoing process of living), it has enabled me to recognise the deep connections I have to the whole of life, which is in itself thoroughly interconnected and complex, while it remains at the same time 'mind-bogglingly' open to further transformation.

In *Virtue Ethics*, Christine Swanton writes that Abraham Maslow (renowned for his 'hierarchy of needs') 'claims that his studies of creativity in subjects rid him of an important preconception about the nature of creativity.'[29] While he had previously categorised creativity by confining it to artists, composers and so on, he realised that in fact it 'pervades life in general'[30]. In the same way, one's attitude pervades everything about them – it is holistic in that it both informs, and is a result of, the workings and interactions of one's subconscious with one's consciousness, and thus encompasses the whole of one's personality.

The Japanese folktale of a House of 1000 Mirrors[31] is a great analogy for the far-reaching effects of attitude: ***One day a puppy climbed up the stairs of a house full of mirrors, and went in. As soon as he entered, tail wagging in happy expectation, he saw reflected back at him countless happy and tail-wagging puppies; delighted to have made so many friends he left in high spirits. The next day another puppy climbed up into the house of mirrors, but he did it in a fearful and doubtful way, creeping in with his tail between his legs and a scowl on his face, seeing all the reflected puppies scowling back at him made him growl and he quickly fled, afraid that the growling puppies would hurt him.*** This tale clearly illustrates the circular way that attitude can work for or against us, with an attitude of creativity being the one most likely to enable growth and transformation.

Lederach points out that to be willing to work and move with creativity involves risk, as it requires that one be open and vulnerable and let go of any need and desire to control the process. Yet at the same time, it is this very vulnerability and openness that allows us to see past danger, by bridging the gap beyond fear and the unknown, 'back to humanity and the building of genuine community'[32]. Being very aware of the necessity for creativity to be present within the work of peace-building, Lederach suggests that our creativity be nurtured, anticipating that the result of this may lead to significant insights as well as to an increased mindfulness of the perceptiveness of groups and individuals, '[o]ver time, I believe, we would keep our professions alive with a sense of wonder and awe, and we would replenish our work-as-craft with art and soul.'[33] In other words, while being part of the indivisibility of the 'whole', creativity is also an intrinsic part of us and if, rather than ignore it, we acknowledged this and nurtured it, we would be able to fully integrate it in our lives and make use of it.

Looking specifically at creativity in business, in *Welcome to the Creative Age* Earls discusses how creativity has been relegated to minor sectors of this serious and 'hard-nosed' world by being given no 'voting rights'. From this position of diminished value, the only input creativity is usually allowed to have is a superficial one of embellishment and design, which prevents it from interfering with 'a 'command and control' culture'[34] that's not well disposed to taking creative risk, because of course any sort of risk is seen as not being 'good' business sense. This is not only a great waste, but it's also a basic denial of our human nature. 'Creativity is our greatest inheritance', says Earls, and it enables us '[t]o refuse to believe that what is given is what is given. To believe that things might be otherwise. And then to make them so ... to make it a world ... we might want to live in.'[35] What he says is very empowering; by allowing our creativity to be part of the world of business we would be able to more clearly see what is not sustainable and does not serve us; this would then assist us to make creative changes to benefit us all – to turn this into a world we would be happy and proud to live in, a world encompassing all the wonder and brilliance we are capable of.

In following the direction of both Lederach's and Earls' reasoning, yet another way creativity could be described is as a potential ability we all have, both individually and collectively, to contribute to the survival, advancement and wellbeing of our society of human beings. Since a 'potential something' only becomes a reality when it's acknowledged and turned into action, this then clearly points to the usefulness, and indeed to our current vital need, of immersing ourselves fully in a holistic approach to whatever we're trying to understand. If we continue to limit acceptable comprehension to only the intellectual level we will persist in leaving much of our potential 'on the shelf' as it were, largely ignored and unused, as so many PhD theses are.

A pertinent question at this point might be: why then, if we are all inherently creative, does it appear that so few of us have been able to fulfil this potential to date? Are we still in the process of fulfilling it? Or have we perhaps not recognised that we have already fulfilled it? Or could it be that we're mostly ignoring our creativity? And might this be due to an underlying stubborn belief that true, or 'big', creativity is a rare gift possessed only by a few? In *Unlocking Creativity*, educator and author Robert Fisher lists some of the qualities exhibited by people in touch with their creativity[36]:

- they are flexible;

- they connect ideas;

- they are unorthodox;

- they show aesthetic taste;

- they are curious and inquisitive;

- they see similarities and differences;

- they question accepted ways of doing things.

These are also qualities that young children (before school age) use when playing. As children's play is largely self-generated, rather than directed, the process of creativity is clearly evident in it. Playing is the child's way of discovering all about life and being alive; young children approach most things in life through play. Totally absorbed by whatever they're involved in, there is a fresh sense of wonder constantly present in their interactions with their environment and they are not afraid to show their delight or displeasure, or indeed to drop some things altogether and move on to something else. What's more, they appear to do this seamlessly, by paying attention and following an inner motivation that only they can perceive.

When an adult, or older child, tries to teach a young child the rules to a specific game, these are invariably questioned and many creative attempts to alter them are made; if this isn't successful then the child may end up refusing to play, rather than acquiesce to play in a prescribed 'restrictive' manner. This was exactly what happened when my youngest was taught the game of Monopoly at the age of four, and I have seen it occur with other children as well. Though in these occasions, in order to justify a child's non-compliant behaviour, adults tell themselves that the child is obviously too young to understand and follow rules, this is a reductive assumption. It is more the case that young children recognise that there are no benefits to following these rules. They don't see the point of forgoing the open-ended exploration of possibilities in play, to instead accept a fixed approach where winning or losing are the only two alternatives; it doesn't make sense to them, and perhaps it shouldn't make sense to us either.

The sort of perspective that adults, perhaps unwittingly, try to impose on children when they teach them competitive games (and this includes all competitive sports children learn in schools) is so restrictive that a young child's viewpoint cannot possibly operate from it. Why trade a big picture with enough room for all to have fun and achieve fulfilment, for one where the majority have to lose in order for only one (or one team) to be the winner? Why stop playing with each other to instead play against each other? While a child may not be able to explain this as I have, their feelings about it are crystal clear. The win-or-lose way of playing is only useful to a culture of control that survives by keeping us separated.

From these beginnings, what happens as children grow up? While they may or may not have a supportive home environment, many of their traits are likely to be discouraged once they reach school age. Most of the creative qualities listed by Fisher are liable to be frowned upon at school, where students overtly displaying them are apt to be seen and labelled as 'disruptive', 'naughty', 'attention-seeking', and so on. Similarly, these characteristics would also be discouraged in most other institutions that value a hierarchical structure of control. Looking back to Damasio's explanation of creativity as a complex interplay of both nature and nurture, it follows that the potential for creativity can hence be affected by a myriad of factors that would see it flourish in an ideal environment, but be stifled in an overly prescriptive one.

The premise, which neuroplasticity confirms, is that we are all potentially open to our brains 'wiring' themselves in any of many possible ways, and we are also open for this process to be repeated over and over, in forever new ways. If, however, we are not in an environment that's holistically supportive of creativity (that is socially, culturally, physically and spiritually) then we may ignore our potential to be open to the new, and make do instead with prescribed 'wiring'. We would mostly choose to do this subconsciously so as to fit in and render ourselves acceptable. With repetitions of the same experience over time, this 'prescribed wiring' is reinforced in us and becomes rather rigid and more difficult to overcome. In fact, with endless repetitions it can feel like we're constantly following a script. Interestingly, this is the same with compulsions and obsessions, for in these cases, as Doidge states, '*the more you do it the more you want to do it; the less you do it, the less you want to do it.*'[37] This means that the more we conform, the more we want to (or need to) conform, and likewise the less we use our creative potential (for whatever reason), the harder it becomes for us to be open to being, or becoming, more connected to our creativity, and this is even if we long to do something different and new. It follows that from these practices and experience comes the belief that we're not creative.

Mihaly Csikszentmihalyi, leading researcher in positive psychology and creativity, and proponent of 'flow', has outlined that an environment supportive of creativity consists of 'openness, positive attitude to novelty, acceptance of personal differentness, and willingness to reward divergence.'[38] To this, Cropley added the very relevant 'absence of rigid sanctions against (harmless) mistakes'[39], which is a truly necessary condition for a society wanting to provide support for creativity. An environment, or a society, rich in these attributes, could easily foster the blossoming of creative qualities, like those listed by Fisher above. If open-ended inquiry were allowed to unfold, without having to follow unyielding directives about the 'right' way of doing something (anything), and without fear of repercussions, then people might feel encouraged (and allow themselves) to be curious, inquisitive and flexible. Similarly, an environment that encouraged people to question accepted ways of doing things, would also be accepting of personal diversity and have a positive attitude to novelty. On the other hand, a hierarchical institution or organisation, or indeed a hierarchical society, whose structure is therefore based on an inflexible linear model where policies are implemented and followed in a top-down manner, would not find it easy to be supportive of creativity. In fact, it would be difficult, if not downright impossible, for a hierarchical structure to be associated with anything that might truly nurture creativity.

Further inquiry into an environment congenial to creativity reveals that much of what it would be dependent upon is ultimately related to one or other, or both, of two main factors. These are time and trust, both of which I see as being intrinsically linked to creativity and to each other. In researching educational settings Fisher found that: 'Creativity thrives where there is time to explore, experiment and play with ideas.'[40] By considering this in the context of a congenial environment, it follows that an attitude of 'openness' (and therefore of trust) would prevail in regard to time as well; practically speaking, this simply means being more flexible with time. It's harder to imagine, however, where one might actually be able to find such a place that was flexible regarding time, especially given that modern society is constantly claiming to be extremely time-poor.

In a world where we are invariably reminded of just how important it is to plan to reach specific set goals (outcomes), it might seem counterproductive that we would also purposely stop ourselves from being able to achieve them, but that is precisely what occurs when we are inflexible with time. To explore this through a tangible example, we might look at time in relation to education. If we liken a desired outcome to the destination in a journey, which in the case of education would be a learning outcome, it makes sense that the journey would need to take all the time that was necessary to get to the destination. To do this, rather than setting timetables and deadlines of varying inflexibility (which is what mostly occurs in the majority of schools), a time plan could be structured to be open and above all respectful of the actual time it took the learners to learn; importantly, this would not always mean that more time would be required but indeed might also mean that less time would be needed to learn. When the focus is mainly on the outcome, it is like wanting to get across a 'finishing line' in a race, no matter what. While not many athletes would even get to the finishing line if they neglected to pay attention to their journey towards it, treating learning in such a linear way renders it very flimsy, making whatever one purportedly learnt at school not easy to remember. Rather than on the outcome, if we instead shifted the focus more on the process of learning – which is where the living and the creating happens – then the topics of study might be allowed to develop according to students' interests and abilities, and this would result in a very different long-term retention of what was learnt.

In setting out to reach a goal, or achieve a learning outcome, a teacher and class of students would journey through unknown territory. This is the process of learning, which is unknown because although it can be planned for, it cannot exactly be predicted nor controlled how this plan will unfold. Although there is much potential for learning, the unknown can be the cause of anxieties and fear; however, it can also elicit a sense of excitement and adventure. Whether the unknown is faced with excitement or with fearfulness largely depends on attitude, as illustrated in the story of the house of mirrors, told above. Consciously harnessing creativity can help us to face the unknown with a positive outlook. Neuroscience considers creativity as the most complex function of human beings, one that has especially evolved to provide us with a 'vision of novel contexts'[41], so that we might give meaning to what we encounter in life and find usefulness in what we discover. Yet in order to make use of their creativity on their journey, the teacher and students in our example would need to be provided with a supportive environment. This is where trust comes in since, together with time, trust is needed to maintain an open perspective.

By journeying through the process of learning (the unknown territory) with a conscious attitude of creativity, this teacher and students might ultimately find what they learnt to be different to what was planned, in other words, the outcome could change. It is vital to be open to this possibility, because in fact the unplanned-for learning may be even greater and of more benefit than the planned-for learning would've been. *The thing that I like about having an idea that you build your creativity on is that your little seed not only grows, but it might grow in a direction you never planned it to, but that is really, really, positive for the students* (educator). This is because as the learning journey changes from what was originally planned, often in response to all sorts of unexpected contexts and dynamics, an attitude of creativity (being holistic) will ensure that the outcome is adapted to the best possible learning given the circumstances. Thus the trust that is spoken of here is mainly trust in our own creative process, and having this trust often simply means being able to overcome being 'frozen', and prevented from making progress, by the fear of making 'mistakes'.

I have found that there is a direct connection between how long it takes me to open to an attitude of creativity, in regard to whatever I am doing, and the trust I invest in the activity. I'm also able to recognise when I'm wholly connected to my creativity because that's when I experience what Csikszentmihalyi calls 'flow' – a feeling of being outside, or beyond, time and totally immersed in and enjoying what I'm doing[42]. What occurs for me is that the more I trust myself and what I do, then the more trust I feel and the less time it takes me to open to the creative process, which is to *be* creative and let myself go to being in the 'flow'. Being 'in flow' seems to sharpen all my senses, including my sense of inner vision, and I find as a result that I'm able to be open to and trusting of my subconscious. It's as if I were part of a complex juggling act, with my conscious mind ready and able to catch everything that my subconscious throws to me, which is all I need for whatever I'm doing. On the other hand, the less I trust myself the more uncertain I become, and this affects the ease with which I can connect to my creativity. I have found whenever I've felt mistrust, anxiety and doubt, that this has made me disconnect and feel completely locked away from my creativity, and despairing of ever being able to reach it again.

If we truly believed that we are creative beings, then creativity would be a natural perspective for us to have and we would be familiar with operating from it. Sadly, the reality we inhabit in this world seems to indicate that many of us still doubt that we have an innate creative potential, despite all the evidence pointing to this. According to psychologists David Fontana and Ingrid Slack, this lack of trust in our abilities is due to the constant criticism that we received as children, where adult judgement taught us to place little to no value on activities that engaged our creativity, like self-directed play. Unfortunately, this has remained an ongoing practice, as children are still being distanced from their creative abilities through their education[43]. What's more, this not only prevents children (who then grow into the adults we are) from fully expressing their creativity, but as Fontana & Slack alert us it is also deeply injurious to their psyche:

> The mind feels restless and unfulfilled, searching for something without knowing quite what it is. There is a feeling that some undefined potential is going to waste, and that something precious is being denied the light of day.[44]

From these experiences, it is easy to feel hopelessness, which then leads us to not trust ourselves, and further develops in us the habit of holding back from flowing with our creativity; eventually many of us end up damming it in some deep and dark recess of our psyche, to which we may even lose the key. Then inevitably, because we haven't experienced what it feels like to be creative for what seems like a lifetime (except in vague memories of a distant childhood), we stop believing that we're actually creative. Through the value judgement imposed by our hierarchically structured education, we have been very successfully taught to repress our innate urge to be creative, and so we've learnt not to trust our creativity, which in most cases we don't even recognise as something that's intrinsic to us. Trust is a curious concept; while we don't usually give much thought to being trusting when we're following rules, policies, or specific procedures set out by the hierarchical structures in our lives, however, that is exactly what we're doing. We may think that we're merely complying with requirements, but in fact, we are at the same time placing our trust in them so completely that it doesn't even cross our mind to question any facet of the procedures we are following. We trust them blindly and we rely on them totally, all the more so because we are not in the habit of being self-reliant or trusting ourselves.

The more unquestioningly we follow exterior structures that are laid out for us, the less likely we are to trust ourselves, and this stops us from connecting to creativity. Bohm observes that 'what we learn as children, from parents, teachers, friends, and society in general, is to have a conformist, imitative, mechanical state of mind.'[45] Even those who rebel against this are often trapped into 'projecting an opposing or contrary set of ideals ... [b]ut evidently such conformity is also not creative.'[46] By giving in to the pressure to conform that we're faced with from childhood, we basically end up allowing an imposed order to take over our minds, and this order precludes creativity. I have named this way of perceiving *institutionalised perception*, and it is the perception that results from conforming to the way institutions dictate we should behave, ways that are based on accepting the hierarchical viewpoint of our society while disregarding everything else. In the next chapter, I delve into a more thorough explanation of this way of perceiving.

Robinson tells us that those in the business sector are frustrated with an education system that pushes conformity; he's been told that people going through education and joining the workforce seem to be incapable of thinking 'outside the box', or out of a straight line.[47] Yet this has been caused by the strict adherence to the traditional hierarchical corporate/managerial model that has reinforced conformity to an extreme point, and indeed education systems worldwide have but set out to emulate this.

In his conclusions to *Welcome to the Creative Age*, Earls discusses how it's the way that companies are structured for control that stifles creativity:

... we love specialization, hierarchies, department siloes and serial processes, which reinforce these structures of control ... we have to remove these structures in order to 'network' our companies properly ... Without these changes, we cannot create a work environment that gets the most from our people or gives them the most rewarding experience. Without these changes, we cannot build a Creative Age company, a place where people want to work.[48]

However, to be able to make the structural changes Earls suggests, we need to become conscious that we live in a world ruled by a hierarchical structure that is so central to our way of life that we no longer even 'see' it, taking all that comes from it as totally 'normal'. It is this hierarchical structure that instils in us the *institutionalised perception* I have discussed, which is then merely reflected in our society in countless ways, including by many of the companies or workplaces where we make a living. This structure is called patriarchy. In order to begin to understand patriarchy, much more exploration and uncovering is needed; over the next two chapters I look at and discuss this complex topic, which is laden with controversy and emotional baggage, as dispassionately as possible.

We are constantly being told that the world needs leaders, and leadership courses, seminars and workshops are frequently and copiously offered worldwide. This belief is one that is inherent to growing up within hierarchical structures – leaders are the ones that give the directions, from their placement at the top of the hierarchy, which are then followed by all those below them. Ian Plowman, an evolutionary psychologist and social researcher, tells us that '[l]eaders discourage creativity, but they don't even realise they're doing it.'[49] Those we recognise as leaders are people who invariably hold positions of responsibility, and hand in hand with responsibility is a reasonable amount of power. Interestingly Plowman also adds, '[a]ll high-ranking persons are generally driven by a need for power ... and the need for power is in direct contradiction with the ability to be creative.'[50]

Though this is a generalisation, and there are usually many exceptions to generalisations, what Plowman says nonetheless makes sense. While people in touch with their creativity naturally thrive from the interaction with like-minded others, leaders (or at least those who particularly identify themselves as such, and enjoy wielding their power) are not likely to be very interested in creativity. What leaders seem to want ranges from simply being the ones who others follow and look up to, to a yearning for glory and adulation, with this appealing especially to those with narcissistic tendencies. Interestingly, research on narcissists has found that they're intrinsically attracted to leadership and highly pressured jobs. Indeed, author of *Emotional Intelligence* and *Social Intelligence*, Daniel Goleman, tells us that our society has quite a number of narcissistic CEOs.[51] Condoning narcissistic behaviour even to a minor degree undermines creativity as much as demanding conformity does. And this again perpetuates the hierarchical order, as Goleman confirms: 'Unrealistic self-inflation comes more readily in cultures that encourage individualistic striving rather than shared success.'[52]

Although narcissistic behaviour can include charm, flamboyant expression and creative ideas, the main difference between this and 'real' creativity is that the 'surface' creativity of narcissism is unable to share (or even include) the context of the big picture, but rather it is aimed at self-promotion within a hierarchical structure. As such it's simply meant to impress others quickly for self-gain; true creativity, on the other hand, is not about making an impression but more about having a lasting and positive transformative effect in the context of the business project being undertaken. A popular notion in business has been that there is somehow a need for business people to have some sort of narcissistic self-centredness in order to survive the ordeals of setting up and being in business.[53] This view is incredibly narrow; rather than acquiescing to this self-limiting 'need', by considering the bigger picture a business could instead be set up to creatively turn these 'ordeals' into adventures.

Indeed, business ventures grounded in the context of the whole – of the self interconnected to others and to the environment – would be more likely to attract both clients and partners with genuine creative interests, and this would then result in more sustainable and successful enterprises. An article in the Harvard Business News in December 2012, titled 'Today's Best Companies are Horizontally Integrated', explains how successful businesses are those able to provide more satisfying experiences for their clients.[54] Delivering this, however, seems to be beyond the capability of most companies due to their internal structures – hierarchical and compartmentalised with 'cultures that do not value collaboration.'[55] Sohrab Vossoughi, the author of this article, in 1984 founded Ziba Design – an international innovation and design consultancy. In the article, he further elucidates that calling managers '*integrators* is to encourage collaborative behavior ... a messy, ambiguous undertaking.'[56]

If we look again at the qualities of those in touch with their creativity, we can see how being curious, inquisitive, and questioning of the accepted ways of doing things would make it difficult for these people to be led into anything that they didn't actually want to do or be a part of. Furthermore, they would not be able to be easily controlled, as they wouldn't want to be 'team players' if they didn't agree with what was being asked of them. They would instead want to have an input into the things they were involved in, with this making them negotiators rather than followers, as well as more self-reliant and able to see many different possibilities. A leader interested in power would want to discourage these qualities, as they are not the ideal qualities of followers. On the other hand, a creative leader, for whom 'facilitator' (or even *integrator*) would be a better term, would understand the creative needs of self-reliant people, and instead of controlling them would support them.

True facilitators would be constantly operating from an attitude of creativity and trust, and they would implement a constructive and creative form of decision-making together with those they were facilitating; this would form an egalitarian system from which could flow positive action able to establish positive changes. According to Bohm, such a creative state of mind is where:

> ... interest in what is being done is wholehearted and total, like that of a young child ... always open to learning what is new, to perceiving new differences and new similarities, leading to new orders and structures, rather than always tending to impose familiar orders and structures in the field of what is seen ... This kind of action of the creative state of mind is impossible if one is limited by narrow and petty aims, such as security [certainty and the avoidance of risk], furthering of personal ambition, glorification of the individual or the state...[57]

We have all experienced what it is like to be in a creative state of mind (at least as young children); we now need to consciously return to it and claim it as the birthright we all share.

* * * * * * * * * * * * * * *

REVIEWING THE JOURNEY OF CHAPTER ONE

This chapter begins with the explanation (both mine and others') that creativity is too complex a concept to be defined simplistically or rigidly, or even elaborately. No matter how involved a definition of creativity one is prepared to give, it is still likely to leave out some aspect of how creativity is seen and experienced by different people.

By starting from one's own meaning of creativity and sharing this in an open dialogue, a fuller understanding of creativity can gradually be garnered. This is especially the case because creativity is best viewed from a holistic perspective, being one of the indivisible 'things' that Bohm refers to. Analysing, by dividing and grouping, what is indivisible, causes fragmentation and works against improving comprehension. The example I give here is the dividing of creativity into 'big' and 'small' creativity, which is shown to be reductive to the overall understanding of creativity. It is not predictable how something as complex as creativity will develop in different people and situations, so what may for some be 'big' creativity – defined as 'when something of enduring value is contributed to an existing body of knowledge, thereby transforming it'[58] – might be only 'small' creativity for others, and vice versa.

Identifying theories by whatever they are meant to explain invariably ends up making the theory more important than what it was supposed to clarify. In other words, the reality of the concept, 'thing', or process can no longer be seen without the theory that was used to explain it. With this substitution trick, rather than simplifying the understanding of the process, or 'thing', it is trying to explain, the 'theory' ends up obscuring it and rendering it inaccessible. Despite this, the gathering of necessary evidence to support theories as the way to make sense of the world is something that became paramount some four hundred years ago with the 'rise of reason'[59]. This has served to validate patriarchy's methods of ruling by dividing and grouping according to an order of hierarchical values. Internalising this – this *'institutionalised perception'* – as 'the way' to perceive the world leaves little room for creativity or for the connections to wholeness that creativity requires.

That is why so many adults don't believe themselves to be creative.

To counteract the demoralising effect of no longer believing in an intrinsic part of ourselves, we end up placing our trust in methods and other prescriptive ways that we are taught, which we would otherwise not necessarily trust, while it is really trust in ourselves and in our abilities that we need. Trust is something that needs time to be acquired and built on; trust and time both facilitate the nurturing of creativity to such an extent that they could be said to be catalysts for its development.

Creativity has been recognised as being important in diverse fields of study and human endeavour, from reconciliation to business, education to environmental sustainability. This has made it the subject of many books, articles and discussions, and we are often said to be living in, or be approaching, the 'Creative Age'. It is not surprising that creativity generates so much interest, as it's intrinsic to us. Above all, I see creativity as being an underlying attitude in us that can, if we allow it to guide our perception, *become a way of 'being' in the world, as well as a way of seeing.* To reach this state, which Bohm calls 'the creative state of mind'[60], we have to let go of our preconceptions, which the *institutionalised perception* has led us to internalise through our socialisation and education, and choose instead to actively nurture our creativity by cultivating the qualities that can help us to do this.

Chapter Two

STEPPING OUT AS THE SELF

It is strange to be here. The mystery never leaves you alone. ... Everyone is an artist. Each person brings sound out of silence and coaxes the invisible to become visible.[1]

–John O'Donohue

In recognising that creativity is at the heart of transformation I began a journey, one that I'm still travelling. Over this time, my understanding of creativity has been crystallising before me as a concept that's becoming ever clearer and more in focus. The experience of nurturing my own creativity has helped me to see myself from a wider perspective, and this has also led me to a better understanding of some of the causes for the inner discord and conflicts that have hindered my self-awareness. As a result, I have gained a more holistic knowing of who I am, including who I emotionally, spiritually and physically feel and sense myself to be, as well as of who I intellectually believe myself to be. What happened was that I actually regained this awareness and then began to expand on it, given that in retrospect I realised that this had already begun to develop within me as a young child. This was prior to years of socialisation in formal schooling and other institutions I frequented. It was in my dealings with these institutions that, led by a natural desire to belong, I more or less conformed to expectations, and in doing so concealed for a time my holistic awareness of myself.

Centring the awareness of myself (of my sense of identity) on the wholeness that I am, and feel myself to be, is an immense shift to how I used to relate to myself.

Primarily, it means that I no longer explicitly identify with the many roles with which I have been labelled: consumer, mother, wife, teacher, daughter, sister, electoral constituent, patient, and so on. Though it might seem 'natural' and 'logical' to label ourselves with the roles that we acquire through the definitions of our relationships and connections, and which therefore play such a big part in our lives, it is the over-identifying with them that limits how we relate to ourselves. This is especially true if we also allow the socially accepted values of these roles to impact on our self-worth and direct how we live. While we might not be aware of this as something we actually do, it nonetheless appears to be a matter-of-fact occurrence in our specifically hierarchical society.

To better explain this, and because it is vital to understand what can so drastically 'freeze' our creativity, some deep digging and uncovering needs to be done. Our hierarchical way of living, that thousands of years of practice has turned 'normal' for us, needs to be revealed so that we might see it in a new light. This means taking a good look at 'patriarchy' – the particular hierarchy we live by that gets hidden in plain sight, like an elephant in the room that nobody will mention, yet at the same time carefully avoids even accidentally bumping into.

Discussing patriarchy is a complex undertaking, which is made even more difficult as all too often 'man', 'male', and 'masculine' have been used as common substitutions for it, as if it were simply a gender-based issue. Although the absolute rule of the father – the senior male – is the original meaning of the term patriarchy, it is indeed quite obvious that men, as well as women, have also been oppressed by it, and are still being oppressed by it. Ecotheologian and cultural historian Thomas Berry points out, in 'Patriarchy: A New Interpretation of History' (where he draws from multiple works of feminism, ecology and ecofeminism), that patriarchal institutions which control our way of life 'have become progressively virulent in their destructive powers, until presently they are bringing about the closing down of all the basic life systems of the planet.'[2]

Though Berry makes a very valid point, I find this statement so extreme that it raises in me deep emotions of fear and anger. While these emotions are warranted given what is at stake, they are so strong that they overwhelm me to the point that I find myself unable to react usefully. My gut feeling is to lash out and smite these patriarchal institutions that are threatening our very existence – I want them gone. Yet looking at the current occurrences that make the daily news around the world, as well as the ongoing discussions in many different circles, from social media to talking over dinner, it seems that many people are allowing themselves to get worked up about a myriad of different things and then letting the same sorts of violent feelings as mine drive their conversations and actions. Though this could at times be thought of as justified and often feels satisfying, all evidence shows that it only leads to more cycles of endless fighting, misunderstanding and frustration. This is where holistic and creative ways of looking at things, so as to better understand them, are more useful.

By creatively making use of what's more accessible, analogies can help us comprehend things that are too big for us to otherwise relate to. In this case, an analogy can better enable us to see what the workings of patriarchy have wrought in the world: imagine awakening, after a particularly mad dress-up party had got out of hand, and was still ongoing, to find that our home had been totally trashed by many of the 'grown-ups'. This would be quite a shock, especially given the expectation that the 'grown-ups' would be responsible and caring ones who would look after things, yet we would still need to clean, fix, throw out, rebuild, and do anything else that needed to be done. Because ultimately what would matter, what would drive us to making our home habitable again, would be that it is *our home*. We would want, and indeed need, to live in it, and so we would want and need it to be the best that we could make it – an environment conducive to the sort of living we wanted – all the more so because this would also free us to pursue our creativity. To be able to do this, we would need to be willing to look and clearly see all the mess and damage that had been made as well as understand its context (the bigger picture) – like who had done this – so as to prevent any further damage from occurring. This action of looking deeply at 'what is' is the best choice we could make, better than denying it and living with it, or ignoring it by going to live in the cubby or the shed, or even focusing on who was to blame with the intention of punishing or fighting them; none of these latter options would be very successful in fixing any of the damage done, nor in restoring harmony.

Currently in the world (our huge home where we live with all the people in the world, and many other living beings) there seems to be a combination of all three of these reactions going on – denying, ignoring and blaming. These reactions are also most likely due to the type of world that patriarchy's institutions have built, which according to Berry is one that is inherently tragic; from this, the dawning of understanding 'that so much ...has been misdirected, alienating, and destructive beyond anything previously known in human history is a bitter moment indeed.'[3] The thing with an analogy is not to take it too far, since it is simply meant to be a story of sorts that helps to provide us with greater comprehension. In order to build a bridge to a broader and fuller understanding of 'patriarchy', I give many explanations of it throughout this book. In this, my guiding focus is on what its significance has been, and still is, to both the nurturing of creativity and to my own journey of transformation.

In a history that is principally about who has gained dominion over whom throughout the ages, patriarchy is the hierarchical 'tradition' that has been instrumental in setting the rules of 'civilised' society, as such this has resulted in a patriarchal culture that champions patriarchal ideals – mainly those of 'conquest and dominion'[4]. These ideals, and the rules that have come from them, have become so ingrained and accepted as being normal that they are no longer recognised as having stemmed from patriarchy, a fact that's strengthened by patriarchy not often being named in current times. As feminist philosopher and theologian Mary Daly points out, starting from: 'the late nineties ... [the] nonnaming of patriarchy narrowed vision, so that connections couldn't be seen.'[5] When something we live with constantly is not explicitly talked about or recognised, it tends to fade from consciousness and becomes tacit. This makes people assume that it has always been present and is therefore beyond questioning, or even worse that it is an inherent trait of 'human nature' that we cannot change; either way, it will exert even more influence on us, without us even realising it.

In *Relating Narratives*, philosopher Adriana Cavarero reminds us that this is the tradition that loves 'the abstract and its definitory logic'[6]. In other words, it is through the patriarchal tradition that the use of labels, which define and create mental constructs, has become widespread. This makes sense, as it's the emphasising of borders, as well as statuses, mandates, authority, and conformity that together maintain the patriarchal tradition. On an individual level, this encourages a focus on the hierarchical values of the roles that one is labelled with, which then makes it commonplace to disregard the wholeness of 'who' one actually is.

The patriarchal tradition is a hierarchical system of social order that is insidiously present in our everyday life. If we pause and consider the meaning of this for a moment, we will realise that hierarchies are in fact present in almost every facet of our social life. In addition, they are reflected in the amounts of money people earn, and in the ways they earn it. All our institutions – from schools to nursing homes, from our businesses to our religions, to our political structures and so on – are all specifically hierarchical. In most cases, a hierarchy is also present within our families and extended families. Scholar, teacher, and writer Dale Spender speaks of this hierarchical system of social order in *Man Made Language*:

> ... patriarchy is also a frame of reference, a particular way of classifying and organizing the objects and events of this world; it is a form of 'order' which patterns our existence (Cora Kaplan, 1976, refers to it as 'patriarchal order').[7]

According to this 'patriarchal order', everything and everyone is placed very specifically, so that there is a constant perception of an order where those who are 'better', 'greater', 'richer', 'worse', 'lesser', 'poorer' and so on, can be easily recognised. These comparisons are made according to the different values assigned to, and so perceived in, the roles that individuals are identified with. For example, surgeons, medical practitioners and dentists, are considered to be higher in the hierarchy than home cleaners and babysitters, and this is reflected in how much money they earn for their work (an amount which differs greatly even when the recouping of educational costs is taken into account) as well as in the prestige of the social status they are assigned. This is interesting and warrants some consideration, since although it could be argued that this monetary return relates to the responsibility and liability attached to their different roles, nonetheless all of these roles carry considerable responsibility, as all of them are actually supportive of people's health and wellbeing. While surgeons, medical practitioners and dentists are commonly associated with health and wellbeing, babysitters and cleaners are instrumental to preventing (and/or relieving) stress by providing people with a clean environment, and recovery time from the often tiring task of attending to the needs of children. Although as the saying goes 'prevention is better than cure', in our society this appears to be rarely backed by monetary value.

With 'logic' having been revered since the time of the Greeks and 'reason' championed since the Enlightenment, it is the roles linked to the 'rational' use of the mind that have been placed at the top of the hierarchy and assigned the highest values, with this also equating to monetary value. Those aspects of self that are given roles at the bottom of the hierarchy are those too difficult to be rationally understood and/or explained and controlled. Among these are: our inherent creativity, intuition, humour, emotions, the body (unless it is being looked at medically, as within illness diagnosis), playfulness, and many unpaid (or underpaid) roles that include caring and nurturing, and so on. Interestingly, there is also the idea that something can be 'invaluable', meaning that it is too valuable to have monetary value assigned to it. While this prevents the invaluable things (like nature, a healthy environment, loving carers, and so on) from receiving any monetary recognition at all, it also often means that they are greatly devalued and disregarded, or taken for granted.

Looking at what CEOs earn confirms this hierarchical division; in 2007 the ratio of average CEO remuneration to average salary in the USA was deemed as having increased to 275 to 1 from around 35 to 1 in 1978[8]. This information came from an article written for *Time* magazine in 2010, by Christopher Hayes, called 'The Twilight of the Elites'; Hayes then went on to write a book by the same name that was published in 2012. Yet by 2018, which was the first year in the USA when publicly listed corporations were required to reveal the ratio of their CEO to average worker pay, the 25th annual *Executive Excess* report (published by the Institute for Policy Studies in Washington DC) reported that this ratio was as high as 339 to 1 (as gained from the first 225 U.S. companies to release this information)[9]. What applies to American CEOs is likely to apply to all CEOs, since we live in a global economy, especially at the CEO level, with multinationals being their main employers.

At face value, these figures are well and truly beyond comprehension, particularly when one considers that even many of the people living in the same countries as these CEOs (let alone in third world countries) are struggling to survive from day to day and that homelessness in our Western societies is ever increasing. This gap between a CEO's and a waged employee's yearly earnings, however, begins to make more sense when it is looked at through the lens of the hierarchical value placement in our system of social order. As already mentioned, everything in this patriarchal system is given a specific, and often speculative, monetary value: home environment, education, food, health care, entertainment, and so on, with this majorly influencing what people can access, as well as how they are perceived because of what they can access. Inevitably this also has an impact on how people see and judge themselves, since when so much in life seems to depend on one's roles it becomes easy to strongly identify with the values that these roles are hierarchically deemed to have. This includes what opportunities are available, but even more importantly the respect or lack of respect that one is treated with, which directly influences one's self-worth.

When it comes to the roles with which this order defines me, I fulfil the majority of them in most of the expected ways; this is because many of these roles refer to the relationships I'm in, like daughter, sister, wife and mother. However, what became different for me once I began to nurture my creativity is that I stopped allowing these roles to fragment my perception of myself; this was something that for a long time I wasn't even aware I had been doing, yet the effects of it were stultifying (I discuss this in more detail in Chapters Four and Five). In other words, I no longer accept, or maintain, the constructed boundaries that delineate each of 'my roles', nor do I accept their professed value.

Rather than allowing my roles to define me, I see them as forming an interconnected web of different contexts. These contexts then become for me 'performative spaces' that my body and *beingness* can animate from the depth of my centre. Effectively I am 'playing' these roles, and inhabiting these performative spaces. The main difference between this perception of myself to one that accepts the labels and values of roles is that rather than allowing the roles and their attached hierarchical value (as dictated by any outside authority) to continue to identify me, I instead identify myself as being *whole*, and it's this *whole me* who plays the roles I choose, in the way I choose. Though this difference may seem subtle, it is very deep and has far-reaching consequences. Seeing myself in this way has made quite an impact on me; its most significant effect being that this holistic self-perception has enabled me to nurture my creativity, something that would hardly have been possible through a fragmented self-perception induced by labels.

Seeing myself as whole means that I primarily identify with my '*beingness*' – my awareness of being – that (as explained in the Introduction) I experience and see as the continuity of myself as a living being. As well as all the aspects of myself that I am aware of, my *beingness* also includes those that I'm not conscious of, and since these latter ones are nonetheless a part of me, I acknowledge that one day I may become aware of them. In this way, my sense of *'beingness'* is very close to what Jung refers to as the 'Self', described 'as the totality of the whole psyche ... an inner guiding factor that is different from the conscious personality.'[10] In addition, I experience my *beingness* as intrinsically connected to my physical sentient body. This is not necessarily a common experience, given that our patriarchal society regularly urges us to separate from our body. We are guided and encouraged to follow 'expert' opinions to look after our bodies, which includes what we feed them, how much rest and exercise we give them, and how to cure any ailments they might suffer. Instead of paying heed to this, in identifying with a *beingness/* body fusion that makes me aware of my holistic self, I'm better able to both become aware of and respond to my body's needs as they arise. In *The Spell of the Sensuous,* cultural ecologist and philosopher David Abram looks in-depth at the concept of the self as connected to the body, through the philosophy of Merleau-Ponty:

> If this body is my very presence in the world, if it is the body that alone enables me to enter into relations with other presences ... if without this body in other words, there would be no possibility of experience – then the body itself is the true subject of experience. Merleau-Ponty begins, then, by identifying the subject – the experiencing "self" – with the bodily organism. ... without this body ... you could neither speak nor hear another's voice. Nor could you have anything to speak about, or even to reflect on, or to think, since without any contact ... any glimmer of sensory experience, there could be nothing to question or to know. *The living body is thus the very possibility of contact, not just with others but with oneself* [my emphasis] - ... Merleau-Ponty invites us to recognise, at the heart of even our most abstract cogitations, the sensuous and sentient life of the body itself.[11]

Here Abram thoroughly explains what Merleau-Ponty is saying – that it is the corporeal reality of the body which, by bringing together all that the body perceives through its sensing abilities, allows for the abstractions of thought and reflection to be made possible. Being aware of this necessitates a holistic perspective of the self.

Yielding to a fragmented self-perception, including the commonly accepted fundamental division into 'subject' for our thinking conscious minds, and 'object' for our corporeal sensing bodies, limits us to also perceiving the world around us as fragmented. It is through this practice that a young child is taught about 'opposites', and so starts making sense of the world through the use of common opposite pairs – light/dark, good/evil, tall/short, happy/sad, or as Hélène Cixous, feminist philosopher and writer, refers to them: 'dual, *hierarchized* oppositions ... Wherever an ordering intervenes, a law organizes the thinkable by ... oppositions.'[12] This 'universal' use of ordered opposites has resulted in a perspective driven by the hierarchical values of patriarchy that is rigidly myopic.

The dichotomous perspective of 'oppositions' doesn't take into consideration the reality of 'what actually is' – the more or less gradual scale of increase or decrease between two extreme opposites; yet it is nonetheless the perspective that most social structures in the world function from, and as such it forms the basis for the majority of institutional decisions regardless of how central these decisions might be. An example of this is how in education most exams have a pass/fail cut-off line, whereby individuals achieving scores on one side of this line are 'passed' while those achieving scores on the other side of it are 'failed', yet all the while it is quite clear that the scores just either side of the line are very close. In the majority of cases, the pass/fail results are so absolute that they can completely change the future of individuals, with untold societal repercussions of which we might remain quite unaware. Whenever I have pointed this out, the answer has invariably been: 'There has to be a cut-off line'. Why does there have to be a cut-off line? And why are exams – artificial situations where questions have to be answered within a specified amount of time – the way our Western society has chosen to ascertain whether someone is capable of doing something? I have met many students who are so negatively affected by exams that the resulting stress severely hampers their knowledge recall as well as other vital abilities; as a consequence, while the implication is that exams will find the 'best person for the job', they could be doing the very opposite.

In our prevailing societal perspective, for one of the pairs of opposites to be 'right' the other must be shown to be 'wrong' (as in the pass/fail example in exams). The result of this, as physicist David Bohm stated back in 1980, is that 'each individual human being has been fragmented into a large number of separate and conflicting compartments ... to such an extent that it is generally accepted that some degree of neurosis is inevitable ...'[13]. Not surprisingly this propensity to neurosis has grown and worsened since then, with depression being considered the main cause of both physical and mental disability worldwide[14].

In *Linked: How Everything is Connected to Everything Else and What it Means for Business, Science, and Everyday Life*, physicist Albert-László Barabási sheds some light on how our obsession with detailed fragments has led us to this predicament:

> Reductionism was the driving force behind much of the twentieth century scientific research. To comprehend nature, it tells us, we first must decipher its components. The assumption is that once we understand the parts, it will be easy to grasp the whole. Divide and conquer; the devil is in the details. ... Now we are close to knowing just about everything there is to know about the pieces. But we are as far as we have ever been from understanding nature as a whole. Indeed, the reassembly turned out to be much harder than scientists anticipated.[15]

'Divide and conquer' sounds like a maxim more suited to warfare than to the understanding of the nature of which we are a part. For as philosopher, writer, and speaker Alan Watts put it, '[t]he hostile attitude of conquering nature ignores the basic interdependence of all things and events—that the world beyond the skin is actually an extension of our own bodies—'[16]. To better understand his words, we need to take a closer look at the perspective, or point of view, which enables me to see and experience myself as being *whole*. This is a perspective closely connected to the nurturing of creativity, as it both enables it and is in turn engendered by it. It is the perspective from which I'm writing this book; it's a holistic perspective, a holistic approach. But what does that actually mean?

A holistic approach is quite different to the analytical/hierarchical combination that has been (and still is) largely the preferred approach in most non-fiction writing, from academic research to business literature, governmental texts, and even many self-help books. While an analytical approach can be very useful for arriving at the 'heart' of whatever is being looked at, when used in conjunction with a patriarchal perception of value (as explained earlier), this approach not only examines what is being discussed through inspection and dissection, but also separates what has been cut up and then firmly excludes some parts while setting up boundaries around others to render them more valuable, or elite.

In *On Creativity*, Bohm explains this analytical process by connecting the occurrence of fragmentation to how we use thought and language, for although:

> ... there is a real need for thought and language momentarily to focus attention on one thing or another, as the occasion demands ... [however,] when each such thing is regarded as separately existent and essentially independent of the broader context of the whole in which it has its origin, its sustenance, and its ultimate dissolution, then one is no longer merely focusing attention, but, rather one is engaged in breaking the field of awareness into disjoint parts, whose deep unity can no longer be perceived.[17]

There is nothing wrong with an analytical approach that is in context; a holistic approach can then make use of it, and both are needed to make sense of the world. It is through the exclusive use of an analytical focus that is kept separate and disconnected that our awareness is fragmented; instead, once we've focused on a specific part, we need to 'snap' back to seeing the whole, like we would do in completing a jigsaw puzzle. A holistic approach looks at the whole picture, with its myriads of parts, and sees the connections because they are inherent to the meaning of the picture, and to what the picture is. A holistic approach includes all that it can see by integrating parts together, but at the same time, it is also aware that there is still much that it can't see and remains open so that what cannot be seen might gradually become known, no matter how long this may take.

An example of how these different approaches would work in a real-life situation would be looking at the study of life in an environment that's not easily observable (such as marine life). In this, an analytical/hierarchical approach would be unlikely to disapprove of removing creatures from their environment (by putting them in aquariums) to study them, and perhaps even dissecting them to try and work out how they function, or pinning them to boards (as many, now extinct, butterflies have been) just to classify them. A holistic approach, however, understanding that the most important 'wholeness' about living things is that they are alive (even though it cannot easily see where this comes from), would observe them in their natural habitat, taking into account as many different contexts as it could in the given circumstances of the study. What makes a holistic approach even more useful, as author and speaker Daniel Pink points out in quoting Denning in *A Whole New Mind*, is that it doesn't do away with the analytical approach. 'Storytelling doesn't replace analytical thinking ... it supplements it by enabling us to imagine new perspectives and new worlds ... Abstract analysis is easier to understand when seen through the lens of a well-chosen story.'[18] It is by being open and inclusive that a holistic approach is therefore also inclusive of abstract analysis.

Even though we can't totally perceive something's wholeness – like not being able to physically see the whole of a tree (or whatever else we're looking at), since we can only see one side at the time – we can nonetheless perceive its wholeness through an inner storehouse of knowledge, an inner 'knowingness'. This inner knowingness helps us to perceive wholeness by critically making use of our experience, while at the same time also utilising creativity and imagination to communicate its findings to us. Because we can imagine it, we can in effect 'see' the whole tree even while seeing only a part of it; we trust our knowingness of a tree because it is connected to our experience of a tree. In other words, the more trees we've seen from different views and angles, the more readily those experiences help us to perceive the tree we're viewing as being whole. It is this holistic process – a complex combination of both analysis and creativity – that allows us to tell the difference between a real tree and one that's been constructed to be part of a theatrical set.

Gestalt psychology explains this very process of perception. Developed by German psychologists in the early 1900s, the reasoning behind Gestalt psychology is that the nature of the parts is secondary to the whole, because it's the whole that determines the nature of the parts in the first place:

> Gestalt psychology ... accentuates concepts like emergent properties, holism, and context. In the 30s and 40s [it] was applied to visual perception ... to investigate the global and holistic processes involved in perceiving structure in the environment ... [and] to explain ... how [it is that] we perceive *parts* of objects and form *whole* objects on the basis of these.[19]

It is through the familiar experience of ourselves as 'whole' – the daily combination of our mental, emotional and bodily functions working together in concert – that we are able to utilise a holistic perspective to perceive the whole of whatever we're looking at. That is to say, our ability to perceive the whole could be explained as a subconscious extension to our experience of being whole – we live in a holistic universe.

Though complex, this 'whole picture approach' process of perception isn't difficult for us, and takes us very little time to navigate; being as familiar to us as breathing and eating, it doesn't have to be consciously broken down into its component steps (many of which happen simultaneously) for us to make use of it. In fact, it is instead the breaking down (or fragmenting) of this process into separate steps, like the description of viewing a tree given earlier, that actually makes both the understanding and telling of it more difficult. A holistic perspective allows for deep understanding as it is consistent with who we are, the 'self' as a whole person – an inherent *beingness* extended through the physical body in such a way that it presents, and 'is', a continuous whole. This is especially important because, as already mentioned, within the hierarchical order we live in (patriarchy) the 'self' has been fragmented into many different hierarchized roles and functions.

In our society, rather than discussing and considering people as whole beings, for all sorts of decisions that have to be made, it is particular fragments of people that are commonly focused on – like the specific cancer or illness someone might have. Due to this fragmented viewing, the various roles and functions of the self are often set up against each other, and this creates inner conflict. We might become aware of this on the occasions when we feel 'torn' towards two, or more, directions of 'duty' – like wanting to spend time with children who are unwell or upset rather than sending them to school, but feeling unable to do so because of work commitments; or even pushing ourselves to fulfil social obligations regardless of needing and wanting to be with family, friends, or even simply alone.

Despite our inclination as human beings to see things holistically, and the difficulty we have in comprehending them when they are fragmented, Western society insists on breaking down teaching and learning into a series of steps accompanied by detailed instructions. Students, trainees, and learners of all kinds are made to methodically and repeatedly practice and explain the individual steps of a process to be mastered, rather than hone it as a whole. The belief that learning requires such linear breaking down and explanation to occur (as for the writing of a computer algorithm) likens humans more to machines than to other living systems, and at the same time, it disregards the holistic way in which we first experience learning as children. The result of children being subjected to this method of learning is that they then come to expect it (even though it's a hindrance to learning), and little by little as they grow into adults they also come to rely on it; this is because it appears 'easier' to learn things in the way they are *expected* to be learnt – with few (if any) connections.

Renowned philosopher Ludwig Wittgenstein discusses in *Philosophical Investigations* how it is that children learn to speak through our speaking to them; we don't need to explain what language is first.[20] We first learn to speak by being spoken to; from talking to walking, to exploring the world around us, as children we learn it all by delving into each experience fully and holistically, not by fragmenting it into details that are then taken out of context. In *The Power to Transform*, educator and author Stephanie Pace Marshall states this discrepancy explicitly:

> Although learning is the creative process of life, our current learning story conceives it as a mechanistic, prescribed, and easily measured commodity that can be incrementally and uniformly delivered to our children. This narrative could not be more wrong. Learning emerges from discovery, not directives; reflection, not rules; possibilities, not prescriptions; diversity, not dogma; creativity and curiosity, not conformity and certainty; and meaning, not mandates.[21]

This quote succinctly reveals that while it's natural for us to operate from a holistic perspective as children – where everything in our world flows almost seamlessly – in growing up it becomes virtually inevitable for us to internalise an *institutionalised perception*. As discussed in Chapter One, this is what I have named the way of perceiving that is primarily based on conforming to the way institutions operate, a perception that only accepts the hierarchical viewpoint of our society while it disregards everything else. By extension, this way of perceiving accepts the value labels that this ruling hierarchy defines things with, as well as its established use of language and thought along the existing paradigms – the status quo of the way things are 'normally' spoken and thought about.

As we grow up, the *institutionalised perception* we acquire invalidates our previous holistic one, which results in internal conflict between our minds and our senses, since our senses retain our childhood ability for holistic perspective. In growing up, in order to conform so as to fit in, we choose (mostly subconsciously) to put aside our holistic perspective of open communication and relationship, and so we leave *our* world behind, a world where we, and what we perceive, are all part of the whole. As soon as we begin to be formally taught, which can happen while we're still very young, we start adopting a view of the world that is dichotomous and fragmented into 'subject' and 'object', and this completely changes our perception. Because this new way of perceiving doesn't agree with what our senses are telling us, rather than synthesising the sensual input from our environment, we start ignoring the messages from our senses and believe instead that there are parts of ourselves that we can't trust. We are presented with, and are made to adopt, a reductive binary view of the world that results in a forced division into pairs (like black and white). For one who could initially see the many hues of colours bridging these, the absolutism of this forced division renders meaning elusive, as well as quite bleak; so it's no wonder that there's so much depression in the world. As Abram puts it:

> To define another being as an inert or passive object is to deny its ability to actively engage us and to provoke our senses; *we thus block our perceptual reciprocity with that being.* By linguistically defining the surrounding world as a determinate set of objects, we cut our conscious, speaking selves off from the spontaneous life of our sensing bodies.[22]

There is an old story, re-told by Buddhist Abbot Ajahn Brahm in his book *Opening the Door of Your Heart*, that not only helps to illustrate the restrictiveness and obstructiveness that the *institutionalised perception* imposes on us, but at the same time also demonstrates the importance of a holistic perspective.

The story is from long ago in a far away place, where a king had some troublesome ministers who argued constantly. Nothing would ever get done, as they didn't agree on anything, each one claiming to be right while the others were wrong!

Then one day the King decreed a public holiday that was to include special performances in a spectacular show. Many people came to see the event, including of course all of his Ministers who were given the best seats. At the end of the show the King brought his royal elephant into the amphitheatre followed by seven men who everyone knew had been blind since birth; they had never seen an elephant and didn't even know what it was. The King guided the first man's hands to feel the elephant's trunk and told him that this was an elephant. He then placed the second man's hands on one of the elephant's tusks, and the third on its ears; he had the fourth man feel its head, and the fifth its torso, the sixth a leg, and finally he had the seventh man feel the elephant's tail. In a loud voice he then asked the men to take turns and tell the audience what they believed an elephant was.

Still feeling the trunk, the first blind man stated that he was certain that an elephant must be a species of snake. At this the second blind man, holding a tusk, was outraged and declared that an elephant must undoubtedly be a type of plough. Feeling an ear, the third blind man announced that an elephant could be none other than a palm leaf fan. By this stage the fourth blind man, who had been feeling the head, was doubled up in laughter and hollered that only fools could mistake a large water jug for all those other things. With his hands still on the torso the fifth blind man interrupted and proclaimed that an elephant could only be an enormous rock. The sixth blind man jeered at this description saying, while feeling a leg, that clearly an elephant was a tree or maybe even just a trunk. The last blind man, who had been feeling the tail, derided them all exclaiming that an elephant was indisputably some sort of flywhisk.

Shouting over each other, the blind men began arguing so vehemently that they got into a terrible fight. It didn't seem to matter to them that they couldn't see who they were hitting, 'They were fighting for principle, for integrity, for truth. Their own individual truth, ...'[23]. As the King's soldiers pulled apart the fighting men, everyone present looked to the ashen Ministers, as all understood the meaning of the King's lesson.

As Brahm points out, '[e]ach one of us can know only a part of the whole that constitutes the truth.'[24] While we ourselves are whole (like a living cell), though nonetheless made up of many parts, we are at the same time also part of much bigger wholes – a whole ecosystem, a whole world, and so on. Abram reminds us, 'the boundaries of a living body are open and indeterminate; more like membranes than barriers, they define a surface of metamorphosis and exchange.'[25] Yet, if instead of recognising this we hold our limited knowledge to be 'the truth', and what's more we believe that this truth can be proven 'right' by proving another's truth 'wrong', then we're acting like the blind men in the story, making the assumption that our own incomplete experience is the only real truth while that of others is a mistake. This is the sort of belief system maintained through the *institutionalised perception*, where whatever is analysed is taken completely out of context by being severed from the whole. When we embrace a holistic perspective this allows us to accept wholeness and complexity, and through openness and dialogue with others, we might together with them get closer and closer to understanding truth. To be understood, wholeness needs to be connected; the 'wholeness' of the elephant, though difficult to perceive by each blind man alone, could have been more easily arrived at if each detailed description had been added to the others, in a dialogic and collaborative way, until understanding had been reached.

Similarly to how in the story the seven blind men represent the King's ministers, it is easy to imagine them as also being representative of: academic faculties, government departments, political parties, schools of thought, or even different industries, scientific sectors, and so on. The majority of the members of these 'bodies' or 'entities', depending on how narrowly focused they were, would most likely be concerned only with the specific aspects of things as deemed to belong within their entity's boundaries and domains, and so most of the time they would hardly even be aware of the interconnection existing between entities. What's more, believing that only their perspective of reality should be followed, the members of these different entities would also feel justified in arguing for the supremacy of their particular point of view. Taking a holistic approach, on the other hand, would enable anyone to look at the whole 'big picture' and include all that they could currently be aware of.

Despite a holistic approach being related to the big picture, this does not mean that the details are glossed over. Chaos theory gives a perfect example of this, with the 'butterfly effect' explaining how minute changes are known to be able to affect very large and complex systems. In 1961, mathematician and meteorologist

Edward Lorenz discovered that the difference in tiny details could substantially affect huge and complex systems. The basic explanation behind the 'butterfly effect' phenomenon is that theoretically even the flapping of a butterfly's wings in somewhere like Tokyo could conceivably and significantly impact on air currents, thereby possibly causing a hurricane later on somewhere as far as Brazil.

In *The Collapse of Chaos*, biologist Jack Cohen and mathematician Ian Stewart discuss how the idea of complexity, where the complexity of something is seen as increasing the more information is required to describe it, is now much more popular than the idea of chaos.[26] Complexity theory is an interdisciplinary science that's connected to chaos theory; it's been defined as 'a chaos of behaviours in which the components of the system never quite lock into place, yet never quite dissolve into turbulence either.'[27] Another way of explaining this is that a complex system is a dynamic system, which despite appearing chaotic doesn't ever actually degenerate into chaos. With no easily discernible patterns, a complex system is difficult to understand well enough in order to accurately predict its next stage. In this sense, a complex system is one that resists systemisation, or any predictable order, as it is in a constant state of flux with its behaviour varying in response to changing environmental conditions[28]. This variability essentially shows us that complex systems are always adapting to the environment that they find themselves in.

These descriptions of complex systems clearly also suit most natural phenomena and living things, including human behaviour, interaction, and creativity. This then likewise fits the 'self', especially if one looks at the whole complete self, rather than just at the fragmented and bordered parts of the self as seen through an *institutionalised perception*. In fact, regardless of our differing individual beliefs of how humans first came to be on earth, we would be hard put to argue that we're not an intrinsic part of the natural physical world, and that the human being, this 'self', is not indeed a natural phenomenon. And yet, given the endless resources of time, energy, lives, and so on that have been used to raise 'man' (I use this term intentionally) above the rest of the physical world, one could easily be led to believe that being part of the natural world is an unacceptable state of affairs for many in our society. Indeed, the way that this 'raised man' seems to be bent on achieving the destruction of the physical world – wide-spread pollution with far-reaching consequences, unsustainable mining and use of natural resources, destruction of many animals' habitats, destruction of old-growth forests, and so on – reflects the successful and almost total disconnection from nature, including the disconnection from our own human nature. This is the legacy of patriarchy, wrought through an *institutionalised perception*.

Throughout my life, I have found that whatever has countered nurturing, while also preventing even just the 'idea' of the possibility of an egalitarian joyful life, has invariably had patriarchy behind it. Patriarchy is the bedrock of things such as war, profit (usually only for shareholders) as the main reason for work or enterprise, and the misuse of power in countless situations. A better understanding of patriarchy might help reveal just how endemic patriarchal culture is in our society, and how it is responsible for blocking creativity by prohibiting it in countless ways, though all the while paying lip service to it. This plays out in our daily life, whenever we are faced with decisions (even seemingly small ones) and we find we are drawn away from following what our heart whispers to us because that choice is not supported in any way, or it's hardly made visible, as it is simply not given as an option that we can choose.

Although philosopher and novelist John Ralston Saul doesn't name patriarchy in *Voltaire's Bastards*, he nonetheless accurately describes its rule in oppressing women and rendering them subordinate. Being traditionally the main holders of 'feminine' roles, women have most often been the ones to display qualities of nurturing, and they have, especially in the past, held none to little power:

> Today ... women are occupying [some] positions of influence ... in the past they have been the exceptions to the rule and they were usually obliged to hold on to their power by deforming themselves into honorary men or into magnified archetypes of the female who manipulated men. It is still not clear that women can successfully become part of the established structures without accepting those deformations ... the realities of Western rational civilization ... [are] male realit[ies]. Women might well want to change that ... Even if they do so, it is difficult to see why women would want to claim responsibility for what has gone before. [29]

Saul is one of an increasing number of male writers (Thomas Berry is another) who openly acknowledge the general exclusion of women from what Cavarero ironically calls 'the glorious accomplishments of Man'[30] – those feats deemed by society to be what really matter according to the hierarchical values of patriarchy. These include many of the victories and defeats of wars and battles told of in history books, and endlessly retold through mediums like movies, non-fiction and fiction books, and so on, over and over again, tirelessly. This also explains why war stories are so popular, and why our children are made to learn so many of their gruesome details at school. Although we're usually told that the reasons children are made to endure this is to teach them about the horrors of war so that these may never be repeated again, wars are in fact intrinsic within a society run according to the traditions of patriarchy. This sort of society cannot help but be drawn to war and conflict, notwithstanding whatever other justifications might be given.

For evidence of this, one has only to look at what the Australian War Memorial official website writes about Anzac Day:

> Anzac Day ... is one of Australia's most important national occasions. ... When war broke out in 1914 Australia had been a federated nation for only 13 years, and its government was eager to establish a reputation among the nations of the world. ... Although the Gallipoli campaign failed in its military objectives, the actions of Australian and New Zealand forces during the campaign left a powerful legacy. ... the "Anzac legend" became an important part of the identity of both nations ... [31]

Since I first visited this website in 2010 when it still claimed that Anzac Day was 'probably Australia's most important national occasion', it has toned down its use of superlatives considerably. This shows some progress, however, I'm surprised that a significant historical fact is still not being reported on the site – that Australian society was vehemently divided during World War I as to whether to take part in the war at all, with the referendum on conscription twice returning a 'no' majority. There also isn't so much of a comment or hint about how horrific it was to send so many young lads to their deaths or, for those who didn't die, to subject them to trauma that most never recovered from and which affected their families and ultimately all of Australian society.

According to patriarchal values, it is an unspoken part of a soldier's duty to be ready to die in war for your country and commanding officer, in whatever mission the governments involved deem appropriate. Given that wars seem to be always ongoing in a number of places throughout the world, with the one in Syria considered one of the worst conflicts of the 21ˢᵗ century, it is reasonable to assume that many in positions of power (of which women only make up a small minority[32]) still uphold these patriarchal values.

In Australia, persuading 'future soldiers', as well as the rest of society, to accept these patriarchal values begins as early as primary school. Here, war is presented in a way that is somewhat alluring; with primary school children being taught about the 'virtues' that being an Anzac gave rise to. I have even known of primary schools where the Anzac dawn ceremony was one of the most important dates on their calendar (among these was a school attended by one of my children). This sort of event is organised with military precision and is rendered incredibly suggestive with candles and beautiful music. Ironically, instead of recognising the full majesty of the dawn for the natural spectacle that it is, the beauty of dawn is used to add to the allure and romance of having died for one's country. With this sort of 'spin' on war not being questioned, the recruiting of 'fodder' for wars to be manned is likely to continue, especially while the fact that our society is still ruled by patriarchy is ignored. Though what I describe is only about Australia, this is undoubtedly very similar to what occurs in other countries, especially Western ones where, as is reported by many (including John Ralston Saul), armaments constitute an important and stable trading commodity in the economy.

The economic value of war is the focus of a video that a friend shared with me on Facebook while I was in the process of doing the final editing of this book. Published by the Veterans for Peace on YouTube in December 2016, it is titled *Ex-Soldier Speaks Truth; "The Real Enemy is here at Home, the Rich"*. In it, a young ex-soldier from the USA passionately explains how young people are duped into joining the armed forces and then into believing that the enemies are the poor people they are sent to kill in places like the caves of Afghanistan. He further clarifies that the government that's sending them to do this does not have their best interests at heart because it's actually the government of the rich, of Wall Street, of the oil giants, of the defence contractors; he states '... you have no reason to put your life on the line and kill and die for profit ...it's crystal clear now that these wars are going to continue and expand, and go into other countries, that is the trend, that is what we know, that there is perpetual war ...'[33] What this video shares is not surprising in a world where most of society is ruled by patriarchy. I did find it interesting, however, that the Veterans for Peace Organisation doesn't make the connection to 'patriarchy' obvious, even though according to their website they seek to '... inform the public of the true causes ... and the enormous costs of wars ...' and work for the '... dismantling of the war economy, ... and most significantly, ... to end all wars.'[34]

But let's return to Anzac Day in Australia; what is in fact espoused in its remembrance is a masculinity imbued with all the hubris of a Greek hero. Constructed by patriarchy, this masculinity has the qualities that are valued highest by this hierarchical order – the virtues of the 'Anzac legend', where war is at best looked upon as a sad but inevitable part of human nature. Thomas Berry calls them 'the male values of conquest and dominion'[35], and they are patriarchal values. These 'values' are in fact reinforced as values by all those who maintain the patriarchal order – all those who follow an *institutionalised perception* regardless of whether they're even aware of it, men and women both. The simplistic substitution of 'male' for patriarchy is an easy one to make, especially when over five thousand years of patriarchy's rule and traditions have placed mostly men (as opposed to women) in positions of power. So that patriarchy might be more clearly seen for the hierarchical system and culture that it is, it is therefore very important to make a clear distinction between 'male' and 'patriarchy', to ensure that the two terms do not continue to be confused as they so often are and have been.

Cavarero reminds us that 'man' is seen as 'a universal'[36]; in its idealised definition 'universal' is mostly taken to be a title, and it can entice ordinary, though unique, men to trade in their uniqueness so that they may identify with the idealised universal – Man! By enabling some of the men who value conquest and dominion to wield the most power by force, patriarchy supports the ideal of the grandeur of universal Man. What's more, the prestige imbued in the power that patriarchy bestows on those at the apex of the hierarchy (usually men) can also be easily mistaken for this idealised universal. Hence patriarchy and Man can become (and have been) interchangeable, and this filters down to all men, trapping them within generalisations that they might find almost impossible to see their way out of without 'losing face' – from not acknowledging feelings, to going to war.

It is by identifying with this generalised universal Man, that individual men allow themselves to be fragmented. They then reconstruct themselves so that only those fragments deemed to have patriarchal value are included, while the other parts of the self are repressed. That is, by not being acknowledged and owned they end up hidden in the subconscious, or in other words (as Jung tells us) they are cast into the 'shadow'. Jung describes the 'shadow' as consisting of 'everything that the subject refuses to acknowledge about himself [sic]'[37], and because the shadow is disowned, so as to gain the illusion of being whole, its contents often end up being projected onto others. Psychologist Harville Hendrix explains the process: 'we project whenever we take a part of the disowned self or the lost self and send it out like a picture onto another person ....'[38]

The projection of a repressed trait that one considers negative can cause dislike, or even hate: '- the negative trait that had seemed so intense when I first saw him was really a part of me. I had taken the part of me that is arrogant – ... that does not fit with my image ... and thrust it onto Robert.'[39] This process of denial and projection applies to both men and women and is one of the main causes of oppression, including the oppression of women in a patriarchal society. In denying parts of themselves so as to be a better fit for patriarchy's values, many men (and women) are no longer whole, yet at the same time, they yearn (even if often only subconsciously) to redeem these denied parts so that they might feel whole again. This longing makes it even more likely for them to project the repressed parts of themselves onto 'others'; these are then mirrored back to them so that they may get to experience what they've rejected, which subsequently becomes what they both hate and love in 'others'.

For patriarchal Man (the universal societal Man) the 'Other' is most often and easily seen in women, and so women are hated and persecuted because they embody, through projection, what Man believes he should not value. At the same time, this 'Other' is also the cause of attraction precisely because this 'Other' is seen to embody, still through projection, all that deep down (subconsciously) Man feels that he has lost, including the qualities of nurturing and caring. Although it could be argued that women are also somewhat a part of this, as I have discussed they have mostly been excluded from identifying with this universal Man behind which stands a concealed 'patriarchy'. This has been a blessing in disguise, as it has protected many of us women from the allure of fully accepting the *institutionalised perception* as our own view of life.

I have found growing up in a patriarchal world that does not openly show itself for what it is to be often bewildering and frustrating. There were times when I felt I had been wronged, impeded or coerced somehow, yet I didn't know how to even begin to stand up for myself. Though each incident itself might have seemed quite small and insignificant, it was as though it heralded something much bigger and more sinister, and I could sense beneath it a morass of wrongness that would immobilise me so completely that I felt I could at best only tiptoe around it, as I was too frightened of literally being obliterated if I didn't at least appear to be conforming. Although this feeling has eased within me somewhat through experience gained with age, because our society still lives under patriarchy it is nonetheless still present and can at times result in a lack of assertiveness, or timidity, on my part.

A recent occurrence showed me just how easily this can be manifest. While driving, on my way to visit a friend in hospital, I noticed the fuel light was flashing. I was in a huge hurry because I was to hold a workshop after visiting my friend, so I felt a great sense of relief when I spotted a petrol station. I pulled in and saw that the pump in front was the only free one; to get close enough to it in order to get petrol, all the while avoiding hitting the car parked by the back pump, I ended up being somewhat diagonal rather than straight. I checked that there was enough room for cars to drive past me, including the one behind me, which had ample room to leave. Everything checked out (I have a small car), but just as I was about to fill the tank of my car with petrol, the owner of the car parked behind me walked towards his car, and on seeing how I had parked he exclaimed in a disgusted tone, 'What a terrible way to park, you could at least have gone forward a little to straighten up!' He was a self-assured man, perhaps a little older than me, and spoke with clear authority.

I wish I could report that I stood up for myself with an appropriate comment, or that I at least ignored him. But no, to my surprise I got in my car (although annoyed to be wasting time I didn't have) and straightened up my parking, thereby 'fixing' something that had not even inconvenienced anyone. Having been judged as being 'wrong', I had felt the need to prove myself capable of 'doing it right'. I pondered on that for a long time after, and could only surmise that I have obviously been 'trained' by the rules of patriarchy to be more deeply obedient than I had ever imagined. At the same time though, I felt that it was good to become aware of it, as it is only by becoming aware of 'what is' that we can make changes, hence the importance of raising the awareness of our culture of patriarchy.

There is a short story by H. G. Wells – *The Country of the Blind* – that I had read years ago, and came across again while doing my PhD. Re-reading it greatly helped me to understand my fearful and confused reactions in growing up under patriarchy as a child very much in touch with her creativity. In this story, a mountaineer finds himself in a hidden valley and discovers a village of people that appear to be an idyllic society, however, they are all blind and have been for generations. Realising that he's different from them, the elders finally offer to 'fix' him – by removing his eyes – as the condition for him to be allowed to remain with them and marry the girl he has fallen in love with, and who has also fallen in love with him. It's a very powerful story that serves as a great analogy about the harm that can be (and often is) caused when limited perception is imposed on those who reveal their holistic perspective of creativity.

I was almost four when I first consciously became aware of my 'self'. I remember it vividly; my white wardrobe was decorated with colourful pictures: they were pink and blue drawings of plush fluffy bunnies and bears, and they looked as real to me as cartoon characters appear to children. I spent a lot of time playing and having conversations with them; I remember that one minute I was playing with them, and then all at once (or so it seemed to me) I became firmly aware that I couldn't swap places with them – I was 'myself' looking at them, and that was that. At that moment it was as though something within me had shifted, like a door opening and another one closing, and all I can access of my existence prior to then are just a few fragments of colourful memories. Among them are those of my younger sister, by eleven months, who had died before I turned three. I had not been told about her death when it occurred, so for me, she just disappeared. It was the convention at the time not to include children in grief, and as young parents mine followed this convention, thinking it was the right thing to do.

From that time, whenever I played, I knew I was pretending, and all of the memories of my childhood since then are from the inside looking out – from the place where thoughts and feelings happen. I spent a lot of time there, observing and reflecting, and also listening to, or eavesdropping on, adults' conversations about things they didn't think I heard or understood, as they thought me engrossed in reading. Having learnt to read when quite young, settling in an armchair with a book made me feel magical – it was as though I was invisible, for nobody interrupted my reading, so I was careful not to move or make a noise, or in any other way draw attention to myself. From as early as then, I began to become aware of much around me that didn't make sense, not because I couldn't understand it, but because it seemed conflicting, absurd, or just plainly untrue. I didn't know then of patriarchy or the concept of *institutionalised perception*; I just saw adults who looked as though they were playing at 'pretend', but then pretended they hadn't.

By the time I reached my late teens my frustration had turned to rage, in itself not an unusual thing for a teenager. I remember feeling that I wanted to physically shake people out of their complacency, as too often they seemed to me to be accepting of a confused jumble of unfair events within a dreary existence that was only occasionally lit up by brilliance. Altogether in my school career, I had frequented ten schools, in six different cities and towns, and in two different countries – Italy and Australia. This had served well to maintain my role of 'observer', as I had never been in one place too long for any of them to appear normal, or for me to take them for granted. Ideology has been said to be 'a set of practices which make inequality seem as natural as the air students and teachers breathe.'[40] I didn't find unfairness natural, and its occurrence (in the classroom or in world events) as well as my ongoing reaction to it, which was to feel personally affronted, irked me greatly. On the whole, I thought of adults as liars, whether through intent or circumstance. Hungry for fairness, beauty and peace, I fluctuated between cynically seeing 'conspiracies' everywhere, to taking the weight of the world on my shoulders in wanting to right all wrongs.

It wasn't until I had children of my own that my view of life became softer and more joyous. Nurturing my children and watching them grow led me to reconsider many things deeply. It also made me realise that there is a lot more brilliance to be seen in the world when looking through a holistic perspective. There's an adage that says that children are sent to those who are ready to learn from them; I believe this with all my heart, as in the process of raising my children I learnt more than I ever thought possible, and this led me to become aware of new ways of learning that I could access every day. Having children and nurturing them has rekindled in me much of the curiosity I had as a child, allowing me to rediscover myself. Most importantly, it also brought home to me the reality of the interconnectedness of life, and the importance of nurturing creativity.

* * * * * * * * * * * * * * *

REVIEWING THE JOURNEY OF CHAPTER TWO

In this chapter, I introduce the sense I have of myself, which is of a *beingness*/body fusion that I experience as my whole self, and I explain how I've come to identify with this from a combination of personal life influences as well as communal social influences. While the specific life experiences I have had are unique to me and are part of what makes me who I am, it is also how I've responded to communal influences that has shaped me – every decision and choice I have ever made set me up for the next one, and the next, and so on. I see the social order, or culture, of 'patriarchy' as one of the major influences of our social context, and I have endeavoured to communicate the extent of its hiddenness and complexity. Complexity itself is also discussed, since a holistic perspective reveals complexity wherever it looks – the self, creativity, the interconnectedness of life, and so on ...

In this chapter, I explore what a holistic perspective is, as this perspective is vital for the nurturing of creativity. I therefore explain it in various ways: firstly, I contrast a holistic approach to a reductionist approach, then I look at it through Gestalt psychology, and show how the intrinsic holistic perspective we have as children is inevitably replaced by an acquired *institutionalised perception*. This is the name I have given to a perception that is guided by the values set by the hierarchical viewpoint of patriarchy, which also makes use of a specific analytical perspective to provide a convenient way of including whatever supports patriarchy, while excluding all else. Reductionism can cause us to 'lose sight of the forest for the trees', for by taking the 'trees' out of context we run the risk of completely forgetting that they're growing in a 'forest'. This, combined with a carefully applied analytical force of 'rationality', can be a very useful tool to convince the general populace of the intrinsic 'rightness' of the hierarchical values of the social system we live in. This conviction is particularly necessary to enforce patriarchy's ideals of conquest and dominion within the entire social and personal practices that this entails – from war to self-fragmentation.

A holistic perspective, on the other hand, is based on connections and enables those utilising it to be open to the new, while at the same time being aware and accepting of their limitations, as in being able to acknowledge that there is still much that they don't understand. Through a holistic perspective one can clearly see that there are 'wholes' and also 'bigger wholes', or in other words, something can at the same time be whole (though being made up of many parts) and yet also be part of a bigger whole. Moreover, a holistic perspective encompasses a holistic perception of the self, a perception that is vital to the enabling of creativity, as only by being aware of the self as whole can creativity be given sufficient scope to unfold.

Chapter Three:

NETWORK OF SUPPORT

What you have to do in this world you cannot do alone. Every successful human enterprise is a collaboration – a drawing together of diverse resources and energies...[1]

– Barbara Sher & Annie Gottlieb

Creativity has been recognised as being vitally essential by many, while many others maintain the essence of what this means, even while not specifically mentioning 'creativity'. In this chapter, I explicitly link to an eclectic mix of different voices (most of which I use throughout the book) that foster creativity in different ways, through theories, ideas, writings, practices, or other means. For my thesis it made sense to connect these voices together, to form a metaphorical loom (as it were) in order to provide support for the weaving of my discussion, and this is still relevant to the non-fiction book this has now become. Some of these voices are veritable linchpins, including: scholarly personal narrative (SPN), appreciative inquiry, various types of feminisms, Adriana Cavarero's theory of the 'narratable self'[2], and Mikhail Bakhtin's notion of 'dialogic discourse'[3].

As I shared in the Introduction, I chose scholarly personal narrative (SPN) as the main methodology for the writing of my thesis. Apart from enabling writing to be more holistic, SPN is also backed by Jung's philosophy of the 'Self', which stresses the importance of self-knowledge – working towards an understanding of all parts of the self as much as possible. Coined by Robert Nash, a professor at the University of Vermont, and taught by him there for a period of time as a course by the same name, SPN supports the practice of openly including the self in academic writing. In *Liberating Scholarly Writing: The Power of Personal Narrative*, Nash maintains that:

> As an author, you are always an insider; not omnisciently removed from what you write, but caught up personally in every word, sentence, and paragraph; in every statistic and every interview; ... The inclusion of the self in research and scholarship is inescapable, even more so when writers try intentionally to excise the self from their research. The "I" voice always has a way of seeping into an "objective", third person text.[4]

Although the traditional academic convention of strictly removing the traces of the self is finally beginning to be relaxed, as Nash's and many other academic books attest to, the belief that a treatise needs to be 'authorless' to command greater authority still seems to prevail. There is of course the postmodern idea that while the 'author is dead'[5] the text is everything, and yet at the same time the authority of those in the literary canon and those deemed to be experts in their disciplines (even though they may literally have been dead a long time), continues to be revered. Indeed, one could be forgiven for believing that in some way death actually bestows distinction. Yet it is useful to remember that once upon a time those scholars, who are now looked up to, were forging new ground and opening up new vistas with ideas never heard of before. Indeed, it took some of them a very long time to be celebrated, or in some cases to be even accepted. Ken Robinson comments on this in *Out of Our Minds*:

> There have been countless scientists, inventors, artists and philosophers who were ridiculed in their own times but whose work is revered by later generations. Think of Galileo ... Galileo's work was denounced for not being science at all. ... There are many examples of artists who died in penury, whose work now changes hands for fortunes.[6]

It's also worth remembering that no matter how much acclaim anyone receives for what they've brought forth, there were (and still are) those with different or even opposing points of view, and this is the case for most theories, beliefs and practices. From a holistic perspective, it's more a case of all of these points of view (or at least most of them) being necessary in order to get closer to the 'whole picture' of reality, since each of them is just a part of the whole, as the fable of the seven blind men in Chapter Two suggests.

Ultimately, though one might hope even primarily, writing is all about communicating – an experience, idea, thought or discovery. Although there are many mediums through which to communicate, writing as an extension of talking is all about making sure that the message is rendered more accessible to countless people that we may never get to meet, as well as to future generations, so it's reasonable to suppose that clarity might be one of its most valuable qualities. All too often, however, academic writing is anything but clear, and much specialised writing in all fields suffers from jargon use. As Nash points out in his paraphrasing of Keyes, 'The more a scholarly piece of writing needs translation, the higher evaluation it receives from scholars ... Use lots of insider words, complex syntax, and endless referencing, and you will be ... celebrated ... in no time.'[7] Traditional academic writing seems to encourage an obfuscating sleight of hand, or I should say sleight of pen. To draw an analogy from a well-known children's tale, it's as if academic writing were written by the likes of the Wizard of Oz, who not wanting to be seen for the human he really is hides behind a curtain and speaks into a microphone so that his voice may sound more commanding. Only by doing this can the sought after authority be achieved, and this is also the case with policy writing in both the corporate and governmental arenas. This appears to ensure that the final text is somehow accepted as being greater than any of the authors, and for policies and laws this certainly makes them less questionable.

On the other hand, by revealing that the writer is human, scholarly personal narrative (SPN) enhances the clarity of academic writing and serves to make it more accessible to readers, this can also apply to the best of non-fiction writing. This kind of writing is imbued with more authenticity than any so-called objective and authoritative expert voice could ever have, as it touches a chord with readers by connecting to their humanness. Authenticity evokes validity, legitimacy and empathy, whereas authority often carries with it a certain obligatory coerciveness that can irritate readers, as it often implies that the reader is somehow a 'lesser' being. Scholarly personal narrative is effective writing, since by fostering the communicating of ideas in ways that are more widely understood it also allows them to be shared and built on. This makes it particularly useful for writing about creativity, which is all about possibilities and open perspectives.

Nurturing creativity entails being willing to pursue exploration and follow an unforeseen path. In much writing this straying from a set course is not tolerated, and it can be very quickly labelled 'a mistake' before it is even allowed to show us where it can lead. In *Writing from the Heart*, Nancy Aronie, who is greatly supportive of creativity and of bringing the personal into one's writing, describes what it's like to be open to making mistakes:

> Living creatively for me means being willing to screw up, to play the fool, now and again ... the one who makes the error, the one who can be wrong, the one who understands he will mess up, the one who doesn't know everything, the one who can be lost. Because I know that my biggest mistakes become my best teachers, and my biggest mistake might be my best piece of work. Of course it's not really a mistake. It's just the moment I get out of my own way. It's the moment my ego takes a coffee break.[8]

Though we are told that schools are places of learning, it is at school that most of us first experience what it's like to be constantly judged, as nearly everything we do at school is measured and labelled with specific values. As Jane Tompkins shares in *A Life in School: What the Teacher Learned*, once she became a teacher she relived the terror of when she was a student, consequently she found herself attempting to keep this terror at bay by somehow passing it on to her students: 'If I alternately intimidated and placated the students it's because I was threatened and felt afraid, afraid of my students, and afraid of the authorities who had stood in judgement on me long ago.'[9] If we feel judged it stands to reason that even the thought of making mistakes becomes too risky to contemplate. And with this being so terrifying, following a safe and proven way is preferable, which then leads to a stricter adherence to ways of doing things that have been 'tested', even (in many day to day cases) if these have been simply 'googled' on the internet. The fear of being judged invariably prevents students from sharing opinions in the classroom; the more voices remain silent, the less a classroom can become a vibrant place of joyous discovery, and this is true for all classrooms, from primary school to university.

Even out of school, it is the fear of being judged that stops much from being shared, with this including many ways of doing things that would be more useful and more fun than the prescriptive and accepted (or traditional) ways of doing things. The resultant inflexibility is not a very good state of affairs in a world where one of the surest of things is that circumstances, people, and almost everything else will change. Rigidity is also an especially untenable proposition in regard to creativity, as it counteracts any possibility of nurturing it; Daniel Goleman explains this in *Working with Emotional Intelligence:*

> Teresa Amabile, a psychologist at the Harvard Business School, describes four "creativity killers ...:
>
> • *Surveillance:* Hovering and constant scrutiny. This stifles the essential sense of freedom needed for creative thinking.
>
> • *Evaluation:* A critical view that comes too soon or is too intense ... [can lead] to a preoccupation with being judged.
>
> • *Overcontrol:* Micromanaging every step of the way. Like surveillance, it fosters an oppressive sense of constriction, which discourages originality.
>
> • *Relentless deadlines:* A too-intense schedule that creates panic ... deadlines and goals can focus attention [but also] they can kill the fertile "off time" where fresh ideas flourish.[10]

This provides a likely explanation as to why many of the people I interviewed from the educational community were disillusioned with high school: *In the public school teachers don't really care, they tell you what to do and then they don't really help you if you need help* (student). *The teachers are too interested in control, because they need to be. The school system seems to me to be above the students, they are not treated as equals ... it's not a safe environment* (parent). *At this time creativity relies on teachers' personal initiative, it is not really nurtured nor is it encouraged* (teacher).

As a place where evaluation and deadlines abound, and where surveillance and over-control are likely to be practiced regularly (depending on the sorts of relationships and dynamics present between administration, teaching staff, and students) a high school is not apt to be able to genuinely foster creativity. This can also apply to primary schools, though perhaps to a lesser extent, as well as to higher educational institutions like universities. In fact, the potential for cultivating creativity is seriously jeopardised in all formal schooling where the emphasis is on standardised assessment and reporting. This is something that has been steadily increasing all over the Western world (perhaps the whole world), and when testing carries so much weight then the 'right' answers are sought out above all else. Professor of cognitive science Margaret Boden draws a clear picture of how this is translated into classroom attitudes that stifle creativity:

> First, an unbending insistence on the 'right' answer, and/or the 'right' way of finding it; second an unwillingness (or inability) to analyse the 'wrong' answer to see whether it might have some merit, perhaps in somewhat different circumstances (think of the 'failed' glue recipe that led to Post-it Notes); and third, an expression of impatience, or (worse still) contempt, for the person who came up with the unexpected answer.[11]

Another reason we are so afraid of committing errors is that we've been taught, from when we were at school, to strive for intellectual victory by proving others wrong, with this also being supported by popular media and television shows. Not surprisingly, given that we live in a hierarchical society, the patriarchal ideal of conquering through defeat is mirrored and validated even in academic institutions (where it is the preferred writing style) and in popular entertainment media like most blockbuster films. Through this way of writing, ideas and theories are proven wrong and then 'deposed' so that those proposed may take their place.

At other times writers suggest no specific alternatives to what they are removing, and when this occurs the focus remains on the sowing of doubt, destruction and fear, rather than on creating and building. With so much controversy there is basically a constant state of 'fighting' maintained. This is exacerbated by the attention being given to problems, mistakes, and generally all that is negative; a critiquing style is therefore frequently viewed more favourably and considered a safer approach to take than the pursuit of creative ideas. Yet there's actually no need for destruction in order to show the validity of something: one method may be good and proven, and yet another may at times be better, depending on circumstances. More likely still there might be aspects of one method that if merged with parts of another would transform current approaches to create new ones, with these being more versatile and adaptable and so more useful to our changing lives and environment.

The academic world doesn't need to be a war-zone in order to be rigorous; as

Nash puts it, it can be:

> ... about loving ideas so much that we are willing to play with them, to take
> chances with them, to express our passions about them, to deliver them in
> some fresh, new ways; to nurture and care for them; and to continually test
> and challenge them in the company of others ... to make ideas live, ... and
> ...[to] become wiser.[12]

Rather than competitiveness, we could engage in collaboration, and so transform
competitive academic discourse to dialogic discourse; this is what Mikhail Bakhtin
(social theorist and semiotician) called:

> ... a multiplicity and diversity of voices, a "heteroglossia," ... an act of
> (and an active) listening to each voice from the perspective of the others, a
> "dialogized heteroglossia." Its purpose is to test our own and others' ideas
> and ourselves and thus to determine together what we should think and how
> we should live. Its characteristic forms are the expression, juxtaposition, or
> negotiation of our individual and our cultural differences.[13]

The sort of openness and willingness to dialogue that Bakhtin calls for would,
if pursued, allow for theories and ideas to be transformed as necessary to meet
our changing needs. Having experienced the centrality and importance of this
through years of working on peace-building and conciliation, John Paul Lederach
states that 'A key to constructive social change lies in that which makes social
fabric, relationships, and relational spaces.'[14] In his work, Lederach supports a
holistic approach, together with the use of creativity, for positive and effective
social change. Rather than a problem-oriented approach, this sort of relational,
positive and creative approach is precisely what appreciative inquiry also puts into
practice.

First proposed by David Cooperrider and Suresh Srivastva in the late 80s,
appreciative inquiry is a generative form of action research, which was developed
in response to the authors' recognition that most action research had failed to
enable social transformation due to its intense focus on criticism and problems.[15]
Social change and transformation require new ideas to be put into practice, yet
criticism can prevent this; as Daniel Goleman points out, '[n]ew ideas are fragile
and all too easily killed by criticism. Sir Isaac Newton is said to have been so

sensitive to criticism that he withheld the publication of a paper ... for fifteen years, until his main critic died.'[16]

Action research is research that's grounded in practice though still linked to theory; it therefore bridges practice and theory. This means that many of the findings of this type of research are arrived at through the process of actually putting ideas into practice, as well as taking into consideration the input and reflections of those participating in the research. In the *Handbook of Action Research,* action research is described as 'the whole family of approaches to inquiry which are participative, grounded in experience, and action-oriented.'[17] Rather than analysing things in a critically destructive manner and searching for solutions from the viewpoint of the problem, appreciative inquiry looks at what's positive, as in most things that would benefit from change there are nonetheless often some aspects that are useful, and so would be best kept. As an analogy, if we wanted to remove some stains from a brightly patterned favourite scarf or t-shirt, we would do well to focus on the design just as much as on the cleaning so as to ensure that it wasn't damaged by the detergent/s used to remove the stains; if we paid attention only to the stains we could easily make things worse and ruin the garment.

Although it's a cliché, not 'throwing out the baby with the bathwater' aptly conveys the usefulness of appreciative inquiry. By focusing on aspects that are precious or even just useful and we would therefore want to keep, these can be taken as starting points for generating changes that are constructive; in this way instead of destroying and vetoing, the emphasis is on transforming and building. This doesn't mean that problems are ignored or deemed irrelevant, but they are only given secondary importance to anything that is working well, because it is what works that can better inspire us to make positive changes. Although the idea that fear is a great motivator is still quite prevalent, we really do our best work when we're inspired and believe that what we do can actually make a difference and improve things. Essentially, what this means is that problems are disempowered so that they can no longer be overwhelming, or in any way prevent us from taking positive action. This is especially useful when, as Bohm suggests in *On Dialogue,* what is viewed as a problem is in fact not really a problem at all but a paradox, as in the cases when 'the problems' we perceive end up being 'problems with false or self-contradictory presuppositions.'[18] This, Bohm says, happens more often than not, particularly in regard to 'problems' connected to human relations or psychological matters.

Bohm explains that 'problem-solving' is a survival feature intrinsic to us. It is this particular characteristic in us that has helped us to solve problems such as how to get food, find shelter and so on, '[o]nce the mind accepts a problem, then it is appropriate for the brain to keep on working until it finds a solution'.[19] Sometimes, however, a problem isn't a problem at all but a paradox, and this is crucially different from a problem that can be solved. In this case, if 'the mind treats a paradox as if it were a real problem, then since the paradox has no "solution", the mind is caught in the paradox forever'[20]; it is like being trapped in an endless loop. This sort of dilemma appears to be incredibly widespread in our modern society and is mostly due to the label of 'problem' being assigned to anything that presents any kind of difficulty or doesn't proceed as smoothly as we would like. While this tendency we have could be taken to simply be language shorthand, nonetheless it is important to be aware that by using the term 'problem' we are in fact gravely undermining our capacity for real comprehension, and this can cause much ongoing confusion and misunderstanding.

Appreciative inquiry is able to help us overcome all sorts of challenges because instead of focusing on what's problematic, it looks at what is positive. As a positive form of action research, appreciative inquiry provides perfect support to the nurturing of creativity and transformation; as James Ludema, David Cooperrider, and Frank Barrett state, it:

> ... can unleash a positive revolution of conversation and change in organizations by unseating existing reified patterns of discourse, creating space for new voices and new discoveries, and expanding circles of dialogue to provide a community of support for innovative action. ... More than a technique, appreciative inquiry is a way of organizational life – an intentional posture of continuous discovery, search and inquiry into conceptions of life, joy, beauty, excellence, innovation and freedom.[21]

I discovered appreciative inquiry soon after commencing my PhD journey and I immediately adopted it for my project. I chose it because I could see that its life-affirming and integrative approach to research is fully compatible with the nurturing of creativity, as although it's been tried and tested it hasn't become rigidly attached to a specific methodology, but is instead open and welcomes diversity. The process of appreciative inquiry, depicted in the figure of the 4D model – showing its different phases – is so supportive of creativity that it would be easy to imagine that it had been designed especially to elucidate the nurturing of creativity.

PHASES OF APPRECIATIVE INQUIRY – THE 4-D MODEL[22]

Indeed, the nurturing of creativity and appreciative inquiry share many similarities both in theory and practice. Like appreciative inquiry, creativity could also be said to be a deliberate attitude of a constant questioning of life in order to look for and find 'joy, beauty, excellence, innovation and freedom'[23]. However, a difference is that appreciative inquiry is also described as 'a way of organizational life'[24], meaning that it's been specifically structured in a certain way. This structuring allows it to be systematically explained and followed and further ensures its ease of use within organisations and institutions. Looking more closely at the individual phases of appreciative inquiry (illustrated in the diagram) helps us to gain a deeper understanding of it:

- Its first stage, *Discovery*, explores, researches, and generally looks for the positive that's already present in the current situation. 'Valuing the "best of what is" opens the way to building a better future by dislodging the ... dominance of deficit vocabularies.'[25] In relation to the nurturing of creativity, this entails recognising, from among all that is at present, those qualities that allow, encourage, and open the way for creativity. These could be environmental factors or the attitudes of particular individuals, or they could emerge as a combination of these, and among them would be included: flexibility, openness, humour, connectedness, the establishing of a sense of safety, inspiration, caring, support in risk-taking, and so on.

- Its second stage, the *Dream* stage, allows for the 'painting of a beautiful picture' through imagining and sharing how things could be if they were allowed to grow and be nurtured from the best of what currently is. In this stage 'new ways of seeing and understanding the world begin to emerge. ... vocabularies used ... are creative and constructive in the sense that they invite new, positive alternatives.'[26] Having started with some of the best of what has been experienced, more can be added to the whole at this point in order to work towards an ever-improving vision. As it is often the case that like begets like, those recognised qualities and situations that nurture creativity are expanded on, so that more are included in the vision that's being shaped. As perspectives open, there could be even more positive qualities to be discovered among all that can now be more clearly seen.

- The third stage, the *Design* stage, combines what has been discovered and appreciated together with what has been envisioned; making this connection engenders something new that can be put into practice. 'The key to this phase is to create a deliberately inclusive and supportive context for conversation and interaction.'[27] This is tantamount to nurturing the creativity that's essential for planning the implementation of the dream, which is what also ensures the best likelihood of success. As with the *Dream* stage, which is still open to any 'discovery', this phase may also re-visit and expand the work of the previous stages, since retrospective discoveries in planning could in fact lead to a greater vision.

- The last stage, the *Destiny* stage, is the synthesis of all the cycles of the previous phases. 'Appreciative inquiry accomplishes this by including ever-broadening circles of participants to join in the conversation ... [as they] translate their ideals into reality and their beliefs into practice.'[28] This clearly connects to Bakhtin's idea of dialogue, and further develops into a tangible process that allows the melding of individual and cultural differences and similarities into a best-practice scenario. Similarly with the nurturing of creativity, if this were to be accepted as a prevailing way to approach much of what we do in life, or at least in our work, study and community life, then this would continue expanding and growing in new ways from strength to strength. It also links to what Bohm suggests can be made possible through open communication and participative creative dialogue, which he explains allows for 'the possibility of transformation of consciousness, both individually and collectively ...'[29].

As can be seen from this detailed explanation, both appreciative inquiry and the nurturing of creativity are much more complex than what a linear (though circular) diagram of phases could ever depict, and this is true of any process. Predominantly, a process that is being explained by diagrams in a linear way (unless it's a description of a manufacturing factory assembly line) has been conceptualised, or in other words, reduced into its principal components; this means that it has been formalised by being defined, and then labelled to fit this definition. As such, this sort of explanation can only be useful if we understand that it is in fact merely a depiction of a process (which in practice is a lot more complex) that has been simplified to help us understand it. Consequently, it is important to be aware that diagrammatic explanations are almost invariably reductive.

If we focus on the explanation or methodology of a specific process in a literal sense, we run the risk of 'fixing' this in our minds as the 'right way' that the process should unfold, and this raises in us the expectations that this must be rigidly adhered to. This is not a useful proposition, mainly because the expectation of having to do something in a particular way can greatly hinder any possible creativity or newness that might arise in us, and this prevents the process from being developed and transformed. If, however, a labelled diagram is recognised as simply being the explanation of a process – an explanatory part that describes the whole – then instead of becoming a controlled prescribing of how a process should unfold, it can be an avenue of creative expression for all those involved as it helps to render a clearer understanding.

In their research, Ludema and colleagues found that:

> ... when groups study human problems and conflicts, they often find that both the number and severity of these problems grow. In the same manner when groups study high human ideals and achievements, such as peak

experiences, best practices and noble accomplishments, these phenomena, too, tend to flourish. In this sense, topic choice is a fateful act. Based on the topics they choose to study, organizations enact and construct worlds of their own making that in turn act back on them.[30]

That is to say, any sort of research seems to cause an effect both on the researchers and on the topic in question. A new world comes into being for the researchers and what they're looking at, precisely because of the research that's being undertaken, and so the brand new perspective that governs this is then shaped by the way the research is enacted. It could therefore be said that all research is action research; I have in fact experienced this in my own research – with my thesis being about *the nurturing of creativity as the basis for transformation*, and my approach to it being the creative process itself, this set me up to be open to creativity. What's more, it not only affected me, but it also had the potential to affect all those with whom I came into contact through the project, as well as all those in some way connected to me. In practical terms this meant that both change and growth were facilitated by the choice of topic in my journey; this enabled me (and others connected to me) to learn even more about creativity than I had anticipated, and also provided numerous possibilities for applying this learning. The amazing result of this was that I saw unfold around me a considerable number of creative endeavours (many unexpected and seemingly 'out of the blue') that were undertaken by many of my friends, family members and colleagues.

Being informed by numerous theories, in its practice action research draws from these simultaneously. In 'Uneven Ground: Feminisms and Action Research', Patricia Maguire speaks of 'feminisms' in the plural, reflecting the feminist understanding that there's a multiplicity of feminist perspectives included in feminist scholarship. This connects the concept of 'voice' to egalitarianism, since by creating spaces that allow marginalised voices to speak and be heard (and not just those of women) it fosters inclusivity. Self-expression nurtures creativity and can lead to personal meanings being uncovered; this also eases the frustration that has been experienced with modes of expression being controlled and limited (or even silenced), which has often resulted in meaning being denied and stultified. In contrast to the patriarchal value system traditionally embedded within institutions, which functions on the hierarchical principles of elitism, feminisms greatly value lived experience and the transformation that this can bring about, as Maguire explains:

> Embracing this call to transformational action, personal and structural,
> has always been a bedrock of feminism and feminist scholarship (Mies,
> 1983, 1986, 1991; ...). As Liz Stanley asserts, feminism is not merely a
> perspective (way of seeing) or an epistemology (way of knowing), it 'is also
> an ontology, or a way of being in the world' (1990:14). ... Both action and
> feminist research have centred the voices of the marginalized and muted in
> knowledge creation processes by starting from their everyday experiences
> (Barsley and Ellis, 1992; ...). ... as a source of legitimate knowledge (Barrett,
> Chapter 27; Gatenby and Humphries, 1999; ...)[31]

This clearly shows that, similarly to scholarly personal narrative, feminisms also
declare the importance of allowing experience within scholarship. Nash suggests
a mantra that might encourage academics to be more open to valuing experience:
'*The discourse should reflect people's experience*'[32]; this is a mantra that also supports
the feminisms' egalitarian notion of allowing and encouraging all voices to be
heard. If, rather than principally linking research to theory, we chose to insist
in also grounding it within experience then perhaps we might look at writing,
and especially academic writing, very differently. Given that any text can only
be as useful and valid as the writer's understanding at the time of writing it, it
seems reasonable for texts to be altered and updated as more is learned through
lived experience, and this goes way beyond the common updating through 'new
editions'.

I find it difficult to believe that, as a society, we continue to allow ourselves to
be bound by traditions and philosophies that have been written down in texts
by writers who had not the slightest idea of the world we now live in, nor had
any awareness of the challenges we would be faced with. An example of this is
Cartesian duality (the body-mind separation), which, though shown as flawed by
countless scholars, obstinately remains a basis for many of our social constructions.
This body-mind separation is probably still being used because it has served the
patriarchal tradition so well, and even now it still does so by providing a convenient
distance between discourse and action, thereby preventing the status quo from
being able to be actively challenged to any great extent. In *Voltaire's Bastards*, Saul,
who is invaluable for establishing the historical context of many of the theories

according to which our society seems to operate, tells us that Cardinal Richelieu (who was also Prime Minister for Louis XIII, and a contemporary of Descartes) was the first to restructure government to be 'rational', incorporating 'into the first real modern state ... all of Descartes's deductive ideas.'[33] It was at this time that he set a precedent for many of the occurrences of our times:

> The degree to which he was creating our future can be seen in such details as his restructuring of the educational system in order to produce more graduates in scientific, practical professions and fewer in the general arts ... He was obsessed with detail ... placing himself at the centre of the flow of information in order to control or collect it.[34]

Cartesian dichotomy served Richelieu's patriarchal method of 'divide and conquer' very well, and it's not surprising that this way of operating is still apparent in our modern-day politics and public service sectors.

The dichotomising of discourse and action can present side effects that have given rise to dangerous ironies. Among examples of this are the many climate summits that have been held, like the 2009 Copenhagen Climate Change Summit, the irony being that with all the participants needing to fly to the Summit they increased the amounts of emissions produced just so that ways for the reduction of these emissions could be discussed. Despite living in an era when technology allows us to organise and carry out distance conferencing, there has been nonetheless major and constant travelling being undertaken for the supposed purpose of discussions and agreements to be reached, and this did not seem to ever be questioned. Only with the COVID-19 pandemic halting travel and gatherings at the beginning of 2020 did we finally start making use of technologies (that we've had available to us for decades) for virtual meetings over the internet. Hopefully, the benefits of virtual meetings will be acknowledged so that they may continue, even when all restrictions on travel cease.

From within 'feminisms' Maguire provides yet another clue as to why theories such as Descartes' are still being upheld; she quotes feminist philosopher Sandra Harding:

> '... we are forced to think and exist within the very dichotomizing we criticize ... These dichotomies are empirically false, but we cannot afford

to dismiss them as long as they structure our lives and our consciousness' (1987: 300-1)" [35]

Here Harding seems to be saying that although we recognise dichotomy as being an imposed social structure that doesn't reflect reality, at least not in the way things actually are, we nonetheless choose to remain within it because we somehow can't afford to reject it. Yet how could that be so? What can we possibly lose by rejecting it? Rejection of it would not need to be in the guise of any kind of revolution. This predicament seems to be due to the sort of thinking that in revealing the overwhelming weight of a problem-based perspective also believes that we are somehow stuck with it. In fact, it has been through the acquisition of an institutionalised perspective *(institutionalised perception)* at the individual level (from when we were very young) that we have become caught within this problem-based way of seeing (even though ironically we call it problem solving). This can eventually become so overwhelmingly crushing that it totally prevents emancipation from occurring, or even any type of positive action being taken.

Feminist perspectives are very successful at uncovering unjust power relations and the nature of oppressions, yet like much activism, they mainly focus on the negative – on the problems. The use of an approach like appreciative inquiry would benefit these perspectives immensely as, rather than remain trapped in a 'struggle mentality', it would enable them to more easily transform the oppressions that they can so clearly see. By basing its research on a positive approach, appreciative inquiry gains strength, and therefore is able to present very different possible outcomes from its recognition of the limitations imposed by Descartes' theory:

> Ever since Descartes, the Western tradition has suffered a form of epistemological schizophrenia (Popkin, 1979) ... [given that its] starting point of doubt and negation undermines its [supposed] constructive intent. Appreciative inquiry recognizes that inquiry and change are not truly separate moments, but are simultaneous. Inquiry *is* intervention. The seeds of change ... are implicit in the very first questions we ask. For the questions we ask set the stage for what we 'find', and what we find becomes the knowledge out of which the future is conceived, conversed about and constructed.[36]

In utilising a holistic perspective that acknowledges the intrinsic connection between investigation and action, between learning and experience, appreciative inquiry is able to assist us to set aside the limitations of dualism so that a best-practice action, or 'way of being', can flow almost seamlessly from a holistic 'way of seeing'. By starting with a positive question that stems from comprehending that both investigation and action are part of the whole, appreciative inquiry cuts through any expectation of struggle, which is what we most often experience when we are faced with a problem. This sort of practice enables the nurturing of creativity that encourages what we can see – all of the positive and passionate things that we might find within ourselves, as well as in our relationships and in the world around us – to 'bear fruit' so that this can then nourish, and further nurture us, in an ever-flourishing cycle of growth and transformation. Ken Robinson highlights how crucial this way of nurturing is:

> We need the right conditions for growth, in our schools, businesses, and communities, and in our own individual lives. ... Some of the elements of our own growth are inside us. They include the need to develop our unique aptitudes and personal passions. Finding and nurturing them is the surest way to ensure our growth ... [37]

I first encountered Robinson's work when a friend attended the *Backing our Creativity Symposium* in Melbourne in 2005. As at the time I was just finalising my PhD proposal, reading Robinson's keynote presentation helped to further coalesce my ideas and I made the connection of how vital it is to nurture creativity. My focus then developed and transformed over the course of my research journey, from looking at the nurturing of creativity within formal education, to creativity as a journey of transformation for the 'self' and of 'itself'.

The importance of creativity and its nurturing has remained the main message at the heart of my work, which then expanded to accommodate a more holistic micro/macro view. After this shift in direction within my research, I noted with interest that the focus of Robinson's book at the time, *The Element*, was also on the power of nurturing creativity within the self, and that, similarly to me, he sees this as being interconnected to that of others, as he calls for us to 'move beyond linear, mechanistic metaphors to more organic metaphors of human growth and development.'[38] This idea of replacing rigid linear metaphors with flexible organic ones so as to make more sense of our lives, as well as to construct meaningful ways for reaching decisions on the directions to take, connects back to SPN's invitation to include the personal in the scholarly. For of course much of our lived experience is essentially organic already, coming as it does from the interaction of a unique organic entity (the self) with an organic world. David Abram, who in *The Spell of the Sensuous* reconnects the body and mind with the natural world through the philosophy of Merleau-Ponty, explains this well:

> If ... we wish to describe a particular phenomenon without repressing our direct experience, then we cannot avoid speaking of the phenomenon as an active, animate entity with which we find ourselves engaged. It is for this reason that Merleau-Ponty so consistently uses the active voice to describe things, qualities, and even the enveloping world itself. To the sensing body, *no* thing presents itself as utterly passive or inert. *Only by affirming the animateness of perceived things do we allow our words to emerge directly from the depths of our ongoing reciprocity with the world.* [39]

It is the acceptance of this personal and related way of being in the world, the acknowledgement of the relationships we have with all that is around us as we engage with it, which allows us (if we are open to it) to build specific unique meanings that can nurture our creativity. As Stephanie Pace Marshall points out in *The Power to Transform*, in education '[w]e have become almost blind to wholeness, connections, relationships, and the vibrant and healing energy of our senses and creative imagination.'[40] It is by paying attention to the way our relationships mirror our own selves back to us that we can gain an understanding of our uniqueness that in turn can cultivate our creative self-expression. This enables us to be 'who' we are – the creative unfoldment of our unique selves, rather than just 'what' we are – a series of disconnected roles we've been labelled with by the definitory hierarchical system we live in.

In *Relating Narratives*, Adriana Cavarero makes a strong case for this creative self through her complex and multifaceted theory of the 'narratable self': 'Every human being, without even wanting to know it, is aware of being a *narratable self* – immersed in the spontaneous auto-narration of memory.'[41] She tells us that it is this narratable self that is able to construct the meaning of 'who' we are:

... narration 'reveals the meaning [of the self] without committing the error of defining it.' ... narration reveals the finite in its fragile uniqueness, and sings its glory. ... The one who narrates not only entertains and enchants, like Sheherazade, but gives to the protagonists of his/her story ... a design, a 'destiny', and unrepeatable figure of ... [their] existence, ... [42]

Sheherazade is the narrator in the story framing the magical *Tales of the Thousand and One Nights* (or *Arabian Nights*), as she tells stories to her husband, the Persian King Shahryar, to stop him from slaughtering women. The back-story to Sheherazade's quest is that fearful of women's unfaithfulness, having been betrayed by his first wife, the King married virgins only to have each one killed the morning after their wedding night. Through her connection to Sheherazade, Cavarero reveals narration as being a feminine art imbued with the power of the orality of its beginnings, and she contrasts this with the mostly written 'philosophical discourse on the universal – the definitory art that loves the abstract'[43], which has supported patriarchy extremely well. Orality is connected to wholeness because that's how stories were first told and passed down through generations before writing was developed, and even now that's how children first learn of any stories. So orality is apparent to us from the beginning in its full life context, whereas writing is connected to fragmentation especially as its context is not necessarily revealed, with this being particularly the case with 'universal' discourse, which has therefore been generalised and made abstract.

Looked at symbolically, the framing tale of the *Arabian Nights*, with the murderous and misogynist King, can be seen as an apt representation of patriarchy, with its values of oppressive authority that, as Thomas Berry explains, has 'little regard for the well-being or personal fulfilment of women, for the more significant human values, or for the destiny of the earth itself.'[44] Sheherazade is instead placed 'as the symbol of a feminine knowledge capable of giving the lie to the misogynist prejudice, and capable of overcoming its violent effects.'[45] Through her character, Sheherazade symbolises the nurturing power of feminine wisdom. The King and Sheherazade are not, however, just an archetypal symbolic representation of a separate dichotomy of masculine versus feminine, or male versus female. Rather, through her storyteller role Sheherazade stands for the creative impulse, which is actually the synthesis of both the masculine and feminine archetypal principles; in other words, she stands for the masculine and feminine connected in a harmonious relationship, which constitutes a life-affirming whole.

The archetypal feminine and masculine principles are perhaps best explained by the ancient Chinese symbols of yin and yang, which are said to be the complementary creative energies present in all that is. They are spoken of in Lao Tzu's *Tao Te Ching* as 'a metaphor for all that exists'[46]. Pictured in the familiar Tai Chi symbol ☯ yin and yang represent the interconnectedness of the nature of the universe and its dynamic and transformative rhythm of ebb and flow. The black dot within the white, and the white dot within the black, show that within each is the seed of the other, and that one cannot exist without the other. Clearly the archetypal masculine isn't the same 'masculine' that is promoted by patriarchy, as the only masculine that patriarchy recognises is one that's been warped to be brutal, misogynist, and issuing of a 'phallocentric' discourse – centred on the phallus, or penis, as a symbol of male dominance – upheld by the belief that power (whether through physical strength, money or status) is for taking whatever one wants, without any concern for anyone else. Cavarero explains how narrative can artfully rescind this symbolism:

> Contrary to the law of the sultan, which makes death follow sex, the law of Sheherazade makes a story follow sex, disconnecting sex itself from death and from the rite of deflowering. Narration and conjugal love go together, step by step, for one thousand and one nights. The tale not only stops death, but also gains the time to generate life. ... "after the last story, Sheherazade is able to avoid death by showing the children (sons, it seems) born from the conjugal loves of the thousand and one nights."[47]

The creative impulse, embodied in the 'feminine' (Sheherazade), is asserted through its generative unfolding of creativity (the narratives and lovemaking). This dissolves a distorted 'masculine' championed by patriarchy (the bloodlust of King Shahryar), thereby restoring the harmony of the connected masculine and feminine archetypal principles – the very keys to life – which is demonstrated through the children born of this union. Re-union into unity cannot be achieved through a reductionist and problem-based approach, but only through a holistic approach. In fact, as Cavarero tells us:

> [Importantly] Sheherazade does not tell her first story to the sultan, but

rather to her sister ... [who] had permission to sleep on a bed lower than the nuptial bed in the room of the couple. At the request of her sister, Sheherazade thus begins a tale before sunrise that enthrals the sultan until the sun comes up and which makes him postpone the death of the narrator until the next day. ... [So rather than being] the explicit addressee of a tale that is requested by him ... [he is] only a listener knowingly seduced by the narrative art and her strategy of *suspension*.[48]

Bohm informs us that suspension is the very approach that is necessary when we are faced with any sort of violence or problems that are paradoxes. As an example, he suggests that in dealing with anger we neither demonstrate it nor suppress it. 'What is called for', he says, 'is ... suspending them [both] in the middle at sort of an unstable point – as on a knife-edge – so that you can look at the whole process.'[49] Sheherazade's narration provides this knife-edge suspension for a thousand and one nights, and during this time the creative nature of the self is able to both find expression and gain awareness through time and trust. Thus creativity is nurtured through the connective and participatory process of narration, which in turn has a nurturing and transforming effect on all who come into contact with it.

* * * * * * * * * * * * * * *

REVIEWING THE JOURNEY OF CHAPTER THREE

This chapter brings theories, ideas, writings and practices together into a framework that supports creativity through a holistic perspective. At the same time it continues to develop the theme of nurturing creativity, as well as moving further along the journey of personal transformation. Included in what is discussed are: scholarly personal narrative (SPN), action research – specifically, appreciative inquiry – and feminisms' theories. These three concur on the importance of admitting lived experience within research, and at the same time they bring into question the rigid conventional research methodologies that, due to patriarchal control, hold prime positions in Western thinking and continually stifle creativity.

In 'spreading' the fear of making mistakes, coupled with promoting a 'war-like' outlook, the patriarchal tradition keeps institutions focused on finding problem-based solutions. This is not only overwhelming, but can frequently lock us into trying to solve problems that have no solutions since they are actually paradoxes, and this is more often than not the case, especially with human issues and concerns that are looked at reductively.

This chapter includes the voices of many authors whose work extends the insights and explanations I share. Included among them are those I see as being largely supportive of creativity and the holistic perspective I put forward. These are: Ken Robinson, Nancy Aronie, Daniel Goleman, Mikhail Bakhtin, John Paul Lederach, David Bohm, John Ralston Saul, David Abram, Stephanie Pace Marshall, Thomas Berry, and Adriana Cavarero. Quotes from most of them are found throughout this book.

Bohm is particularly helpful for his lucidity and exactness of expression in describing a holistic view of reality, which he also connects to creativity. Bakhtin's idea of the importance of dialogue, as a point of connection for individuals in the creation of a best-practice way of living, is connected to the appreciative inquiry approach (the work of James Ludema, David Cooperrider, and Frank Barrett) of encouraging 'ever-broadening circles of participants to join in the conversation.'[50] Bohm also promotes the idea of the importance of dialogue, as he suggests a creative dialogue of open communication; he goes even further in letting creativity lead this by proposing that there be no specific theme or topic and that dialogue might be simply allowed to emerge. This he advises could be better achieved if we were able to 'suspend' any kind of emotional or intellectual reactions – even just our urge to respond – by simply observing, so that we might regain our ability to be aware.

Through her theory of a 'spontaneous narratable self', Cavarero is closely linked to theories of feminisms as well as to the nurturing of creativity. By recounting the narrative of Sheherazade, the narrator par excellence, she provides symbolism that unmasks the false masculine, constructed by patriarchy, thereby revealing that the feminine and masculine life principles are harmoniously connected.

Indeed, all the threads introduced in this chapter are already connected; it is as if they were already woven together and I simply had to shed light on them to be able to both see this and show it. They each provide nurturing for creativity and are at the same time led by creativity to unfold and develop through my journey of transformation.

Chapter Four:

THE GROUNDING STRENGTH OF TIME AND TRUST

Nature does not hurry, yet everything is accomplished.[1] – Lao Tzu

... something arose in me, a trust that something in my life itself was the teacher.[2]
– Anderson & Hopkins

Being familiar facets of everyday living in both conversations and thoughts, it may seem redundant to ask, or even reflect on, what 'time' and 'trust' are. Still, the familiar often risks being taken for granted and so can be overlooked; meaning that it's not likely to be thought about deeply or even receive more than cursory consideration. Although familiar, time and trust are also incredibly immense concepts, so much so that, similarly to creativity, they defy definition. While on my PhD journey, I discovered that a more mindful way of engaging with them better enabled me to both nurture my creativity and express it more joyously. In other words, in the process of remaining open to learning and discovering more about time and trust, through observation and experience, I found them to be powerful catalysts for the nurturing and expressing of creativity.

The personal insights that I share in this chapter were gained through the reflection of life experiences – mine, as well as those who related their stories to me. Some of these experiences were quite significant, and I have found that their impact continues to unfold even long after their occurrence, and perhaps may never cease. As Nash, author of *Scholarly Personal Narrative* (SPN), writes: 'The ultimate intellectual responsibility of the SPN scholar is to find a way to use the personal insights gained in order to draw larger conclusions for readers; possibly even to challenge and reconstruct older political or educational narratives, ...'[3]. This concurs with taking a thorough look at time and trust and truly seeing them anew. In gaining new understanding, revealed by a more holistic perspective, the conventionally accepted ways of perceiving them (through the *institutionalised perception*) can be recognised as being irrelevant, and this makes it easier to release this sort of perception, which can then cease to encumber our growth and flow.

If considered in an academic sense, time and trust might be discussed through in-depth analytical use of philosophy; otherwise (and this is much more frequently the case) they are mostly ignored or taken for granted. At the same time, however, their lack is routinely bemoaned as they are constantly referred to as being scarce. Phrases like 'Because of time constraints ...' 'We don't have enough time ...' 'I would love to do it, if only I had time' are frequently heard and used, while the majority of 'risk management' and insurance sales constantly push 'not trusting' and 'things not being trustworthy' as the only sensible way to function in a modern world. All of this has a significant effect on us, as these 'normal' fundamental constraints cause our potential to be limited. By investigating our perception of time and trust a little more closely, it is interesting to also note that they seem to have been basically set up as measures of trade – most work and projects are quoted by the hour, while insurance and risk management vary the cost of all sorts of things considerably, and even put a stop to some creative projects by declaring them too risky.

Time and trust are intrinsic parts of our lives, and as such it is important to reflect more deeply on our experience of them so that we may better understand them. If we could see more clearly how the routine way we perceive them and talk about them impacts our everyday experiences, we might be willing to embrace them more holistically, and this would help us to open the door to our innate creativity and allow us to flow with it more easily.

It was with trepidation that I embarked on the writing of this chapter when I initially wrote my thesis. With an inner knowing, backed by experience, that to be able to successfully face the challenges in our lives we need to make use of trust and time in ways that engage our creativity, it was frustrating not to be certain that what I was setting out to explain would be understood. Given the anxiousness I felt, I suspected that it would have been easier (certainly less fraught with apprehension) to follow my original plan of writing a thesis on 'Nurturing Creativity in Education'. Doing so would have meant elaborating on my findings and interviews to produce yet another 'original' scholarly critique of the education system. Yet from my experience, as well as from all that I have researched and heard on the subject, problem-focused critiques are not very likely to facilitate much social change or transformation. Ludema and colleagues state that:

> As people in organisations inquire into their weaknesses and deficiencies, they gain an expert knowledge of what is 'wrong' with their organizations ... but they do not strengthen their collective capacity to imagine and to build better futures ... [4]

When the spotlight is on what is wrong with something, the critical voice is so strong that it literally drowns out the possibility of the new taking shape. Focusing on the negative makes it impossible to trust – putting 'risk management' under a totally different light – and trust is what is needed for taking action in building, or indeed re-building, the new.

As I was first writing this chapter I realised that 'I' also needed trust to overcome my concern at continuing along the path I had chosen. I needed to trust that I would be willing to give myself enough open time, as in unmeasured time without pressure, to sufficiently untangle the complexity of my experiences, so that I might be able to express them in ways that would be best understood by readers. Furthermore, I also needed to trust that I would be able to deal with whatever happened. This all meant trusting myself, which is not necessarily an easy thing to do.

In *Trust: Self-Interest and the Common Good*, author Marek Kohn points out that 'Like love, trust is involuntary ... Although you can't make yourself trust, you can act in ways that help trust develop ...'[5]. Through practice and experience I have learnt that I can get to a place where I feel more trusting and safer than how I started out. This means that I can help myself to feel safe enough to deal with whatever fears might arise, while knowing that I will be able to do the best I can for myself. I have learnt, however, that to get to this place of trusting I need time. This requires me being aware that I am only physically present right now, at this very point in time, while also being mindful that this time is flowing and so will pass. Time is always 'moving', as the future becomes the present and then the past; the best thing to do is to flow with it, for doing so ensures that I am always consciously present in the here and now.

A new day – dappled sunlight, playing with the jacaranda and bougainvillea, shines through the garden bay window in the kitchen, and drips onto the translucent blooms of the begonias. It's perfect. Full of colour, the day stretches before me fresh and inviting, with just a hint of mystery to be revealed. Hovering in this moment, I feel suspended between the mundane and eternity; I'm in a magical threshold world, where by being fully present the desires of all my senses feel fulfilled, and I'm enveloped by a sensation of peace and contentment. I belong in this world, ever-present to the now; time is my friend here. It is here that I do my deep thinking, much of my writing, and all of my happy living, fully connected with everything in my environment. I slip back here whenever I can, in between measured time slots, that as a member of Western society I seem to have agreed to keep by default. Yet, there was a time when feeling present and connected was not a frequent occurrence for me.

Before I consciously chose to nurture my creativity, my access to the world of 'the here and now' was sporadic and seemed to happen only by chance. Though aware that I was more than the sum of my roles – daughter, sister, girlfriend, university student, friend, information officer at the Australian Bureau of Statistics, air traffic controller trainee, and so on – I did not actually know how to go beyond these separate roles so as to connect with the bigger 'self' that I felt, and knew, I was. Although I had freely and willingly accepted these different roles, I was fragmented by them and their specific definition, and furthermore I felt pressured to fully identify with each of them so as to be a 'good daughter', a 'successful trainee', a 'high achieving student', and so on. They weighed me down with guilt, which I felt because I believed I wasn't totally fulfilling the unspoken expectations that each of them required. More than anything, it was ironic that despite the clear labels of these roles I nonetheless felt lost; it was as though my wholeness had seeped through the cracks created by the boundaries of these different roles clashing against each other. I fervently wished to relieve the guilt and pressures that oppressed me, but not knowing how or where to find myself I could not go forward, no matter which direction I faced; I felt overwhelmed, powerless, and stuck.

There are many links I would like to make here as part of this trust-time connection that I'm endeavouring to explain. Seeing them as differently coloured strands of thread, I want to weave them together, and by connecting them create the fabric of this chapter – contrasting side by side, now intersecting and now diverging, each of them important and present in the 'now' of what I want to communicate. This is where the limitations of writing become very clear. It seems overwhelmingly the case that in writing an experience can be explained only one sensation at a time; likewise only one thread of reasoning can be followed at a time, and this is especially true for traditional academic writing, where it is also preferable for each thread to have a clear beginning and end.

To continue my weaving metaphor, I ask myself if it is possible to weave threads and yet 'keep them separate', in accordance with the strictly linear academic convention. Over and over again, I have found a linear dichotomous perspective to be favoured as the prevalent one in many societal aspects of life, as particularly in anything that has been institutionalised it is often touted as the only possible approach. A linear, either/or, perspective limits our ways of thinking as it reduces us to believe that we only have one of two opposite choices; the focus on these two opposite choices is given as being so clear and obvious that all other possibilities are practically rendered invisible.

One such situation occurred for me when my daughter (ten years old at the time) broke her arm just above her wrist. On returning to the hospital two weeks after the incident for a second lot of x-rays to check the progress of the fracture, the young registrar told me rather grimly that my daughter's green-stick fracture had not set right, and that a cast would need to be put on. He quickly added that this had to be a surgical procedure under anaesthetic, as the bone had to be manipulated internally. Given we were at the hospital already, and they just happened to have room to admit her, the registrar said he could arrange everything straight away. All I had to do was sign the papers to give my permission, and then go home to collect what she needed for an overnight stay. He stressed the importance of acting quickly as we had already 'wasted' two weeks, and leaving it any longer might mean that the bone would knit together with a kink, causing all kinds of problems. He also added that it was possible that an infection might occur, since the wound's dressing would not be able to be changed because of the cast, so I was required to sign my consent to relieve the hospital of that responsibility.

By this stage my daughter was crying and begging me not to leave her at the hospital on her own – a quick trip for a follow-up x-ray had turned into a nightmare! What was I to do? Should I go ahead with what I'd been advised by the medical professional or not? Apart from wanting to calm my daughter, I felt quite upset myself, and yet it was clear that I was expected to make a quick rational decision so as to ensure the best possible outcome for her. Among the things that my daughter loved most in the world was ballet – if I didn't act immediately would it ruin her chances of a possible career? I had other fears – of having my daughter go under anaesthetic (as there is always some risk associated with this), and of the chance of infection. I had to choose, yes or no!

I don't know what made me listen to my inner *beingness* that day – among all of the voices that clamoured for my attention in my mind was a voice that came from deep within; it was very calm, and focusing on it for just an instant was enough to win me over. What I got from it was that I could *trust myself* to make the right decision, but to do this I needed to give myself enough calm time – I did in fact have more than two choices. So I left the hospital with my daughter and the x-ray. Within a few days I found an appropriate specialist to give us a second opinion, and then organised for my daughter to have a cast put on by him with only minimal external manipulation, which after six weeks resulted in a perfectly healed arm.

Listening to myself, and most importantly trusting myself, gave me both the courage and the time to move forward with ease, which included handling the objections and fears of other family members. What had appeared to be an insurmountable problem quickly became a lot less complicated when I trusted myself, as possible choices opened up before me, giving me what felt like a sense of freedom, even in such a foreboding situation. In retrospect, the choices I made seemed like the only possible ones I could have made – they had an inherent sense of 'rightness' about them, and choosing one led me to easily make the next choice. From having the almost certain belief that I only had two opposite choices, becoming mindful of trust and time led me to walk a pathway of many interconnected choices.

If we keep seeing each 'thing', 'idea', and 'concept' we come across as something separate and often contrary to everything else, and believe that we need to choose whether we are for or against them, then all we might ever see is a jumble of 'things' – fragments of the whole picture that is in this way likely to remain devoid of meaning. In *Philosophical Investigations,* Ludwig Wittgenstein gives a useful and vivid analogy that I see as being helpful in showing us that seeing things as separate is not a true reflection of life. He explains the intrinsic connection of similarities between things as being 'a complicated network of similarities overlapping ... as in spinning a thread we twist fibre on fibre. And the strength of the thread does not reside in the fact that some one fibre runs through its whole length, but in the overlapping of many fibres.'[6] This is a much more holistic way of looking at the world, which is, after all, whole and made up of many interconnected things. Bringing clear awareness to this also enables us to better make use of the strength of interconnectedness.

Anticipating readers' expectations is another factor that can further complicate the attempt of revealing the whole picture in the process of writing. Indeed, writers are told to always consider their readers' expectations by thinking of the audience they're writing for. My concern in writing my thesis was that the unconventionality of my writing might prejudice how it would be received. I was apprehensive that by not being familiar with the ideas being presented, a reader might not be willing to take them into consideration, indeed a reader might even stop reading altogether, and this would mean the message I wanted to convey would never be received. I felt that this was more likely to be the case if the reader were to strongly identify with the roles of lecturer/tutor, examiner, supervisor, publisher or reviewer – roles of 'gate-keepers' of the status quo, requiring some sort of value judgment to be made of the work, usually in the form of a grade or a decision to accept or not accept the text for publication, with this decision starting to be formed even before the piece was read. As Nash reminds us, 'Anytime you want to do something different ..., whether it requires a drastic or moderate change, you are talking about shaking up established hierarchies of intellectual authority.'[7] This challenging of established and traditional ways of doing things can make people feel threatened.

The realisation of all of this required me to be even more trusting if I was to go ahead and 'risk' writing this chapter. In understanding that I needed trust to write, I also recognised that trust is similarly needed in reading – to be open to new ideas and messages, a reader has to at least momentarily suspend any disbelief and judgement – with more trust being required as the complexity of what is read increases. For my part, I needed to trust (more than hope) that the readers of my writing would approach my work with an open attitude. Indeed, while writing this chapter I envisioned my readers approaching it with a state of mind reflecting the environment congenial for creativity. As described in Chapter One, this includes: openness, a positive attitude to the new, acceptance of diversity, a willingness to see the value in that which is not 'standard', and an absence of the desire to suppress all that challenges conformity and authority.[8] Through trust and openness, readers of my writing would also be able to access other qualities vital for co-creating (through visualisation) the complex whole pictures that the concepts presented in the writing required. These qualities comprise: patience and tolerance of ambiguity, as well as flexibility in going beyond the often quite passive role of 'reader', to one who is actually dialoguing with the written text. These types of readers often mark the text, underlining and writing notes in the margins and between the lines (in pencil, of course), or might be recognised by their animated expressions as they read, as if they were conversing with the author, while others may do it all in their head with little outward sign.

When readers interact with a text they creatively bring in the personal experiences that they've been reminded of while reading. These are the experiences that connect them to what the author is saying, and they serve to make the discussion that the writer has begun more relevant and real. In the case of this chapter, as language theorist Roger Fowler suggests, with writing that poses questions the 'questioning of existing conventions is the basic creative act that is being performed.'[9] The trusting and creative sort of reading I'm suggesting, and wanting from my readers, also requires time. It would be difficult for a reader on a tight schedule to be open to see what non-conformist writing has to say, as this entails accepting the possibility of reconsidering one's perspective and beliefs on how the world functions[10].

As Lederach writes, '*[t]o risk* is to step into the unknown without any guarantee of success or even safety. Risk by its very nature is mysterious. It is mystery lived ...'[11]. However, the more one trusts, the more risk becomes possible, as trust somehow provides an invisible and yet palpable mantle of emotional safety that allows one to be able to courageously face risk. In this way, trust could be said to be somewhat akin to faith, which has given believers the world over the courage to face even martyrdom and death for their beliefs. While it is readily known that faith means the belief in something that the believer is certain of, with trust the 'object' of belief is not often that clear, as we're not usually accustomed to stop and think about what it is we must believe in, in order to trust.

It wasn't until I began to trust more that I became aware of how little I actually trusted. In practicing trust I discovered that it helped me to let go of expectations, with this encompassing the release of the need to control outcomes, while at the same time being totally certain that the best possible outcome was the one that would occur, by being the one that the focus was on. An analogy of this is of someone passionate about tightrope walking, practising and focusing on learning the skill to become a tightrope walker. A big part of that would be trusting that they would not fall, which they would do by focusing on walking the rope and safely reaching the other side. It is this trust and confidence in themselves (besides all the other exercises and practice they would need) that would help them walk the rope nimbly and flowingly. It is this particular aspect of trust – of enabling a total focus on the positive – that can help us to fully connect to our creativity and embody it. This allows us to live the mystery that Lederach speaks of, and to express our creativity in life with an intrinsic openness.

At the start of his book on trust, Kohn looks at the feelings that trust engenders; he points out that the word 'trust' itself 'has the gift of warming the heart and dissolving its tensions.'[12] In the last paragraph of his book, after having looked at the evolutionary origins and development of trust, as well as having explored it from various perspectives in numerous contexts, Kohn sums up with:

> Trust is desirable in itself. When it is placed well, it enhances relations of all kinds. Life is more enjoyable, work is more productive, relationships are more meaningful and rewarding. And it is also part of a complex of factors – association, social capital, community, democracy, equality, health, and happiness – that make for a good society.[13]

In other words, trust improves the quality of human life; when we believe that those we mix with have our best interests at heart, then we find it easier to connect with them in more positive ways and we can relax in these interactions more openly, with this serving to further strengthen our relationships with them as trust begets trust.

In his book Kohn also highlights an important finding by political scientist Eric Uslaner: that societies where there is more equality are more trusting than those where there is considerable inequality. That is to say, equality plays a big part in the levels of trust that are present in a society, especially in the case of economic and social care equity. I use the word 'equity' here rather than 'equality', because equality can often be misunderstood by simplistically being taken to mean 'the same', and the belief that fairness entails equality for all. The truth, however, is rather more complex; for example, the cost of parking in a place like a hospital in Australia is usually the same for everybody, but although the cost is 'the same' this is a perfect example of economic inequality. Depending on their disposable income, some people would hardly notice the money spent on parking while being with a loved one who had to stay in hospital for a week. Instead pensioners, or those on a low income, might have to do without some necessities, or even food, in order to have the parking money required. Bringing about equality (equity) would entail varying the monetary cost of things, like parking at hospitals or the many fines imposed on different situations, according to people's economic means, which would then have more of an equal impact on them.

On reflection it seems quite reasonable and understandable that equality would be an important basis for trust. People who accept each other as equal do not feel driven to compete with each other, and they also do not feel any need to defend themselves; what's more, in knowing that the majority of people in their society have access to the means to properly care for themselves, individuals are released from the often crushing sense of responsibility (usually felt through guilt, and asked from them as money) of having to take care of others. In such societies a stronger feeling of safety prevails, an atmosphere that everything is 'alright', a feeling that would not be commonly found in societies where inequality was prevalent.

As Aronie emphasises in *Writing from the Heart*, a sense of safety is very important in order for people to feel that they can be trusting. As she explains:

> When people aren't pitted against each other, when they are not even mildly competing, when people aren't vying for position (because all positions in this circle are equally important), they jump out of themselves and into their humanity. ... When people feel safe, [when people trust] they

recognize themselves in others, and instead of being threatened by their differences, they are moved by them.[14]

When people feel safe enough to be open to actually seeing the differences between others and themselves, then there is a chance for them to build on what they see; feeling an all-encompassing sense of this also helps their creativity blossom. In everyday society in many (and perhaps most) situations, it is not commonplace to feel safe enough to trust oneself to be open. The reasons for this are the numerous obstructions in place, with these being practically 'inbuilt' in the current way our human societies are structured. Kohn observes with surprise that despite substantial research clearly indicating a strong direct connection between inequality and problems with health and wellbeing, both in individuals and societies, this has not resulted in inequality being addressed and resolved. He remarks that when issues are addressed it is as though inequality is bypassed, as though it's looked straight through without being seen; even when it's mentioned it is still not acknowledged as being a main concern.[15] In revealing this, Kohn has exposed the proverbial 'elephant in the room'.

We live in a society that designates the worth of things and people according to the system of values of the hierarchical social order we live by (as has already been discussed in detail in Chapter Two). The principles of our governing hierarchical system are obviously entrenched within the institutions that have specifically been developed to run society, and as a result these principles are so embedded within us as to have become the accepted 'norm' by the majority of the members of society. To realise this, we need only consider how deeply ingrained in our psyche the war/fighting/conflict metaphor is. Not only does it appear to be accepted at all levels of society that conflict and fighting are a necessary part of our human reality, but this is also most often the metaphor of choice for a wide variety of points that we want to get across. It is the superlative accepted way to communicate that we're in earnest about what we want to achieve. Thus we fight dirt, disease, bullying, recession, poverty, global warming, terror, and anything else we fear (or have been made to fear), dislike or simply don't want. The use of what we call strong words such as 'fighting', 'war', 'warrior', and so on, being an essential component to show that we are serious about addressing these issues, with any other way of talking appearing simply too ineffective or 'wishy-washy'.

That the fighting metaphor is so ensconced within us is a symptom that reveals that we are indeed carrying the values of our governing hierarchical system – patriarchy. They've been grafted onto us by the *institutionalised perception* we have been taught to operate from since we were children, when we allowed them into our psyche more or less willingly because we experienced that conforming was the only way to belong, to be accepted and fulfil our need to be loved. As we grow up, our exposure to the authority of legitimate language, handed down to us through the media, school, government and books, stifles our innate creative inquisitiveness, until ultimately we shut it off ourselves, tired of the negative (or even unsafe) reception it provokes. Finally, by the time we reach adulthood we are hardly aware that what we now perceive as ordinary has actually only slowly been built within us, a social construct that provides us with our sense of what normality is – the familiar everyday things that blend together into a sort of big background canvas that does not require much of our attention because we know it so well. Despite this feeling of things appearing 'normal', Fowler reminds us that 'common sense is not natural, but a product of social convention.'[16]

Much like the background noise of traffic, for those who have grown up living in homes on busy streets, normality (all that we are used to) is not consciously noticed unless it somehow changes. Fowler stresses that we become compliant when we accept the state of things as being normal and natural, since they are in fact anything but. A minor example of this is the wearing of school uniforms. Originally said to have been instigated in the UK so that teachers might not differentiate between students, especially based on their parents' level of wealth or lack, in some countries uniforms are now seen as the dress code of choice for school children, while in countries that don't have this tradition having students wear them would appear preposterous. Although the status quo is arbitrary, by accepting it as 'normal' we believe and internalise constructed meanings without considering what they really mean. The result of this is that we end up living mostly by tacit rules.

In a hierarchy, inequality is considered to be normal, since by its very definition a hierarchical system can only exist through inequality. Were we to actively promote equality in our society, we would instead live in an egalitarian system with 'leaders' who would essentially be facilitators. Rather than place themselves at the top, they would facilitate the positive growth and advancement of society as a collective, with wisdom and care, from wherever they found themselves in our human circle of belonging. I see this as a vision of a very possible future for us, with many others, including most of those whose quotes appear in this book, also sharing this vision.

Returning now to the discussion of Kohn's surprise at inequality not being recognised as a serious concern; it is useful to reflect that it is virtually impossible for inequality to be noticed as something needing to be changed by anyone in a position of authority, especially if this person intends maintaining his or her position. By authority I mean its common definition of the right to give orders and enforce obedience. Maintaining authority within the system we live in, given the way this system currently operates, effectively means maintaining inequality.

The inequality in our society is constantly perpetuated through the regulating (controlling) of everything and everyone, so that each thing and individual is assigned (and often reassigned several times over a lifespan) its 'worth', in line with the hierarchical value system we live under. This worth is what dictates how much something will cost, how much a person will be able to earn and have access to, with this including the means to pursue one's dreams, and so on (as elaborated on in Chapter Two). All of this ensures that the hierarchical status quo is maintained, and that the whole system continues to turn upon inequality. In *Schooling for a Fair Go*, the authors highlight that, according to the relevant conclusion of Tony Fitzgerald's report on *Poverty and Education in Australia*:

> ... people who are poor and disadvantaged are victims of a societal confidence trick. They have been encouraged to believe that a major goal of schooling is to increase equality, while, in reality, schools reflect society's intention to maintain the present unequal distribution of status and power.[17]

Despite all I have pointed out, I have no doubt that the greater majority of people in society genuinely want things to improve for those who are poor and disadvantaged, and are therefore not consciously intent in maintaining a status quo of inequality. In fact, in *Social Intelligence*, Daniel Goleman confirms this from the studies of renowned Harvard psychologist Jerome Kagan, who assures us through his extensive research that human nature is made up of a lot more goodness than nastiness:

"Although humans inherit a biological bias that permits them to feel anger, jealousy, selfishness and envy, and to be rude, aggressive or violent," Kagan notes, "they inherit an even stronger biological bias for kindness, compassion, cooperation, love and nurture-especially towards those in need."[18]

This 'bias' towards kindness, however, is stymied if we don't feel safe ourselves. 'Caregiving flows most fully when we are feeling secure ... [so that] we can feel empathy without being overwhelmed. Feeling cared for frees us to care for others – and when we don't feel cared for, we can't care nearly so well.'[19] In navigating through life we come across many things that cause us stress and worry, and the more of these pressures we have to deal with the less we are able to care for others, especially those others who (unlike our children, elderly parents, and so on) are not directly our responsibility and concern. As Goleman points out, in a hierarchical society there are even more reasons for feeling insecure and stressed:

> In rigid hierarchies bosses tend to be authoritarian: they more freely express their contempt for their subordinates, who in turn naturally feel a messy mix of hostility, fear and insecurity ... because their salary and very job security depend on the boss, workers tend to obsess over their interactions, reading even mildly negative exchanges as ominous.[20]

Interestingly, this applies regardless of the level of education achieved by the 'subordinates'. For example, in many Australian universities, highly educated people in possession of doctorate degrees are more and more likely to be hired to lecture, tutor, and research on short-term casual appointments, rather than be given tenure or any kind of reasonable job security that acknowledges the value of their work. These casual appointments require academic employees to sign contracts accepting the possibility of their position being terminated with one hour's notice, as well as having them fill in timesheets that then have to be authorised by 'supervisors' (quite possibly with a lower level of education) before payment is approved. This can cause the first pay after they start a contract to come through several pay cycles later, although parking payment is required immediately. This sort of treatment of academic staff by universities has been normalised through the growing casualisation of academic work in most of the Western world. This creation of a 'casual academic class' is another way that Western society, through its educational institutions, maintains the status quo of inequality.

A common result of job insecurity is overwork; in response to more and more workplaces looking to maximise their productivity while minimising their expenditure, many individuals end up working long hours and making do with less than satisfactory conditions in the hope that this will safeguard their employment. Added to this are also the ordinary stresses of daily living. These range from major concerns – like ensuring we can take care of ourselves and anyone else in our daily care, including children, pets, elderly or ill relatives or friends – to other minor concerns. Despite being 'minor', when enmeshed by the bureaucratic requirements common to our modern civilization, these concerns can nonetheless oppressively loom over our lives. Among them are complying with requirements for tax returns, seeing to home and car maintenance and repairs, filling in all sorts of forms for all the institutions we come into contact with – medical, educational, governmental, and so on, as well as coping with traffic, noisy neighbours, rude people, and a myriad of other things that both fill and fragment our life without adding to the enjoyment of it.

All that we're required to do and comply with (there are now positions whose job description is ensuring people's compliance), as opposed to what we freely choose to do, holds us captive, with this hold feeling tighter when it causes stress, which is more often than not the case if we allow our roles to dictate our lives. When our attention is taken up with so much to worry about, as Goleman tells us, empathy doesn't stand a chance, in fact we find it extremely difficult to even become aware of the genuine needs of others, let alone have any mental space to care about them. In addition, when we feel overwhelmed by pressures and responsibilities these can impact negatively on us, so that like a downward spiral our stress and anxiety increase. With this sort of experience being commonplace in much of modern society, our capacity to trust becomes easily eroded and our fear of change increases. This is because change would require an investment of time that we feel hard-pressed to provide in our state of compliance, which we invariably believe must be maintained to guarantee our survival. Since without trust it is very difficult to see past the overriding fear that change would make situations worse, we therefore feel compelled to maintain the status quo despite this not being in anyone's best interest.

A timely and synchronistic example of this societal impetus to retain inequality occurred while I was first reviewing this chapter, to submit my thesis. This took place on 24 June 2010, when Julia Gillard was elected as the new leader of the Labor party by a leadership ballot in her favour, and Kevin Rudd was dismissed as Australia's Prime Minister. Rudd had planned to introduce a resource super profits tax on the profits made by mining companies (many of them multinationals) in their Australian mines. This was in line with his principal motivation since becoming Prime Minister, which he reiterated at his final press conference: 'I was elected by the Australian people as prime minister of this country to bring back a fair go for all Australians ...'.

While the details of this tax are quite complex, the main gist is that the Australian Government was committed to introducing it so as to get a fairer share for the Australian people from the mining of Australian resources – this meant a share from the profits which had been going straight to the multinationals and their shareholders. This caused huge retaliation by the multinational mining corporations, who undertook massive advertising campaigns to rally the public's support against the proposed tax, saying that it would cause job losses in the mining sector and result in economic uncertainty. By tapping into people's fear of change, the proposed imposition of the tax looked very dismal and frightening.

In Mr Palmer's (a Queensland mining billionaire) words: 'This is the first time in Australia's history that a prime minister has been defeated by a civil campaign of anger ... Have a look when we first started this campaign where he was, and where he was at the end of it'[21]. The campaign he referred to is the advertising blitz undertaken by the mining industry; he unabashedly stated that the 'mining industry campaign had helped ensure Mr Rudd was dumped as leader.'[22] Although the change in leadership was actually a lot more involved and complex than Mr Palmer claimed, as it had to do with party dynamics and other issues that need not be broached here, the message that came from some of the super-wealthy of the world – those at the top of the hierarchy – was significant. Some of the biggest multinational mining corporations made it clear that they did not want things to change, even though this would have meant just a *little* move towards more 'equality'. The online *Business Spectator* reported at the time that:

> The Association of Mining and Exploration Companies Inc (AMEC) has also called for "an immediate and complete withdrawal of the proposed toxic mining tax in order to restore Australia's reputation as a safe, reliable

and financially attractive place in which to invest."[23]

I find the choice of the word 'toxic' quite ironic, given the literally toxic crises that the world is made to regularly face by following the common 'business before anything else' attitude endorsed by the majority of its most powerful economic entities. If power and profits were not considered as being of primary value no matter what the consequences to anything else, there would not be so many environmental disasters occurring, and actions would be taken to ensure that everything affected by any business endeavour was adequately restored and looked after. Instead, it is the order of the day that in the pursuit of profits and business, the environment is abused and harmed, as are those at the bottom of the Western societal hierarchy, who bear the worst brunt of most environmental disasters, these are those who are poor and disadvantaged, which includes First Nations people.

Valuing 'business as usual' above all else is the basis of environmental catastrophes such as the oil spill in the Gulf of Mexico, which (according to the South Florida *Sun-Sentinel* website) began on 20 April 2010 and was finally capped on 15 July 2010 after spilling some 200 million gallons of crude oil. Less than two years later, the unparalleled Fukushima nuclear disaster occurred; according to the Fukushima Nuclear Accident Independent Investigation Commission it was a 'man-made disaster – that could and should have been foreseen and prevented.'[24] Despite their extensive impact on many of us, these disasters don't appear to be newsworthy for long, and even though they've not been resolved it's not long after they've occurred that interest in them has all but 'fizzled out' in mainstream media, where in comparison to the reporting of political campaigns and various 'scandals' they pale into insignificance.

As stated at the beginning of this chapter, both time and trust have one thing in common, which is that they are viewed as being scarce, and this is in most of the settings and situations of our modern Western world, like its institutions. *It all just comes down to time ... that preparation time and reflection time is just so crucial and most of the time you just don't have it* (teacher). In a productivity race for everything, deadlines are set to push people to produce more and more, faster and faster. Most businesses (especially those with shareholders) tend to work on the previous year's figures of turnover and profit, with the constant aim being to 'improve' on them, to have the business growing and to make more and more profit.

To make sure that the yearly profit growth occurs, by 'seeking to control risks, employers codify what they once might have trusted their employees to decide for themselves.'[25] This means that employees are given less choice on how their time is utilised at work, as it becomes a requirement for procedures to be written down and standardised. With more procedures being prescribed, more trust is therefore replaced with control, and this occurs each time new possible risks are identified, until ultimately more time is increasingly taken up with controlling things and people, for even some of the most obvious sorts of tasks. This results in incongruous but common scenarios of checkout operators greeting customer after customer with exactly the same stock phrase, or question: 'Hello, how are you today?' or baristas asking for peoples' first names so they can call them out when their order is ready... a procedure they seem to follow even if there is only one customer present.

On an individual level, this perception of a lack of time ends up meaning that time is viewed as a constraint, as well as a source of impatience and irritation. While I have certainly experienced this, I have also experienced time being a flowing stream, which once immersed in feels blissful. In listening to my intuition, I hear a quiet voice telling me that no amount of pushing or punishing work is going to get me finished or achieving anything sooner than the journey connected to any particular thing is actually going to take.

Imagine watching a wave wash onto the shore, coming up and up on the sand, right up to the point when it then starts receding, the ocean pulling it back. The intellectual mind cannot work out where that point of stillness will be when the wave will go no further. Obviously, it would be unreasonable to dictate that it should come up to a particular point and take a specific time to do this – the wave will only come up to the point when it will start receding again, and it will take exactly the time it takes to do this. This action of the wave washing onto the beach is akin to the process of doing creative work. Writing is creative work; in fact making or doing anything we do in life is creative work, as it involves transforming both our environment and ourselves through our actions. These actions are a mix of physical, mental and emotional work involving the *creation* of something new.

Having studied how time is viewed differently by different cultures, David Abram points out how Western society perceives the present as 'nothing more than a point, an infinitesimal now separating "the past" from "the future."'[26] It makes sense that we would feel very time-poor given that our preoccupation with measuring time has led us to view it only as a sequence of 'nows'[27], with these quickly evading us as we see them zooming at us from the future and receding into the past. This makes us feel empty-handed and almost cheated, and at the same time it ensures that an attitude of scarcity becomes firmly entrenched within us. It is this sort of attitude that can lead to difficulties or even panic ensuing when we are faced with having to make decisions. If we don't believe that we have enough time to make a considered decision we can feel pressured and fearful that we may make the wrong decision, or miss an opportunity as it 'flies' past us.

There have been times in my life when I have felt invisibly coerced into hurrying the making of a decision over something important, and inevitably this has meant forgoing something I intuited I both deeply needed and wished. While I couldn't have clearly stated what this actually entailed at the time, I strongly sensed that in making a quick decision I was unwittingly depriving myself of even the time to find out what this might have been. It has been at moments like this that I have heard the faintest of whispering within me 'shouting': 'Trust! Trust!' However, I mostly ignored this, caught up, as I was, in the panic and seriousness of whatever situation I happened to be in. I also often found that this uncomfortable emotional state was heightened in me by a sense of guilt, induced by thoughts that I was letting myself down because I should have known what I wanted, but I wasn't prepared enough, or I wasn't good enough, and so on. It was only when I finally started listening to the voice deep within me that I realised that by trusting 'trust' itself, time opened out before me, and I found that I had just the right amount of it necessary to do whatever was needed. Moreover, by trusting I found that I could think more clearly, so that opportunities were more likely to present themselves in ways that mapped out an ideal path for me to follow.

I have already described the situation of when my daughter broke her arm; it was in choosing to finally listen to and trust that little voice within me, the one coming from my *beingness,* that I was able to find the time I needed to more easily decide what the 'right' decision was for me. While my initial identifying and relating to my different roles had resulted in a cacophony of voices that pulled me in contrary directions, centring on my *beingness* strengthened my ability to trust myself. This experience, together with a number of subsequent others, taught me that trust and time are together powerful catalysts that nurture the possibility of a creative response for the best possible outcome in countless situations.

These best outcomes, coming from occasions when trust and time are made use of, seem to apply even to trivial sorts of decisions, like for example home renovating choices, which, although seemingly unimportant and frivolous when compared to many other choices in life, can nonetheless make a substantial difference to our lives. Once the garden bay window, the granite bench top, and the garden path had been installed, each looked right, as if it belonged, as if it had always been there. Over the years these renovating choices have provided my family and me, and also visitors to our home, with aesthetic harmony and pleasure. By creating the sort of beauty we like at home, we can essentially establish a sense of safety and rightness that supports our day-to-day living; by extension this can also impart calm and clarity to the more important decisions we need to make. Basically, the love we fill our homes with is always mirrored back to us.

When we trust, and give ourselves (and others) enough time, we nurture the possibilities, the seeds as it were, of a creative attitude developing; thus trust and time provide the space necessary for creativity to grow in. As Lederach shares: 'Providing space requires a predisposition, a kind of attitude and perspective that opens up, even invokes, the spirit and belief that creativity is humanly possible.'[28] Belief in creativity actually helps us to allow for the trust and time that can then nurture creativity. This connects to Bohm's suggestion of 'suspending action without suppressing it'[29]: trust allows for this suspension, which then allows for time and attention. This also shows how trust and time have an inter-generative connection, which is to say they generate each other. By trusting, we become willing to give more time to ourselves, others, and situations; similarly, time allows trust to grow and deepen through our experiences of the benefits we gain from it. It is this generative process that shapes the space and the attitude for an environment that is supportive and nurturing of creativity, the same sort of environment that Csikszentmihalyi discusses as being conducive to creativity.

A practical example of this sort of approach to time and trust, which goes beyond the personal, is provided by Finland's education system. For quite a number of years prior to the completion of my thesis by the end of 2010, Finland had been coming top, or near the top, in the PISA (Programme for International Student Assessment) study. Run by the OECD (Organisation for Economic Cooperation and Development), PISA has every three years, since the year 2000, conducted testing of fifteen-year-olds on a number of subjects in around forty countries. The main aim of this study is to find out whether the students have gained from their education 'the knowledge and skills essential for full participation in society.'[30] To fulfil this aim, PISA's test results answered questions such as: 'Are students well prepared for future challenges? Can they analyse, reason and communicate effectively? Do they have the capacity to continue learning throughout life?'[31] The results that Finland attained attracted the interest of many countries, with some, like Japan, even adopting part of the Finnish schooling model; interestingly, after doing this Japan also improved their scores of the PISA study.

What was it, and what is it (as Finland's scores in the PISA study continue to be high) about the Finnish education system that helps students achieve so highly? The very informative website *Virtual Finland,* at the time I visited it (in 2007) told the world that '[t]he Finnish school system is based on a culture of trust, not control, and teachers are active in developing their own work. On the job they set an example of lifelong learning.'[32] After completing the required qualification of an Arts Master's degree, teachers in Finland enjoy significant autonomy and, unlike in many Western countries, they don't have to undergo regular evaluations; students call their teachers by their first name and yet this doesn't lessen the high level of respect that teachers have in society.

Exams are rare in the nine years of comprehensive schooling in Finland, since they are clearly seen as creating artificial time pressure; what's more, there's no standardised testing or grading in assessments. Priority is given to creating an atmosphere of safety and motivation at school, and students are encouraged to learn in their own way, with learning by 'doing', and community focus being considered vital to help develop the students' self-reliance. Children's parents are welcome in the classrooms, and all of the adults in the school (that is all staff, not just the teaching staff) are welcome to have an input in the school. A particularly relevant remark on the website, was that 'unnecessary hierarchical structures are avoided among the staff.'[33] Compulsory comprehensive school starts at the age of seven, with one non-compulsory pre-school year available for six-year-olds.

Furthermore, schooling is free for all, being mostly government run and funded.

Finland's website is now called 'this is Finland', and in its section on education is also featured an article by Tim Walker (an American teacher, blogger and author) – 'The Simple Strength of Finnish Education'. Based on Walker's two years' experience of teaching in a primary school in Helsinki, the article shares the acronym he developed to best explain education in Finland – SIMPLE. This, he elaborates, stands for: 'Sensible, Independent, Modest, Playful, Low-stress and Equitable'[34]; reading it confirmed for me that the Finnish school system incorporates much that nurtures creativity in its teaching practices. Furthermore, in an interview about his book – *Teach Like Finland: 33 Simple Strategies for Joyful Classrooms* – released in April 2017, Walker explains how it's a lack of equity that is responsible for much of the difference in education between Finland and the US:

> Before moving to Finland, I confess that I did very little thinking about how U.S. schools might compare to other schools around the world. I suspected that America had its share of "bad" schools, but I largely blamed the nation's social inequality for their failings, not the educators. ... Today I'm convinced, after teaching and living in Finland, that the glaring weakness in American education is, in fact, a basic matter of inaccessibility: too many kids in America lack access to decent schools.[35]

Based on its choice to trust its teachers and students, rather than trying to identify only those who are 'gifted' through standardised testing, the Finnish education system is clearly more egalitarian than elitist. In addition, the choice of trust is invested over enough time to allow for a 'natural' return. To quote Tuula Haatainen, who was Finland's education minister from 2003 to 2005: 'We believe that if we invest in all our children for nine years and give them the same education then we will reach the best results.'[36] This investment also continues with higher education, where tuition fees are government funded. Unlike many countries where students are pushed through university as quickly as possible, something that can often result in underemployment – employment in positions that don't utilise people's abilities or qualifications – the Finnish education agenda allows for the necessary time for people's talents to be discovered and developed:

> School education stretches over long periods of time; most people do not

qualify for their professions before the age of 20, and a significant number of higher education students do not do so before the age of 25. The goal is lifelong learning; there are plenty of further training opportunities supported by the public sector for adults already working in an occupation, and it is by no means a rare phenomenon for people to learn a new profession later in life.[37]

Giving people sufficient time to prepare for a career is more likely to allow them to nurture their creativity, and this can better enable them to find what Robinson calls 'their Element ... the meeting point between natural aptitude and personal passion ... [which] provides a sense of self-revelation, of defining who they really are and what they are meant to be doing with their lives.'[38]

Finland's example clearly demonstrates that by harnessing trust and time it is possible to support creativity in the mainstream, that is to say for everybody rather than just for some 'gifted' few, while still operating within a modern Western structure. If an institution, such as an education system, can achieve this, then perhaps it is possible for all institutions to endorse the nurturing of creativity. After all, institutions operate through the work of individuals, and a community of individuals who choose to base their work on an attitude of creativity could also help to transform the whole system itself, including its institutions.

* * * * * * * * * * * * * * *

REVIEWING THE JOURNEY OF CHAPTER FOUR

This chapter looks at how mindfully engaging with trust and time would facilitate the nurturing of a creative attitude within all of us, so that together we might be able to imagine, and then create, a different reality to the one we currently inhabit. While time and trust are necessary for the nurturing of creativity, many of the environments of our modern Western world (especially institutions) seem to function on a carefully maintained perception of a lack of both. Indeed they also often appear to have us pay lip service to creativity while at the same time it is kept comfortably 'at bay'. Being mostly based on hierarchical control, the structures of these institutions are simplistic and reductionist, and so are unable to truly offer any support to nurturing something that is as open-ended, complex and natural as creativity. In other words, the way these institutions are run is incompatible with creativity. When this is what most of our experience has been, hoping to be able to nurture creativity might seem as achievable as some utopia. However, in my experience, even just a little extra time I choose to give to myself enables me to connect with my *beingness* and gives my creativity a chance to unfold in unexpected ways. This is because by relieving my immediate time-pressure it allows me to start to develop some trust in myself.

Control and risk management are diametrically opposed to trusting and giving time; based as they are on 'what if' scenarios, that employ problem-solving in what are usually seen as escalations of possible conflicts of interests, they block creative perception before it even has a chance to see and sense. Interestingly, the Finnish school system shows us that through trust and time, and thereby through the nurturing of creativity, Finnish students are given a greater chance to both discover and develop their talents and abilities. With this as a model it becomes quite conceivable that 'institutions' could function differently if they were run more according to trust than according to control, and if they were to allow more time for this to develop.

Chapter Five:

SELF-FULFILMENT: AS WITHIN SO WITHOUT

All know that the drop merges into the ocean, but few know that the ocean merges into the drop.[1]

– Kabir

There is an intrinsic connection between the individual and the community, between the inner world and the outer world. For me, this has become easier to see when I have looked at the nature of the relationship between my *beingness* (the *beingness*/body fusion I identify with, first explained in the Introduction) and the nurturing of creativity. By considering the effects of this on my interactions with the outer world, I have found them to be so fully reflected as to be both pleasantly surprising and unexpected. The relationship I speak of is linked to what Jung calls 'the process of individuation' – a 'natural', and almost unconscious, process of growth guided by one's 'Self' in response to an inner 'urge toward unique, creative self-realization.'[2] To discuss this, in this chapter I reflect on how my creativity has been nurtured by the creative endeavours I have undertaken, and on how this nurturing has revealed the connections between my inner and outer worlds.

As I travelled the path of writing my thesis I found myself trying to find a balance between opposite forces, which to a certain degree caused a vortex in the climate of my inner world. One of these forces I have called the *power of conformity*, as it stems from societal beliefs and pressures to maintain things as they are, and to be the 'same' as everybody else. With a need to belong and be loved at its core, this force gives rise to both the fear of failure and the fear of success, with the two of them being complexly interwoven. Concerned at the possibility of failing at what I had set myself to do – successfully completing my PhD – I found that this fear was actually heightened by my belief of how important it was that I not fail. A downward spiral could ensue from that, as the stronger was my belief that it was important not to fail, then the more I felt pressured not to fail, and therefore the more debilitating my fear of failure actually became. Gradually this was becoming so huge in my life that it could have literally paralysed me and stopped me from taking further action. There were times when this caused such an unpleasant feeling that I (or at least my mind) would seek out all kinds of 'legitimate' diversions to relieve the situation: from cleaning that I convinced myself had be done immediately, to paying important bills, to booking a concert that my daughters couldn't possibly miss in the school holidays, or searching to read yet more of what others had said on the subjects I was addressing.

How an overwhelming fear of failure feels was well known to me, as I had originally experienced this in my childhood during my education. In *Out of our Minds*, Ken Robinson tells us: 'Many people have very deep anxieties about education ... it stamps us with a very deep impression of ourselves, and of everybody else, that's hard to remove.'[3] My experience of all the stages of schooling I attended (from primary right through to university), and of what happened there, taught me to expect disappointment regardless of how much effort I put into a formal academic scenario, and despite whether through this I achieved 'failure' or 'success'. With marks being awarded at school in accordance to a competitive hierarchical process, there's constant pressure to be among the best. So as not to fail in meeting the underlying expectation of being a good student (an expectation that my parents and teachers had of me) I found I had to conform, this consequently meant having to forgo exploring profound aspects of myself that I desperately needed to come to light. 'Children with strong academic abilities often fail to discover their other abilities'[4]; these are abilities that are considered to be less important anyway and so not worthy of much time or focus.

In acquiescing to the pressure of concentrating on schoolwork, I simply did not have the mental space available, nor the time required, to dedicate to getting to know myself better. My creativity was therefore hardly nurtured. I remember experiencing feelings of frustration, as well as of anticlimax after anticlimax, when receiving good marks for tests and assignments and then going on to the next one and the next, and so on. Somehow I constantly had the expectation that something amazing was about to happen, something that would make up for all the holding myself back from the self-exploration I desired, in order to produce the kind of work that was expected of me. Surely all the sacrificing I had been doing would be recognised and rewarded! At times I really felt that if something didn't happen soon I would actually explode; it was like having some great energy that was dammed inside me trying to get out. Yet with every piece of work I completed that didn't originate from an impulse of my own creativity I only built the dam wall higher and higher. In explaining how the covert, or indirect, messages that we're given at school warp how we see ourselves as learners, Stephanie Marshall writes:

> YOUR PASSION, EMOTIONS, INTUITION, AND SPIRIT [AND THUS YOUR CREATIVITY] ARE NOT WELCOME OR VERY USEFUL IN SCHOOL. They distract you from the requirements of the curriculum, generally waste time, and get you, the teacher, and the class off track. Besides, none of that stuff is on a test, so it is not very important.[5]

It's the imparting of these kinds of messages, even though this isn't done wilfully or even consciously in most cases, which can make school very oppressive and possibly even damaging. This is the 'hidden curriculum', as Peter McLaren explains in 'Critical Pedagogy and the Curriculum', which 'deals with the tacit ways in which knowledge and behaviour are constructed.'[6] The hidden curriculum is part of the way that schools ensure the maintenance of the societal status quo, and as such, it is promoted by all those in authority at a school, though usually quite unintentionally. The hidden curriculum is:

> ... a part of the bureaucratic and managerial 'press' of the school, the combined forces by which students are induced to comply with dominant ideologies, and social practices related to authority, behaviour and morality ... Often [therefore] the hidden curriculum displaces the professed educational ideals and goals of the classroom teacher or school.[7]

In Chapter Two, I related that I had learnt to read quite early; this strategically enabled me to become proficient at 'reading' adults and my environment, thus I was very good at picking up unspoken messages both at school and at home.

Accordingly, as I wanted to fulfil the roles of being a good daughter and a good student, I did the only thing I thought I could do – I complied with what was expected of me. In doing this I wasn't aware that I was slowly storing a lot of rage at the self-repression I was being enticed into. Of course I could have rebelled and failed at school, but I happened to be good at academic work and I was taught that if you were good at something you did it, and did it, and did it – relentlessly. However, we were never told at school what 'good' all this academic achievement would actually be for us, or for the rest of the world. I was also quite unaware, at the time, what this 'doing' was preventing me from experiencing and creating.

I spent my schooling years (especially at high school) very afraid of failing and disappointing others' expectations. At the same time I was also frustrated with success, though again I probably wasn't very conscious of this, as in my experience success meant being focused and pushing myself into achieving increasingly better results and grades for tests and assignments. This required me to give up more and more of the interesting and creative sides of myself – like writing poetry, or just having spare time to simply daydream and be in my inner world. Perhaps my fear of failure resulted from a total belief that I absolutely needed to do what I was doing, a belief that also helped me to hide the mounting anger at what was occurring. By the first term of my final year, Year 12, which in Canberra (the capital of Australia) didn't require final exams but used continuous assessment in a series of tests and exams throughout Years 11 and 12, my anxiety regarding exams had become almost debilitating. In recognising that I needed to do something about this, before it completely took over my life, I made myself fail a physics test (by not studying) to prove to myself that nothing catastrophic would happen as a result of failing.

That was the same year that I auditioned to be in a school production of Brecht's *Mother Courage* and got the main role. The experience of taking part in this creative work was absolutely incredible. We included the songs in the play, and had music written for them; we also constructed most of the props ourselves and put together our own costumes. It was the first time, in a school situation, that I mixed with students of all kinds of academic ability and from across grades – it was a breath of fresh air! The show was only on for two or three nights, and my friends who came to see it liked it, but my family was instead quite critical. Having lived and breathed the play for a few months, so that I was thoroughly intimate with it, it didn't occur to me that they might've found it difficult to understand, especially with English not being their first language. I was disappointed at their reaction, feeling that even though I had given it my all, I had somehow failed them.

These learning anxieties clearly had an effect on how I faced the completion of my PhD through the writing of my thesis, so that a fear of failure was intertwined with a fear of success that on one level expected 'success' to only mean conforming more and more, in line with the hierarchical order that shapes much of our lives. Yet because of the subject of my research — the nurturing of creativity, and my experiences in engaging with it, including all the positive ones that had come from trusting it and giving it time — I was aware that success might also present itself as a stepping stone to more freedom, in being able to live a life that was more in tune with the whole of me. This connected me to the other force at play that opposes the force of the *power of conformity*, which I've named the *power of the desire to be whole*. Connecting to this force meant seeing the completion of my PhD as a transition that marked the recognition of who I was, and who I was becoming, and furthermore openly told the world, so that I could live the reality of being myself more fully.

In describing what motivates many of his students to write scholarly personal narratives, Robert Nash gives a description that comes close to explaining this force, this *power of the desire to be whole* that I have realised has been such a strong presence in my life. He describes it as something that 'might heal the rifts that exist between their personal and professional lives.'[8] In this, these students' reasons for writing personal narratives are akin to mine:

> They want congruence. They seek wholeness. They are tired of compartmentalization. What they do as professionals is inseparable from who they are ... They think of themselves as being called to service ... they know that, before all else, they are called upon to "profess" a belief or faith in the power of connections and relationships ... [9]

In these relationships, I include as first and foremost the inner relationship that enables me to perceive myself as a *beingness*/body fusion and allows this to unfold and grow. It is the strength of this most intimate relationship that makes it possible for my inner and outer world to be meaningfully connected, so that the flow from one to the other might remain dynamic and able to actualise a self-perpetuating loop. Being visual, the shape that comes to mind when I think of this loop is much like the symbol for infinity, with creativity at the central point of intersection. In *The Reinvention of Work*, Matthew Fox describes this process well:

> When we manifest the inner work we are truly working ... We take in a problem or concern from the world around us and we ponder it, we live with it ... we sleep on it, and we dream about it. Eventually ... Something is born of the problem we have faced, ingested ... The outer work becomes an inner work for a while and then moves out into the world again to contribute its share of healing and truth ... In other words, as representatives of the age in which we live, if we are living with our hearts and minds open, we will indeed take in the struggle and conflict of our times. Our creativity will do its best to wrestle with those conflicts so as to produce some kind of resolution and hope.[10]

What Fox explains is something that is regularly ongoing, whether we're aware of it or not. As we don't live insular lives, we are constantly affected by what happens in the world around us, and in turn we have an effect on our environment. This is true just by virtue of our being part of a complex system of many networks, including ones that are social, ecological, biological, and so on. If we imagine all we do, think or feel, or in other words anything that occurs because of our existence as little drops that fall into a universal pond and send out a series of ripples in all directions, we can start to get a picture of just how complex the system that we're part of is. This is where an attitude of creativity, which Fox calls 'living with our hearts and minds open', plays a big part, and where if we take time to nurture our creativity and allow ourselves to trust it, we can reap the most fulfilment, as our creativity will indeed 'do its best'. We can then make the shift and change this 'outer' work to 'inner' work, which will become more satisfying if we also choose to undertake it consciously and willingly.

The only thing I would change from Fox's quote above, is the image of creativity 'wrestling' with conflicts; rather than fighting, creativity creates. Putting a word like 'wrestle' in the way of creativity can actually hamper its creative power, since even just by mentally preparing to 'fight' fighting we set ourselves up for more fighting – like the outcomes from declaring 'war against terrorism'. As Lederach reminds us, justification of violence (any level of violence) 'narrow[s] or destroy[s] the capacity for creative alternatives ...'[11]. I point this out because the fighting paradigm has so firmly taken up residence within the human psyche (as discussed in both Chapters Four and Two) that it regularly undermines and lessens the effects of otherwise powerful insights (as in Fox's quote). Stephanie Marshall advises us that if we want to create a 'new story' we will need to change the language we use, because our current language 'is rooted in a militaristic, hierarchical, competitive, and command-and-control framework'[12]. These divisive and mostly dichotomous frameworks in our language are the result of a structuring that comes from living in a hierarchy, for as Bohm points out our current language mode is 'playing a key role in helping to originate and sustain fragmentation in every aspect of life.'[13]

Actions are born from thoughts and words, so it is important that we be mindful of nurturing creativity whenever we can; this includes the use we make of language and the metaphors we choose to communicate our thinking. The reality that we are agents of is largely created from what we focus on, as is pointed out by appreciative inquiry (as discussed in Chapter Three): '[W]hen groups study human problems and conflicts, they often find that both the number and severity of these problems grow ... when groups study ... best practices and noble accomplishments, these phenomena, too, tend to flourish.'[14]

What if we were to simply drop our continual and habitual use of the words fight, war, warrior, struggle, conflict, loser, winner, and so on? These words only serve to strengthen our thinking (and then our actions) along the same aggressive grooves that have been etched into our inner landscapes for countless generations, turning them into true obstacles (pits in some cases) that prevent us from taking a different road on a grand scale. What if instead we chose to use colour and music as new metaphors for suggesting the paths to follow? Both colour and music deeply affect our lives, and they have so many nuances that we could go on forever discovering them. This would make them ideal metaphors to adopt for resolving situations that we perceive as being threatening.

Rather than heroes and warriors, or winners/losers, in these new metaphors we would all be artists learning to create colourscapes and soundscapes to reflect our truth and wholeness, where each of them would be a unique part of a dynamic and well-balanced whole picture of reality. Imagine working towards becoming masterful at transforming the picture, sound, or ambiance, of anything that was not sustainable in life – situations, products, relationships and anything else we encountered – so that it might become more harmonious and whole. This would develop in us levels of subtleties that we would have previously been unaware of; depending on the picture that we wanted to create, we could seek out specific 'colours' and 'sound', and blend them together or contrast them, for effect and beauty. For example, when faced with diseases, rather than fighting them, we could look at the bodies and the lives of those affected and really see them as masterpieces (since we are all masterpieces), and we could then work out which tones and colours we could enhance and/or transform so as to facilitate healing. This would help us to face challenges holistically; as artists we would be free to delve in passionately, fearlessly working with the whole complexity of any situation.

Choosing to use new metaphors, while discarding those that hinder our growth, is an example of consciously nurturing creativity, one that can greatly help us along the path of individuation. Briefly described at the beginning of this chapter, the process of individuation is explained in *Man and His Symbols*, by Marie-Louise von Franz, with the analogy of a seed growing and maturing into a unique individual tree. It is not by conscious willpower that a tree is thus able to grow, but through the nurturing of the soil, sun, slope of the land, wind and rain meeting the potential that is held within the seed as a promise.[15] Likewise, the impetus of our growth towards the realisation of our own individual uniqueness arises in us from deep within our subconscious; as such, Jung believed it to be most commonly revealed in dreams. It is not necessarily an easy task to bring to light what is 'hidden', as in this process 'one must repeatedly seek out and find something that is not yet known to anyone. The guiding hints or impulses come, not from the ego, but from the totality of the psyche: the Self.'[16]

This searching within and then allowing what *is* to surface as it will, or in other words, this perfect combination of receptivity and effort, *this* is exactly what is required for creative work. It is not a coincidence that these two processes are linked, for creativity is intrinsically connected to our ability to birth ourselves anew moment after moment. Yet it is only if these insights are consciously recognised that the journey towards wholeness can continue, as Franz points out:

If, for example, I have an artistic talent of which my ego is not conscious, nothing will happen to it. The gift may as well be non-existent. Only if my ego notices it can I bring it into reality. The inborn and hidden totality of the psyche is not the same thing as a wholeness that is fully realized and lived.[17]

In other words, it is by paying attention to my *beingness* (the 'Self' Jung speaks of), by being open and trusting, and allowing myself the time needed for insights to bubble up to my consciousness, that I can become more and more whole. Indeed, I have found that activities that nurture my creativity also nurture the whole of me; these are activities that enable me to stretch my imagination and try new things without being prescriptive in any way, and although they can be challenging they bring me insights that greatly contribute to my self-fulfilment. The process of individuation involves consciously making a choice to integrate whatever comes from our subconscious that can lead us to become more whole and self-actualised.

A sense of self-fulfilment and creativity can no more be pinned down by words on paper than can the ephemeral rainbow I glimpsed today for no more than seconds, before a curtain of grey rain washed it away. But this doesn't make these experiences any less valid, or significant, than those that appear to be able to be logically argued and proven. This sense of the creative is at once similar and different for each of us; Oriah Mountain Dreamer explains it well in *What We Ache For: Creativity and the Unfolding of Your Soul*: 'Our *creativity* is the soul-deep impulse in all human beings to go beyond the perceptions of the senses to the conception of something new. We begin with what is and make something more of it.'[18] Robinson echoes this idea of creativity combining a harmonious blending of the conscious and subconscious:

> Creativity is not a purely intellectual process. It is enriched by other capacities and in particular by feelings, intuition and by a playful imagination ... We all have creative abilities and we all have them differently. Creativity is a dynamic process that draws on many different areas of a person's experiences and intelligence.[19]

Creativity goes beyond what is; it encompasses it but moves further, past the 'perceptions of the senses', past the 'purely intellectual process', and in doing so it connects all of one's fragmented parts, bringing them together into wholeness. Creativity can do this because we are and actually have always been whole; we are just not fully-grown and realised yet. This often confuses us and makes us think we're not whole. Despite the disconnection caused by our intellectual insistence to separately identify with different parts of ourselves, creativity helps us to experientially become aware of our wholeness, while at the same time it also reveals our potential to become self-realised. Fulfilling that potential is more pleasant than we might realise, and we move closer to fulfilment each time we pay more attention to that little voice within that calls out to us whenever we encounter anything that moves us, delights us, energises us and makes us feel alive.

Although writing has been my preferred medium for expressing my creativity since I can remember, I am also attracted to light and colour; in fact, I see writing as painting with words. When I'm paying attention, the play of light and colour upon the corporeal substance of forms can suggest to me specific textures and depths that create harmoniously satisfying and sensually rich combinations that please me to the core of my being. At other times, however, what I have perceived through this same sensual awareness has so negatively overwhelmed me as to literally nauseate me, and I remember instances when a jarring combination of colours and objects almost caused me to be physically sick. Clearly the sense of the aesthetic within me is quite precise, and it is by trusting myself, as I explore what I feel called to, that I discover more about myself.

There is a maxim that says that 'beauty is in the eye of the beholder'; this is a way of saying that it is our inner beauty that is mirrored by all the beauty we see and connect with (remember the story of the house of mirrors and the puppies in Chapter One). I find this especially interesting as I don't have perfect sight – I'm both short-sighted and astigmatic to a different level in each eye, yet I have good peripheral and night vision, and near perfect close-up vision. This means that if I want to see details clearly I need to get in close (in fact, I wear glasses to drive), while with distance, boundaries fade, and at night lights appear more splendid and magical because of the glowing halos that surround them. Having lived with these sight conditions since I was a young child, it could be speculated that by filtering the way I see, they have also filtered the way I perceive things, or might it be the other way round? Could the way I have perceived and still perceive things be that which has affected my sight?

In *Natural Vision Improvement,* Janet Goodrich writes of vision rather than of sight: 'From our physical eyes right through our feelings, thoughts, dreams, creative insights, and spiritual unfolding, vision permeates all our life experiences.'[20] She further points out that:

> Arnold Gesell, who did brilliant studies of the development of children and their vision said, 'Seeing is not a separate isolated function, it is profoundly integrated with the total action system of the child – his posture, his manual skills and coordination, his intelligence and his personality. He sees with his whole being [*sic*].'[21]

According to Goodrich's research, there are many factors that can affect vision including emotions, diet, physical environment, posture, and beliefs as well as the thinking patterns that arise from these. Moreover, these factors are not independent but interconnected, so that each one can reinforce another and be reinforced by it, like in a repetitive domino effect.

In summarising the thesis of Raymond Welch, who offers a sociological perspective for the rise of myopia in America, Goodrich calls attention to the possible effects of events like the Industrial Revolution, the beginning of the optical industry and compulsory public schooling.[22] She describes how eyesight has been steadily deteriorating since our technological advances have been requiring us to be more machine-like in the undertaking of specific tasks. These are things like data checking, flat screen watching, reading, looking at a whiteboard and so on – all tasks which cause our eyes to strain because to do them we have to keep them fixed and rigid. Thus rather than following movement by moving with it, something our eyes are very adept at and attracted to (which is why watching the flames in a fire is so mesmerizing), our eyes are often forced into a 'staring mode' for long periods of time.[23]

Could it be then that to an extent the clarity of my vision reflects the society I've lived in and how I've been affected by it? In posing this question I want to point out the vastness of what might need to be taken into consideration in order to arrive at any kind of comprehensive answer. I would not be surprised if following all the clues would eventually link back to what first led me onto this path of creativity, and that anything connected to and affecting my vision would therefore also connect to and affect how I perceive creativity.

This connection between seeing (vision) and creativity is explained in 'A painter's perspective', where Francoise Gilot notes how:

> Seeing is more than a visual experience; perception is more than a function of just one sense ... The artist's internal passions and power interact with cosmic forces to establish a new way of seeing that is different from – and yet fundamental to – the limited perspective of the ordinary world. To see a new way is to use the full continuum of mind and body.[24]

Gilot's quote is an extension of Gesell's discovery of children seeing with their whole being. While in growing up many of us are cut off from wholeness and this whole way of seeing, through adherence to the *institutionalised perception*, those who allow creativity to lead them, like artists, return to this wholeness and with it find a 'new way of seeing'. In advocating using nurturing and imagination for her suggested path to vision improvement, Goodrich states: 'Creativity and confidence grow as you start nurturing your own well-being and imagination.'[25] There are times when despite my non-perfect eyesight I can see incredibly clearly; this is when all around me is harmonious and pleasing, and I feel that I'm part of a flowing and deep expression of life: I live it, I feel it, I'm in blissful relationship with it!

A year or so into my PhD, I gave a 'Pub talk' entitled *Creativity, Time and Trust* (at the time, our University was hosting a series of informal monthly talks and encouraged postgraduates to participate). Among those attending was a lady who had developed the *Extraordinary Mind Project* – a series of two courses designed 'for anyone wishing to uncover and recapture their natural birthright of extraordinary talents and creativity'[26]. After meeting with her at a café to discuss creativity and being told that she had found out by chance about the Pub talk, which naturally interested her because of the topic, I was convinced that this was a synchronistic opportunity not to be ignored.

First introduced by Jung, the concept of synchronicity is defined as 'a 'meaningful coincidence' of outer and inner events that are not themselves causally connected. The emphasis lies on the word 'meaningful'.'[27] Just as I was considering different ways of nurturing my creativity, so as to go deeper into it, here was somebody who had for some years been doing just that – nurturing creativity. Though it crossed my mind that by having first met her I might feel I had to live up to expectations, I was quickly relieved of this fear after the first lesson of the course.

I used to draw as a child; I remember asking my five-year-old sister to pose for me (I was about eight), and doing a portrait of her that she had truly liked – and younger sisters can be really quite particular about the portrayal of their likeness. But as time went by it seemed to get harder and harder to put pencil to paper; in being focused on wanting to draw something beautiful, I was fearful of marking the paper in an ugly way, until at some point I stopped trying altogether. The first session of the *Extraordinary Mind Project* was very effective at removing expectations from the process of drawing. The focus was on playfulness, deep concentration, and connecting eye with hand coordination by just looking at the object being copied, rather than also checking on how this was developing. Thinking that I could not possibly achieve anything worth looking at in following this sort of technique, I totally relaxed into it. Relinquishing control, I let the eyes and hand do their own thing while I 'just went along for the ride'. At the end of it I couldn't believe that two and half hours had already gone by, and I left feeling 'refreshed' as had been promised.

As the lessons progressed, a peculiar thing started to happen – I found myself getting angry, feeling irritable, yet I couldn't put this down to anything rational. I would become aware of these emotions well into the lesson, but being immersed in the drawing process, I didn't pay too much attention to them. I noticed them but continued drawing; by the end of the lesson they seemed to have lifted, and while driving home I was mostly in the sort of rejuvenated state I had experienced after the first session. It was not till the writing of this chapter, while revisiting the memory of these occurrences, that upon reflection I realised what had been happening during these workshops.

It dawned on me that the reason for those emotions and feelings of anger in many of the sessions of the *Extraordinary Mind Project* was that I had been releasing all the pent up rage from when I had been at school as a child and teen, where I had been kept from exploring my creativity. What enabled me to release this rage was also being in a non-judgmental environment where I felt safe and had a strong sense of belonging, as I was with a group of people who were there for the same reason I was – to reconnect with creativity. In a way it was like being in therapy, art therapy. Not only did the *Extraordinary Mind Project* rekindle in me a stronger relationship with my creativity, but in giving me a sustained experience of being present, and yet non-judgemental; it also allowed me a deeper way of relating with all that was around me.

In discussing Merleau-Ponty's approach to phenomenology, David Abram explains the very experience I had: 'Considered phenomenologically – that is, as we actually experience and *live* it – the body is a creative, shape shifting entity ... [that] is my very means of entering into relation with all things.'[28] It was my physical bodily participation in the drawing, the intensity of awareness of this creative process and the harmonious coordination between eyes and hand, which kept me in the present long enough to allow me to form a deep connection, a fusion-like link with all that I was drawing. There was no separation between my 'self' and the 'other' outside of my 'self'; so strong was my relating to it that I became, and so 'was', that which I was drawing during the process of expressing and experiencing it.

In the Postscript of *On Not Being Able to Paint*, Marion Milner sums up her exploration on the 'problems' encountered in drawing and painting by sharing her discovery that they are directly linked to the incongruence between what we physically experience through our sense of sight and the vision we actually choose to impose on the world:

> Observations of problems to do with painting had all led up to the idea that awareness of the external world is itself a creative process, an immensely complex creative interchange between what comes from inside and what comes from outside, a complex alternation of fusing and separating. But since the fusing stage is, to the intellectual mind, a stage of illusion, intoxication, transfiguration, it is one that is not so easily allowed for in an age and civilisation where matter-of-factness, the keeping of oneself apart from what one looks at, has become all-important.[29]

We live in a society that persistently advocates for objectivity, or in other words a perception of separateness (an *institutionalised perception*), which is contrary and opposed to the holistic perspective necessary for the nurturing of creativity.

Interestingly this is also contrary to what quantum theory suggests actually occurs, as Bohm tells us:

> … quantum theory shows that the attempt to describe and follow an atomic particle in precise detail has little meaning … In a more detailed description the atom is, in many ways, seen to behave as much like a wave as a particle. It can perhaps best be regarded as a poorly defined cloud, dependent for its particular form on the whole environment, including the observing instrument. Thus one can no longer maintain the division between the observer and observed … Rather, both observer and observed are merging and interpenetrating aspects of one whole reality, which is indivisible and unanalysable.[30]

A common saying is that 'seeing is believing', yet we often question what we see and how we actually come to see it. Regardless of what information we gain from our senses, it seems that more often than not we mistrust it and instead rely on the 'rational' powers of the mind. In view of this, it might perhaps be more correct to say that believing is seeing. Our main beliefs, or principles, hold a certain amount of power over us, and they are quite a motivating force that can often cement divisions between 'us' and 'them'. This could be why the establishing of fundamental beliefs in people, through the harnessing of an *institutionalised perception*, is a major preoccupation of those in authority. Indeed, so many wars (perhaps even most, if not all of them) are waged in the name of beliefs, or principles. To bring attention to this, in *Gulliver's Travels*, Jonathan Swift satirised the pettiness of wars over principles by telling the story of a war waged (between Lilliput and Blefuscu) over the disagreement of which was the proper end for an egg to be cracked – the larger end or the smaller end.

Beliefs, even fundamental ones we might not be totally conscious of, are mostly connected to the mind, whereas my sense of *beingness* includes, but transcends, the mind to comprise the wholeness of myself, which also includes my body in a *beingness*/body fusion. As far as I can ascertain, most people relate to this sense of self to a certain degree from quite a young age, as it is this that enables them to speak about themselves as 'I', rather than just as a specific part of themselves, like 'my hand', 'my head' and so on. In the Introduction, I explain this sense of *beingness*, of knowingness, by likening it to an iceberg where the consciousness is the visible part.

I see my beliefs as convictions that arise from meanings that I arrive at myself, based on the awareness or perspective I have. That is to say, in my experience, my beliefs are deduced from how I see the world, while at the same time they help me to live congruent to that vision, yet they don't prevent it from expanding and transforming. Every time that my perspective has shifted and grown during my life, my beliefs have also undergone change. In the quote above, Milner clearly states her perplexity at knowing that to see what one *actually* sees, as in perceiving and becoming aware of what is in fact around you, is not 'so easily allowed' in our society. Having come from a position where she had to unravel much of what she had been taught, so as to freely engage with her 'new' awareness of the external world, she gives experiential proof of living in a society where 'believing is seeing'[31]. In *Anam Cara*, John O'Donohue describes this in another way:

> To the judgmental eye, everything is closed in definitive frames. When the judgmental eye looks out, it sees things in terms of lines and squares. It is always excluding and separating ... It enjoys neither the forgiveness nor imagination to see into the ground of things where truth is paradox. An externalist, image-driven [as in appearance-driven] culture is the corollary of such an ideology of facile judgment.[32]

As described before in more detail, taking part in the *Extraordinary Mind Project* gave me a corporeal experience of what it was like to be non-judgemental. Through a way of drawing that allowed me to explore and also negotiate between what I saw and what I wanted, or needed, to express – a way of drawing that allowed me to flow with the spontaneous creative process – I was able to reconnect to the time when my creative energy had been obstructed and walled up within me. This then brought up in me the emotions of anger and frustration that I had denied myself from feeling at the time, and consequently I was able to start releasing them. This emotional clearing was additionally supported by the nurturing of creativity that, at the time, another activity was providing me with; this was a specific dance practice called Chakradance™.

I have always loved dancing, particularly dancing by myself to music I love. Whenever I allow music to elicit from my body whatever movement I feel totally in tune with, and I focus on this movement, I find myself gently releasing stress that I wasn't even aware of. Aches and pains present themselves and then are let go; this is followed by an arising of thoughts and ideas (that at times come thick and fast) as well as solutions to things I had been pondering. It is like a dancing meditation. I instinctively developed this practice years ago, and since then dancing in this manner has always been a sure way for me to consciously connect with my body. Yet although I know this from experience, I have not made use of dancing in this way whenever I might have benefited from it. In times of need it has not been uncommon for me to lock away my inner strategies for coping, or even thriving, and instead desperately search the outside world for answers. How could I forget something I know so well, just when I need it? Then unexpectedly something might come along, a synchronicity that's closely connected to my inner resources, so that finally (often once I have given up searching) I'll be reminded of them.

In 2006, the year I began my PhD, a friend invited me to take a dance course with her that made use of 'authentic dancing'. This type of dancing allows your own movement to flow from the body in tune with the music, the idea being that the dancer will not think about how to dance but simply accept the body's suggestions unimpeded. As this seemed very similar to the kind of dancing I did, the main difference being that it was in a class group with the dance 'teacher' choosing a particular focus for each workshop, I decided to go along. I'd been concerned about possibly being self-conscious in dancing in front of others, but instead I found that because everybody was so focused on their own process, no one paid much attention to anybody else. Moreover, the atmosphere in the class was one of acceptance and nurturing.

The first effect I noticed from the dancing course was on a physical level, as I found I always had lots of energy after the workshops. Then towards the second half of the course I realised that some kind of creative process was also taking place – I started to imagine, 'see', and experience amazing inner worlds and narratives at each of the workshops. This process felt to be quite deep even though it seemed to remain contained within the time frame of the workshops. Additionally, it importantly reminded me of just how much I loved dancing; this reawakened awareness made me realise that I needed to incorporate dance into my life, and with that decision made it wasn't long after the end of the course that I discovered Chakradance™.

As with authentic dancing, Chakradance™ also allows individuals to move spontaneously. It does this to music that has been chosen or composed for specific chakras and, through the research of founder Natalie Southgate, it is a practice that's been designed to incorporate '[t]he primary aim of Jungian psychology ... to form an ongoing relationship between our conscious mind and our unconscious [or subconscious] mind'[33].

Our Western knowledge of the chakras comes from the yogic system of ancient India. In Sanskrit, chakra means 'wheel' or 'turning', and the chakras are seen as centres of energy, or energy vortices. The seven major chakras aligned along the spine – base, sacral, solar plexus, heart, throat, third eye, and crown – are said to be akin to the endocrine glands of Western medicine that are connected to our autonomic nervous system, whereby they allow energy to be received and transmitted throughout the body. Jung saw an affinity between the Eastern chakra system and the process of individuation, that 'conscious coming-to-terms with one's own inner centre (psychic nucleus) or Self'[34], so he incorporated work on the chakras in the process of individuation through the use of active imagination – imaginative techniques for accessing symbols revealed by the unconscious. He also made use of mandala (meaning 'circle' in Sanskrit) art and drawing, as a way of connecting to, and communicating with, the 'self':

> I had to abandon the idea of the superordinate position of the ego ... I had to let myself be carried along by the current, without a notion of where it would lead me ... I saw that everything, all the paths I had been following, all steps I had taken, were leading back to a single point - namely, to the mid-point. It became increasingly plain to me that the mandala is the centre ... It is the path to the centre, to individuation ... I knew that in finding the mandala as an expression of the self I had attained what was for me the ultimate.[35]

The holistic meaning of what the body expresses through movement in dance has also been studied in performance theory. Peggy Phelan, who was a member of the *corps de ballet* in the New York City Ballet for twelve years, writes about this:

> ... the body can express things that consciousness and its discursive formations cannot. Within psychoanalysis, these bodily expressions are

called symptoms. Symptoms are somatic expressions which signal the work of repression; they are the bodily place holders for material that consciousness cannot fully absorb ... [as they] are condensed indexes of a not-yet-consciously-narrativized event... From a dancer's point of view the symptom is one way of understanding a movement phrase. Movement phrases are somatic expressions ...[36]

From what Phelan points out (while also bearing in mind the explanation of Jung's process of individuation) it seems plausible that if the body is the 'place-holder' for that which the individual cannot yet consciously understand, then allowing the body to express itself freely in dance would help to release these 'symptoms'. Furthermore, these symptoms may also reveal themselves as insights through active imagination and/or mandala art.

Chakradance™ incorporates all of these elements in its practice: authentic dancing while focusing on the chakras, engaging with what Jung calls the 'process of individuation' through active imagination, and integration through the drawing of a mandala at the end of a session. This enables Chakradance™ to be a holistic way of accessing the unconscious Jung speaks of, which by nurturing creativity can then foster growth and self-development.

Another creative practice that warrants a mention is singing, as this has also been a way for me to nurture my creativity, and like drawing and dancing, it has similarly enabled me to access and release my emotions. A time when this was specifically relevant was when I lived in Italy in my early twenties and was dealing with the break-up of a long-term relationship. A friend had asked me to join a Gregorian choir she was part of that met twice weekly to rehearse, and also occasionally performed. Though I might not have necessarily understood this at the time, I instinctively knew that being part of something that required the engagement of my creativity and connected me to others in harmony was what picked me up from myself and literally saved me. I don't know whether it saved me from a breakdown, or perhaps something even grimmer, but I do know that for three months or so I totally lived for that choir. Singing in it gave me an encompassing feeling of being 'swept away', together with an astonishing sense of power and beauty that really brought me back to myself.

Having found Chakradance™ about a year into my PhD, it became for me a regular creative practice. Among other insights, it enabled me to realise that much of my physical pain had been caused by my creative energy being locked in. I had mostly done this myself by holding back from doing creative things through a belief of lack of time. This had stopped my creativity from flowing, thereby damming it rather than effortlessly pouring it out to be shared. Following this realisation while dancing I had a visualisation, or day-dream, of my inner landscape: *A powerful waterfall of love starts cascading and washing over the jagged rocks of jealousy and self-hatred, smoothing them to kinder shapes, tumbling over the pebbles of indifference and complacency, moving and mixing them into more caring formations that do not hinder flow. The waterfall builds up so much momentum that it finally pushes through the rocks, shifting the boulders of fear that have dammed it in for so long.* I continue dancing the sacral chakra and imagine stepping into the flow of that stream: *energy flowing, going from water to fire, hot and cool, cold and warm; as water flows, so the flickering of the fire seems to flow – liquid fire. The sun lights up the water to a beautiful orange hue and the liquid fire spreads through my being, whispering, caressing, lulling, soothing, inspiring me to expand, move, dance, flow.*

It has been both humbling and comforting to discover that simple things like dancing, singing, and drawing have had such a powerful and freeing effect on my creativity. I have found this humbling because it has made me feel like a child again by allowing me to rediscover what it is like to play. And I have found it comforting, because the exuberance of being attracted by the wonder and beauty of flowing with creativity has in effect rolled back long periods of tiredness and jaded existence. Given the strength of this experience, I wonder how empowering it might have been had I been allowed, or even encouraged, to pursue these activities as a child at school. Rather than setting up a prescriptive curriculum to be followed, imagine if schools nurtured the exploration of their students' creative potential more freely, and what a boost this would be to humanity's journey of growth.

Already convinced of this, Robinson is quite outspoken about the importance of adopting a more holistic approach to formal education: 'One of the legacies of academicism is the exile of feeling from education. Reconnecting feeling and intellect is vital for the development of human resources and the promotion of creativity.'[37] 'Feeling' is a word that can mean so much in so many different contexts, because we *are* feeling, sensual beings. Our society's lessening of the importance of the meaning of 'feeling' doesn't change the need that we have to use and develop what we possess – our creative talents. These of course will be different for each of us since we are unique, but what is similar for all of us is the sheer amount of energy and joy that we can gain through the nurturing of our creativity. Furthermore, as I nurture my creativity through various creative practices – Chakradance™, drawing, writing, dancing, singing, playing music, cooking, gardening – by trusting these experiences and giving myself enough time to experience them fully, I find myself gaining clarity of awareness and self-fulfilment, as well as increasing my connection to others and to the world around me.

* * * * * * * * * * * * * * * *

REVIEWING THE JOURNEY OF CHAPTER FIVE

In this chapter, scholarly personal narrative is the main thread (or method) I use to introduce the different facets of my inner and outer worlds – the life of the 'world' within me, and my life in the world – as well as to explore how the nurturing of creativity is able to reveal the connection between these worlds.

Reflecting upon my experience has confirmed what I have found in my research and observations – that while young children's lives might be quite holistic, with their inner and outer worlds blending harmoniously, as soon as education takes over in guiding them (from both parental and formal institutions) this builds boundaries between their worlds. In growing up, one's connections to their inner self becomes difficult to sustain and can appear untrustworthy, and so one's value of their sense of self, and even their recognition of self, diminishes. What instead gains in importance is one's apparent place in our hierarchical society, our social standing or status in other words, which stems directly from the results of tests, reputation, and social status. This can then lead to both fear of failure and fear of success as we learn that in a competitive world there's little room for self-fulfilment, and that rewards are merely tokens that are meant to keep us competing.

This competitive climate is strengthened by the fighting mentality fostered and maintained by the language we use, which severely hampers our creativity. Exploring creative new ways of looking at what is displeasing, while working towards change, opens up many possibilities that would allow us to work holistically and bypass competitiveness, favouring instead cooperation and the building of connections. These new ways could be likened to being the 'artist's ways' as they would make use of feelings, intuition, and sensual perspectives, as well as the intellect. These would enable us to nurture our own creativity and thereby promote self-fulfilment on a deep level, since it is by flowing with our creativity that we can reconnect to our whole self and thereby reunite the inner and outer worlds of our lives.

This working towards recognising the whole of the self is what Jung called the 'process of individuation', which he saw as being one's ultimate path in life. Embracing creative self-expression not only enables us to achieve self-fulfilment and improve our inner world, but also increases the fulfilment of that part of the whole (the whole of reality) that each one of us uniquely holds, which has a lasting impact on our outer world.

Chapter Six:

A CONCERT OF VOICES

... the self is best understood, expressed, created, and re-created in relation to others. Although life continually asserts its self, it never stops seeking connections to other life. ... We simply must be connected and in partnership with others in order to continue to learn.[1]

– Stephanie Marshall

The focus of this chapter is on human connectedness, and specifically on how this connectedness has been, and still is, part of my personal transformation of consciously choosing to perceive with an attitude of creativity. Throughout my research journey I experienced many connections: in feedback gained from papers and talks I gave in the course of my PhD degree, in conversations with colleagues, students, friends, relatives and acquaintances (these are still occurring and many still ongoing), and also from the interviews I held, where I specifically questioned different people about creativity. Being open-ended, these interviews were actually less like traditional interviews and more like dialogues. Reflecting on them, as well as on the whole idea of dialogue, led me to recognise some of the unlikely times and places where dialogue also took place or had been on the verge of occurring. Realising this has been revelatory and has allowed me to draw many insights from my experiences.

I based my method of interviewing on appreciative inquiry, the action research that makes use of the '*unconditional positive question* to ignite transformative dialogue and action within human systems ... [where] selecting a positive topic is an essential starting point'[2]. I chose to formulate a range of open-ended positive questions, and proceeded to consult over sixty people on creativity, including students, parents, and educators – teachers and principals. Using the questions as a starting point to introduce the topic, I then essentially allowed myself to be guided by the respondents' answers so that together we dialogued about creativity. In embracing the strength and interconnectedness of our web of human relationships I also made use of aspects of co-operative inquiry – a form of action research that conducts 'research 'with' rather than 'on' people.'[3] Its developers, John Herron and Peter Reason, present co-operative inquiry as a way of redressing a 'traditional' lack of egalitarianism in research:

> ... there is often very little connection between the researcher's thinking and the concerns and experiences of the people who are actually involved ... People are treated as passive subjects rather than as active agents ... the kind of thinking done by researchers is often theoretical rather than practical ... the outcome of good research is not just books and academic papers, but it is also the creative action of people to address matters that are important to them ... it is concerned too with revisioning our understanding of our world, as well as transforming practice within it.[4]

In other words, given that so much research is focused almost exclusively on the needs of the researchers and of those who are backing the theoretical studies they're undertaking, co-operative inquiry allows for the needs, opinions and creative engagement of those directly concerned and/or affected by the study's outcome to be equally considered. This makes it very much a form of participatory action research, and as such, using it reinforces the message of this chapter – the importance of being open to a multiplicity of voices that allows us to get closer and closer to being able to hear and see wholeness through our interconnectedness.

As human beings we are connected to each other in a web of relationships from when we are first conceived. In fact, the dynamics of these relationships are what begot us in the first place, since obviously if our parents had never met we would not 'be', as in exist; or (depending on your belief) we might not exist in the exact way or form that we 'are' now. Stephanie Marshall points out that to be alive is to belong to a complex network of relationships:

Life is naturally interdependent. There is simply no such thing as an independent living entity. Without the cooperation, partnership, and reciprocity of the other, the self will simply not survive. The cocreative process of life cannot support isolation. The self-regulatory capacity and sustainability of a living system is inextricably connected to the density, diversity, and intricacy of its interlinked and interactive networks and feedback loops ... In a living system, relationships are everything.[5]

The importance of this high inter-dependence for both our survival and wellbeing tends to be somewhat taken for granted in everyday living; in fact, it could also be said to be largely overlooked in Western society, where instead it is individualism that receives constant attention. In *Welcome to the Creative Age*, Mark Earls identifies this bias through a practical observation on the difference between Western and Eastern markets:

... it is easy to assume that the individual is the basic building block. Western culture and thinking has encouraged us for hundreds of years to think about individuals and their needs ... [yet] those who have worked in Eastern markets quickly realize how culturally dependent the nature of the West's obsession with the individual actually is.[6]

Nonetheless, this focus on individualism has been a fundamentally important step in our evolution[7] – Robert Jay Lifton, author of *The Protean Self: Human Resilience in an Age of Fragmentation*, discusses this in detail. By helping us to recognise the desire for getting to know and *be* our own 'self', individualism has also heightened our prospects for developing and nurturing our individual creativity, and so it has fostered our self-awareness and ability to consciously make choices. *In all its diversity creativity can't be restricted. Creativity has to be spontaneous; it has to be something that may change with different influences; it doesn't always have to be right* (parent). When the ideology of individualism is pursued too exclusively and pragmatically, however, it can easily degenerate into competitive and harmful selfishness. The consequences of this state of affairs abound in our current society and are clearly evident; it seems that individualism primarily means a 'self-interest' that is connected to the idea of the importance of profit as the 'bottom line'. It would instead be more balanced for the focus on the individual (on the 'self') to be kept in context, and seen as an integral part in the complex network of social fabric. This would also foster a holistic approach to creativity, as the nurturing (and self-nurturing) of each person's unique potentials would unfold into a whole connected humanity, which could therefore enable us to build genuine sustainable communities. These caring and self-actualising communities are necessary to be able to nurture the creativity of all individuals, as Marshall states:

> Webs, or networks, are the fundamental and sustaining pattern of life. Webs remind us that the perceived fragmentation and lack of connection in our lives is a temporary illusion; that parts have meaning only in relationship to the whole ... and that the self is always illuminated in relation to other.[8]

By living in the world, within our web of relationships, we come to internalise a multiplicity of voices. David Bohm confirms this in stating, 'our thought in its general form is not individual. It originates in the whole culture and it pervades us. We pick it up as children from parents, from friends, from school, from newspapers, from books, and so on.'[9] Thus anyone we perceive as being significant in our lives has the power to instil doubt in us by voicing that we're not good enough, or to teach us to trust ourselves by believing in us. An example of this is given by an observation from a parent I interviewed:

... my eldest son who is very good at drawing, he draws cartoons. At one time in high school one of the teachers just about destroyed his ability to draw, the teacher said 'We are drawing a tree', so he tried to draw a tree, then the teacher said 'No, no that is not how we draw a tree'. I really had to sit down with him and say 'Hey some people just see it that way, some people are just taught to see things that way.'

By believing in him, the parent was able to replace the doubt raised by the teacher with the youth's trust in his own abilities.

Our predisposition for learning, from when we're born, is directly connected to our ability to survive. But because we cannot survive in isolation this learning is driven by a deep desire to fit in, to belong, and it is in order to fulfil this desire that we constantly change ourselves and our behaviour. As Aronie reminds us, the 'others' in our lives are especially important to us when we're young, and it is in trying to please them (mostly the adults) that 'we learned very early how to be who they needed us to be. We learned how to accommodate, assimilate, validate them.'[10] In other words, it's through our need to be connected that we instinctively care and want to help, and because of this we're also very susceptible to others' woundedness. Unless our carers and other significant adults in our lives were very aware and self-realised individuals who fully accepted, loved, and nurtured themselves as well as us (something that's not known to be a common trait in people) then we've had to live with their woundedness. This includes their fears, prejudices, guilt, and anything else that hurt them and held them back from growth. In the process of wanting to help them, which as children we believed we could do by becoming what they wanted us to be, we took on some of their woundedness and needs as our own; at the same time this caused us to put aside our deep desire to find out about ourselves.

This desire is described in Jungian psychology as 'the process of individuation', (discussed in detail in Chapter Five); it is an 'almost imperceptible, yet powerfully dominating, impulse – an impulse that comes from the urge toward unique, creative self-realization.'[11] And so it is that from when we're born we have to deal with forces that pull us in different directions. In discussing my experiences of these in Chapter Five, I have called them the *power of conformity*, and the *power of the desire to be whole*. Where one is outward-pulling the other is inward-pulling, and because of this they could be seen as being conflicting forces. Yet, as I have already discussed at length, metaphors of conflict are reductive and mostly counterproductive. In seeing these forces as conflicting we might see them cancelling each other out, or in other words destroying each other. It is possible to instead use metaphor to see them as akin to the complementary forces of circular motion, or rotation – the centrifugal and centripetal forces. It is through this that Lederach explains the nature of social relationships; he sees 'the invisible web of relationships' held together by 'social energy that is simultaneously centripetal and centrifugal.'[12] In giving examples of this he starts from the family relationship, which:

> ... sends us out into the world, yet we return to it for a sense of identity, direction, and purpose. Faith communities, chosen families, even geographic locations provide a sense of identity and also have this centrifugal/ centripetal capacity. In each of these examples there exists a force that pushes out and pulls in, and in so doing creates a "center that holds."[13]

In physics, the centrifugal and centripetal forces are explained as those forces needed to keep a body rotating, the centripetal force pulling towards the centre of the circular motion – like the force of gravity pulling a planet towards the sun, or the electrical force that keeps electrons orbiting an atom – while the centrifugal force balances this centripetal force by pulling outwards from the centre. In a similar way that these forces of rotation work together, I see the *power of conformity* and the *power of the desire to be whole* as being connected – they need each other for balance, and this makes them complementary rather than conflicting. It would be an interesting exercise to revise what we see as conflicting in the world in light of this bigger picture; perhaps we might find that there is much we have misunderstood, and that rather than conflict it is in fact a lack of adequate communication that prevents us from developing sufficient understanding for cooperation and harmonious living in the world.

As the *power of conformity* and the *power of the desire to be whole* balance each other, stability and strength is achieved; this is what Lederach calls the 'center that holds'. It is by maintaining this balance that a relationship can be nurtured and strengthened to the extent that it can nurture each individual who is part of it. Yet given that we're all unique, the personal point of balance for each individual and relationship will naturally vary. *Everyone has their own creativity and are good at their own particular things ... some people have got good memories, some people can paint really well ...* (parent). Resuming the work we left behind as children, towards the attainment of the desire to find out who we truly are, is not only central to living a fulfilling life but can also enhance our relationships. Most of the parents I interviewed expressed that they would like their children's creativity to be nurtured so that they might be enabled to fulfil their potentials, with one parent enthusiastically summing up this possibility: *I remember seeing on television one time, a school for kids who didn't fit in the system and who were able to excel as artists from a young age; as soon as they got to high school whatever they were interested in they did, and they just excelled and it was wonderful to see.*

A friend who has designed websites for universities, and as part of this had to interview senior academics to include their biographies onto the sites, recounted to me that many of the engineering, technical, and science professors were 'crying on her shoulder', lamenting that they'd not been allowed to follow their passions as youngsters. Parents and other well-meaning adults had discouraged them at the time, or even prohibited them, from pursuing art or music or other things that they really liked, persuading them instead to devote themselves to more reputable and financially reliable subjects. Now as mature adults with successful careers they yearned for what they perceived to be their lost dreams, as they did not feel complete without them. Robinson talks of this in *The Element*, when he writes:

> ... many people face barriers from family and friends: "Don't take a dance program, you can't make a living as a dancer," "You're good at math you should become an accountant," "I'm not paying for you to be a philosophy major," ... When people close to you discourage you from taking a particular path, they usually believe they are doing it for your own good.[14]

Yet nurturing our creativity not only enables us to become self-actualised and whole, but it is also through the realisation of the uniqueness of each of our gifts that our human community can grow and successfully face the new challenges that are constantly arising in the world. *I bring in the older students to help with younger students, in this way they learn about that whole helping and nurturing ... we approach ballet very holistically ... they have to dance brilliantly on stage but then three minutes before they would have been helping with the younger ones* (educator). It is because of this complementary and balanced dance of life, where all living things are interdependently weaving an intricate tapestry, that fulfilling the intent of an inner focus also means fulfilling that of an outer focus.

At some point in our lives we need to converse with the voices that we've internalised so as to discover what they're saying, and whether some of these might be preventing us in any way from nurturing our creativity. In addition, we might choose to engage others in dialogue in regard to the myriads of issues that concern us in life, rather than unconsciously assimilate what the 'experts' (or even those we admire) are saying, only to then believe that these are somehow our own thoughts. To do this we need to take the time to creatively explore nuances of thoughts and feelings on these issues and see where this takes us. Bohm highlights the importance of dialoguing, rather than discussing, saying that a group of people who dialogue:

> ... will make possible a flow of meaning in the whole group, out of which may emerge some new understanding ... something creative. And this shared meaning is the "glue" or "cement" that holds people and societies together. ... a dialogue is something more of a common participation, in

which we are not playing a game against each other, but *with* each other. In a dialogue everybody wins.[15]

The dynamics of a dialogue are similar to the way young children play before they're taught to be competitive (as discussed in Chapter One). *Whenever she has been good at something ... like singing or piano, she would compare herself, so I think competition is an inhibitor of creativity* (parent). Bohm's idea of dialogue is akin to the notion of dialogue that Bakhtin puts forward: 'To be means to communicate ... life by its very nature is dialogic.'[16] The type of communication Bakhtin envisioned unfolds in open dialogues where we might express our ideas, both individual and cultural, and by noticing the shades of differences and similarities between these, work towards more harmonious and kinder ways of living together.[17] The open-ended and informal nature of dialoguing allows for creativity to be nurtured within it, and it is this that can transform us and our way of living. With everybody being pushed to produce more and more and be goal-driven, and with the only alternative given being to take time out through entertainment or any number of excesses that often turn into addictions, our current society appears to offer little to none of the space and time necessary to participate in these sorts of open dialogues, yet they are *now* more vital than ever.

Improving our wellbeing, both individual and societal, is a crucial undertaking given the high levels of mental health concerns we're faced with worldwide. Unhappiness, depression and suicide rates are at an all-time high, and this has become even worse since the onset of the COVID-19 pandemic from late January 2020. In 2009, Robinson wrote in one of his books, '[d]eaths each year from suicide around the world are greater than deaths from all armed conflicts.'[18] Perplexed, I researched this to uncover a little more information. In the World Health Organisation's (WHO) first *World Report on Violence and Health,* released in October 2002, I found what I was looking for. In the abstract is stated that:

Globally, an estimated 815 000 people killed themselves in 2000 ... In much of the world, suicide is stigmatized ... Suicide is therefore a secretive act surrounded by taboo, and may be unrecognized, misclassified or deliberately hidden in official records of death ... In 2000, about 310 000 people died as a direct result of conflict-related injuries – the majority of them in the poorer parts of the world.[19]

There is clearly a prevalence of armed conflict in the world: 'During the 20th century – one of the most violent periods in human history – an estimated 191 million people lost their lives directly or indirectly as a result of armed conflict, and well over half of them were civilians.'[20] With the media readily informing us of this, it's worth considering that deaths by suicide, at more than double the deaths by armed conflict (in 2000), are in comparison hardly ever mentioned. In Australia, the Australian Bureau of Statistics (ABS) reported a decreasing rate of suicide since the late nineties, when it had reached 2,700 in 1997. The approximate suicide rate as given by the ABS in 2006 was of 2,000 a year, which was still higher than the yearly deaths by motor vehicle accidents. Most importantly, however, since then this figure has been disputed and in 2009 it was adjusted to being around 3,000 a year, and possibly on the increase, by Professor John Mendoza, who was at the time the chairman of the Federal Government's National Advisory Council on Mental Health. In June of 2010 Mendoza resigned his position because the government was not listening to him; he told us that '[s]uicide is the number 1 cause of death for men 16-44 and women 16-34 years. But across Australia, life-saving suicide prevention services are starved for funds.'[21] I have included this quantitative information on deaths by suicide in order to juxtapose it to our essential, both individual and societal, necessity to nurture our creativity – that intrinsic need we have to realise our inner potential. Could the widespread suppression of this vital need we have to express and nurture our creativity be somehow related to the rate of suicide in the world?

In the WHO's report, among the factors given as predisposing people to the risk of suicide are depression and a general sense of hopelessness, both of which can also result from having our innermost desire quashed, even as children. In Chapter One, I quoted psychologists Fontana and Slack alerting us that when children are prevented from expressing their creativity this wounds their psyche: 'There is a feeling that some undefined potential is going to waste, and that something precious is being denied the light of day.'[22] Childhood wounds need to be healed to prevent us from growing into wounded adults, who could then easily cause more harm, both to themselves and society as a whole.

Having experienced the frightening darkness of depression as well as a sense of hopelessness, I know that they reinforce each other and that they can often arise from tunnel vision. Yet tunnel vision is also a direct result of singularly focusing on something, anything, and only that 'thing', including achieving goals. These are the goals that we believe we have to reach in order to be happy or even just survive, which we have either been given or have set ourselves, and it is through the reductive perspective (*institutionalised perception*) of our Western institutions (starting with education) that we've been taught that they are of primary concern in our life. Of course there is nothing wrong with having goals, in fact it is useful to have a sense of the direction to be heading in, but at the same time we need to be open to how life unfolds and adjust our goals accordingly so as to be able to benefit from them. By 'looking unidirectionally toward a preconceived process and goal'[23] – the 'light at the end of the tunnel' in a sense – as being the only possible way to reaching a solution, success, or whatever else one is hoping for, if anything irrevocably blocks this way forward then all hope appears lost[24]. By firmly believing that there is only one way out, or only one way to reach an aspiration or dream, the rigidity of that belief can stop us from looking for and seeing other ways; it can even stop us from realising that perhaps the desired outcome we're aiming for is not really what we want or need after all. *Pressure is not good for creativity ... expectations are not good for creativity ...* (parent).

In *Wishcraft: How to Get What You Really Want*, Barbara Sher and Annie Gottlieb advise anyone with dreams to pursue 'the goal that sounds most exciting to you – even if it's the most impossible'[25], as it's the passion we have for something that makes us realise our true way to fulfilment. Fifteen years later, Sher wrote another book – *I Could Do Anything If I Only Knew What It Was*. This was her response to the realisation that so many simply don't know themselves; given the overwhelming focus placed on external concerns, an ever-increasing number of people seem to be uncertain of what they actually want. Another fifteen years after that in *The Element: How Finding Your Passion Changes Everything*, Ken Robinson talks about how people react when they are able to be true to themselves, and find out what they want: 'When people are in their Element, they connect with something fundamental to their sense of identity, purpose and well-being ... and [with] what they are really meant to be doing with their lives.'[26]

Many of those I interviewed acknowledged the creative benefits, as well as the wellbeing benefits, of doing what you love:

I think football makes me creative, because I love it (student).

I think that kids connect far better in the classroom with something that is their own rather than some essential curriculum, centrally imposed by whatever authority (educator).

When you're creative you kind of feel good and you can concentrate more, and sometimes you don't have to concentrate at all because you are that much into thinking about something it's like day dreaming (student).

This last quote is an effective description of what Mihaly Csikszentmihalyi (1996) calls 'flow' – that feeling of being outside or beyond time, which we experience when totally immersed and enjoying an activity[27]. In other words, when we're following our passion we go beyond consciousness and fragmentation and we engage with the world with our whole selves. We find what makes us passionate by exploring the gift that we are to ourselves, as it is by getting to know ourselves that we can be led to what is the natural inclination for the growth and fulfilment of this 'self'. Importantly, this is not necessarily going to be just one 'thing', but a unique combination of the essential aspects of ourselves. As Sher points out, if you believe that you can choose only one of the things you love, even if what you choose is what you like the best, then you're going to really miss all the other passions that are prevented, by that belief, from becoming a part of your life.[28] All too often we're placed (or we place ourselves) in an either/or scenario where we have to choose between things we love. We see this as an inescapable part of life and, having learnt well what we've been taught, we believe that to be our only option.

Dancer and choreographer Twyla Tharp gives an example of this:

> To lead a creative life, you have to sacrifice. "Sacrifice" and "Having it all" do not go together. I set out to have a family, have a career, be a dancer, and support myself all at once, and it was overwhelming. I had to learn the hard way that you can't have it all, you have to make some sacrifices, and there's no way you're going to fulfil all the roles you imagine ... Something had to give.[29]

While I agree that all roles one imagines cannot be fulfilled, the reason for that is because roles are not *real*, they are only idealised stereotypes set by external standards. I have experienced very strong feelings of guilt and inadequacy because I could not aptly fulfil all the roles that I saw myself in, and it wasn't until

I consciously chose to play certain roles a certain way (my way) that I was able to finally release this. Still, the fact is that we *can* (we need to) have it all, although something does have 'to give' first, and this something is the limited perspective that we have internalised, the 'tunnel vision' I speak of above. As Sher reminds us, 'life is not a miser, and you have the right to *everything* you love', it's all a question of timing.[30] Even if you don't have much time in your life you can nonetheless connect with all that you love, in practice this will mean that you only occasionally connect with some of the things you love. Rather than having to choose only one thing, it is simply a case of not being able to have it all at the same time. Having, or doing, many disparate things at the same time would indeed be overwhelming, so appropriate timing is something that only we can know for ourselves, which is where trust and time (as explored in Chapter Four) come into play. What is certain though is that to be able to do, or have, something, anything, we have to *love* it, and this is where knowing ourselves is very important, as all the parts intrinsic to us connect and balance each other.

I have been asked many times how I managed to complete a doctorate degree while being married and looking after a family with two children and four pets (two dogs and two cats). Having a tendency towards perfectionism, I find that the practical realities of daily living help to ground me, and though at times it can be quite frustrating having to put aside writing for a myriad of tasks, it's the living connected to others that enables me to make time for many of the other things I love, as one thing leads to another. Thus looking for ideas on a birthday cake I need to make for my daughter reminds me how long it's been since I have drawn anything and I decide I could set up my easel permanently in my study; looking after a sick child brings me back to the practice of meditation and Chakradance™ which I've been neglecting for some days. What's more, having taken the time to nurture these other creative aspects of myself – dancer, artist, baker and so on – I find I am nourished and led to insights, which I may not have otherwise uncovered, that are beneficial to my study and writing. Citing Isaacson's biography of Einstein, Robinson writes of Albert Einstein experiencing something similar:

> "He would often play his violin in his kitchen late at night, improvising melodies while he pondered complicated problems. Then, suddenly, in the middle of playing he would announce excitedly, 'I've got it!' As if by inspiration, the answer to the problem would have come to him in the

midst of his music." What Einstein seemed to understand is that intellectual growth and creativity come through embracing the dynamic nature of intelligence. Growth comes through analogy, through seeing how things connect rather than only seeing how they might be different.[31]

This holistic way of accepting and understanding oneself and one's associations grows the more it's practiced; just as the individual can become more self-realised by integrating and becoming conscious of all aspects of the self, similarly human society could achieve more by being open and inclusive to all its members. Because each person is a unique and precious part of life, whose contribution is unrepeatable, it is actually in the interest of all to be open to others' voices, especially when conducting research. I have ceased to be surprised when coming back to my work, after having made time to see, talk to, and be with others, even just take a friend's call in the midst of a busy writing schedule, to see that I have acquired one or more pieces to the 'whole of the puzzle' – the name of a useful book or person, a pertinent quote or anecdote, and so on. Life *is* truly connected, and the more we're open to it holistically, the more we can recognise this and make use of it.

It is important to realise, when addressing and thinking about specific topics, that while one is likely to come across the voices of researchers, writers, academics, and those members of society who are vocal and find ways of making themselves heard, it is different with the voices of 'ordinary' people. These voices tend to remain unheard, and paradoxically among them are also the voices of those not consulted on things that concern them directly. This happens for many reasons, cultural and personal, or even because these 'silent' ones speak in ways that are not conventional and so are not considered acceptable, or it might not be recognised that their perspective has been left out; yet it can only happen because we live in a hierarchical society where, based on an *institutionalised perception*, people's value and importance is greatly differentiated. Typically, this means that among the voices excluded are: those of students in matters of schooling, of patients in medical concerns, prisoners and victims in matters of justice, and so on. Not only are these voices mostly unheard within dominant society, but also the owners of the voices tend to be rendered invisible by being kept very separate from the everyday and often considered irrelevant (and not important); they are 'out of sight and out of mind' as the saying goes. This is also primarily the case with the world's

First Nations people as well as other 'minorities', which ironically includes women despite the fact that they make up approximately 50% of the population.

Similarly, although it might seem logical that all stakeholders should be consulted when setting up a service, it appears to be a common practice in our hierarchical society to prioritise the voices of the 'service-providers'. It is they, as well as those with the authority to establish what the services should be – the policy makers – who, together with the financers of the services, are invariably the main ones to profit. Given that they're clearly the ones taking action, it follows they would also be unquestioningly accepted as being 'the experts'. This bias makes it more likely for those who are the passive recipients of these 'services' to be at best overlooked, or at worst consciously ignored, with the latter being the case especially if what is being proposed by the 'service-providers' is not actually in the best interest of these recipients.

Though in some cases it may be argued that the recipients of these services – education, justice, medical care, and other types of care like that for the aged and disabled, or even customers of commercial goods and services – are not sufficiently competent to express a knowledgeable opinion, this is not a valid reason for suppressing or silencing voices. It is this sort of attitude that makes use of hierarchical sense of value to elevate the knowledge, and therefore importance, of the 'expert', and thereby often maintains the status quo even when making lots of 'changes'. Accordingly, all too often Royal commissions end up having to be held as recourse to righting what the so-called experts have bungled, and there have apparently been 135 Royal commissions held in Australia since 1902 (not including those called by state governments). Being 'the highest form of inquiry on matters of public importance'[32] Royal commissions can last a long time and cost taxpayers a considerable amount; for example, the one on the 'Misconduct in the Banking, Superannuation and Financial Services Industry' spanned over a year – from the end of 2017 to the beginning of 2019 – and cost around seventy million dollars. Rather than rely on 'righting wrongs', approaching any venture with a holistic perspective so as to really take into consideration the voices of those who are habitually not listened to would prove invaluable, as it could foster the best possible outcome for all concerned. As Friere writes:

The silenced are not just incidental to the curiosity of the researcher but are the masters of inquiry into the underlying causes of the events in their world. In this context research becomes a means of moving them beyond silence into a quest to proclaim the world.[33]

It is action research, and especially co-operative inquiry and appreciative inquiry, that can best achieve this by actually moving the unheard voices 'beyond silence'. In this, Lederach also reminds us of the importance of peripheral vision (as opposed to tunnel vision). It is peripheral vision, or perception, that gives us a better connection to the big picture by having us pay attention to the voices of those who are usually dismissed as not being competent enough – elders, housewives, workers, and children, among others. As Lederach puts it: 'A simple, straightforward statement of how things are, what they look like, can offer greater clarity than a complexified but misleading analysis'[34] from the 'experts'. This is the equivalent of looking at, and listening to, life as it is actually happening, rather than relying on working out abstractions like averages or complex theories to paint an overall picture. The main point being of course that averages are not real – in a family with 2.5 children, where does half a child 'live' except in the abstract land of averages? Or to share with you an Italian saying about statistics that I learnt from my father: 'Statistics is a "special science" – if I have eaten two chickens, and you have had none, according to statistics we've actually eaten one each.' Looking at the statistical manipulation of life through physics shows us how it tends to flatten things out so that they become almost meaningless; Bohn explains this well by telling us:

> If you try to measure one atom exactly, you can't do it – it participates. But if you take a statistical array of atoms, you can get an average that is objective. It comes out the same no matter who does it, or when. The average comes out, but the individual atom does not. And in society you can also get average behaviours, which are often predictable. But they are not very significant, compared with the thing that really moves us and makes the society come into being.[35]

This means that a result arrived at through statistical manipulation is one that is never in fact observed by anyone, very much like the chicken example above. With experts so often relying on statistics and averages to provide them with justifications to base their actions on, like the results of standardised testing or feedback surveys in the case of education, we may well wonder how any services could ever address *any* of the real needs of recipients. Rather than basing most decision-making on statistics, the recipients' voices could instead be listened to, and this would enable some very useful suggestions (in terms of what would work better for them) to be garnered, which could then be used to significantly improve the particular service. For example, the students, parents and educators I interviewed had some quite specific ideas on changes that could be implemented in high schools for the benefit of all:

You could be encouraged more, because like if kids are naughty they get in trouble but sometimes when they do good stuff, sometimes they don't even get encouraged to do that – it is not recognised. It would help if it was encouraged. It would help your mind, like when you play baseball and you pitch and your team-mates yell out 'Good pitch' and everything, and when you bat they just encourage you to do it better and it makes your mind feel better (student).

...the only thing that prevents good teachers from teaching in a good way is the institutional framework and constraints that they are operating under. My children went to an alternative primary school ... we understood that the kids needed a smaller classroom, a more engaged teacher ... (a parent who is also an experienced teacher).

...it would be good if you could choose what to do more often ... you're the one being creative and you have to think for yourself ... maybe if we could choose what we want to do half of the time ... (student).

The students here need a lot of reassurance that being creative is acceptable (educator).

The smaller the class the more personal it can be, like with teachers and staff so they can help you and encourage you more and you can find out about what you like ... (student).

Fifteen would be a reasonable class ... Surely if classes are smaller and so teachers can spend more time [with individual students] it's got to be good for all the students (parent).

... there is also theory of sport which is an hour [when] we write, this would be more interesting if there were more demonstrations rather than just talking all the time (student).

I would just like the school to get the best out of him, just to bring out the best in him basically and to tell us if you need any help in anything, if there are any problems or anything (parent).

Maybe they [the teachers] could all talk to you as if you're equal to them and they're not any higher than you. Also if they had more trust in you. ... (student).

I see a creative approach as looking at whatever you are teaching holistically, so if the person in front of you isn't happy or isn't part of the group then they probably won't learn, so I believe that happiness is part and parcel of learning ... I believe if you provide a safe environment for somebody then they can develop more creatively (teacher).

... we always read and then answer questions, there are no activities ...we could do group work, something to make it more interesting ... (student).

Most of these suggestions would involve grassroots changes that could be easily implemented if approached from an egalitarian collaborative attitude, rather than a top-down hierarchical competitive one. Brian Schultz describes such an approach in *Spectacular Things Happen Along the Way: Lessons from an Urban Classroom*, where he tells of how he designed a course of study by taking into consideration what his students wanted and needed. The results were impressive and served to validate his faith and trust in his students:

> When the classroom is shared and the curriculum is co-constructed, the participants see common threads among [them] and are able to support one another because they have knowledge of others' strengths and weaknesses as well as likes and dislikes. The ability to support one another in classroom activities is important, and this becomes a life skill that can be transferred outside of the classroom and the school environment.[36]

When students from a housing project in Chicago share with their teacher the dream of repairing their crumbling school building, he calls them to the challenge by integrating this dream into their study programme. By nurturing their creativity he spurs their motivation and is amazed at what they're able to achieve together. In comparison to this, the suggestions from those I interviewed seem much easier to attain: helping to make school a safe environment through the building of rapport and trust, maintaining open communication within the school community to include parents, having less students in each class, giving students more say in what they study, and rather than abiding by traditional academic methods, being willing to try out ways of making learning more practical and creative. For schools to be able to put these ideas into action, the service provider (those responsible for making decisions in the Department of Education in this case) would need to be open to listening to what is being suggested. Rather than enforce top-down changes, they might encourage each school to put into practice its own ways of nurturing creativity, as in Finland. By holding open inclusive dialogues in each school's community, as ideas generated within a school are those most likely to suit that particular school best, each school would be able to develop a number of new creative practices to implement.

I think many teachers would like to nurture creativity, but it's not valued, it's not recognised as worthwhile by administration who would have to provide the time for PD [professional development for teachers], *for creative meetings, for workshops, and so on, as a focus, so that it can be implemented* (teacher and parent). If schools were administratively supported to nurture creativity, they would be able to make use of what Lederach calls 'creative learning', which he says 'is the road to Serendip, the discovery of things by accident and sagacity.'[37] 'Serendip' is the name he uses for the imaginary destination of the journey of learning through serendipity, which means the learning that occurs from happily beneficial events that seem to happen by chance. To enable ourselves to discover things in this way – unexpectedly or almost by accident as it were – rather than setting out a plan with rigid parameters that disregards anything considered to be outside them, we need to be open to all that we might come across, including things that might be seen as mistakes.

Being open to and yet at the same time prepared for discovery, means that instead of drawing up and then following plans that prescriptively guide the unfolding of a process, we could also openly take wisdom into account. Another way of putting this is what Leslie Safran calls using 'creativity as mindfulness'. Seeing creativity as being a mindful practice, she explains that it '[i]s not just about making new connections but continually thinking about any part of life, consciously or unconsciously, looking around life from all angles, and asking questions about what one finds.'[38] This means living with a constant 'attitude of creativity' (discussed in depth in Chapter One), and thereby being open to discover, try out new things, and make connections.

Having made creativity central to my thesis, I was led by 'creative learning' to integrate all that I found in my research, including anything that was unexpected. By being open to listening to others' voices, to their stories and experiences, as they happened to cross my path (no matter where these voices came from), I invariably found that this either provided clarity and validation for my own ideas and findings, or that in challenging my train of thinking it led me to reconsider things and look at them in a different light. The practice of being receptive to others, to either their written work or through engaging in dialogue with them, has ultimately resulted in my perspective becoming more holistic, which therefore helps it to continue to become more and more open.

What to begin with seemed to me simply a personal experience (or an inkling of how something might unfold) has now widened, with what I have learnt and heard from others, to become an increased perceptiveness that gains significance through the similarity of shared experiences. As Robinson attests: 'Creative insights often occur by making connections between ideas or experiences that were previously unconnected. Just as intelligence in a single mind is interactive, creativity is often interdisciplinary.'[39] In other words, this is equivalent to saying that creativity is holistic, regardless of whether it be individual creativity or creativity within society. All of this has also helped me to realise that at any point in time what I see and think of as the 'big picture' can actually only ever be 'a part' of the 'big picture', since being about creativity, life and everything, the big picture I refer to is an immense and dynamic picture that is constantly shifting and growing.

When I began my PhD journey I was working part time in a high school teaching English and Drama to various classes, across most years; for four weeks I also taught a child-care class and a home economics class. This mix of teaching served to give me quite a comprehensive knowledge of how the school operated, and enabled me to get to know the students better; in some cases I felt the beginnings of a meaningful rapport with some of them. Yet, from the moment I had started teaching at that school, there had been something particular about my experience there, as compared to other schools I'd taught at, that I couldn't quite identify.

I remember coming out of the very first lesson I held for the Year 9 Drama thinking, 'Wow, I survived it!' as I felt that I had faced 'raw rage' disguised as teenage students. The school administrator who had hired me had told me that the students there behaved just the same as students in other schools. So at first I thought that it must've been my teaching that somehow brought out the behaviour I'd been experiencing. Not understanding this, I felt befuddled, yet I knew I wasn't seeing the whole picture. It was much later that I realised that the main difference had been my approach, my attitude. This hadn't changed the students' behaviour as such, but rather my perception of it and my response to it, since given my focus on nurturing creativity I was finally beginning to consider and see more of the whole picture.

Constantly mulling things over, I had begun paying more attention, and one of the things I could see was that I was getting on quite well with the students in the Fast Track class. The Fast Track programme was one specifically structured for students identified as refusing the normal mode of teaching; not all high schools offered it at the time, and at this school it was available for the last two years, Years 11 and 12, for students aged 16 to 18. The focus of this course was a practical one encompassing things like life skills and work, rather than a focus on exams. Viewing this as a release from a primary pursuit of academic goals, I tailored the English course to help the students improve their overall communication skills. This meant a much more personalised approach, which worked well, and what's more, by improving communication it enhanced the rapport of all the individuals in the class to each other, thereby also improving class atmosphere and behaviour. Although this was quite positive, nonetheless the school's administration seemed to be concerned about me when teaching in the Fast Track class – I could sense them almost holding their breath to see how things would turn out, and this surprised me. Again it was only much later that I became aware that in fact some teachers considered a number of the students in that class as 'rebels', and had difficulties with them.

Akin to streaming, 'tracking' is a term 'used to describe various schooling practices which sort students into relatively fixed groups for instructional purposes according to perceived shared characteristics ...'[40]. In the Fast Track case, this was the school's last attempt at engaging students who had been refusing the standard approach to schooling and so could not, and would not, be part of a 'normal' class. They were the students who were falling through the cracks, as it were, and so in a sense it was perhaps understandable that they were seen as rebels. Because they chose not to conform to the standard practices and requirements of school, this possibly caused some teachers to view them as threatening to their authority; after all, teachers are the agents who ensure that the standard practices and requirements of schooling are met. It is useful to bear in mind that 'mass public schooling developed with strong regulatory functions and purposes ... [given that] schools were established for the control of populations.'[41] This was around the time of the Industrial Revolution, when school was largely used to prepare people to be factory workers. With that awareness, as a teacher I have always focused on authentic teaching and learning while instead consciously distancing myself from measures of control, which I consider to be an archaic practice – a remnant from the Industrial Age. Added to this, my new attentiveness for nurturing creativity opened me further to wanting to understand the students.

With the Fast Track class there were no hidden or tacit agendas on my part; I was upfront about wanting to help the students improve their communication skills, and they were straightforward in letting me know which of my suggestions they were willing to try and which were of no interest to them. This enabled me to plan ways for their creativity to be successfully nurtured, and as a result much was learned and accomplished. For example, gifting them with a journal to be taken on a camping trip engaged them in a process of self-reflection, and also led to further positive interactions within the class. One of the students, who was considered to be particularly difficult, really took to journaling and in doing so reconnected with some very deep feelings that revealed themselves in the poetry he ended up writing. Equally nurturing was allowing students to focus on materials that were of interest to them, like the video *Super Size Me*, about eating exclusively at McDonald's for a month.

Feeling that I didn't have this sort of freedom in other classes, I found that teaching them required a lot of effort. This was mainly due to the clash between what I knew was expected of me in my role as teacher – delivering content that was to be covered in a set time – and what I could sense that the students needed to focus on. This was of a more personal nature and connected to 'real' life, which given the low socio-economic background of many students was probably much more urgent. In other words, the pressure I felt to make the students perform in a certain way prevented me from acting according to the needs I identified the students as having.

One day, after a particularly awful session with the Year 9 drama group, where everything I had planned had basically 'gone out the window', something clicked into perspective for me. My understanding crystallised, and I found myself seeing things in a different way. I realised that the 'grief' that high school students 'give' teachers is not personal, it only seems that way because high school teachers play the role of 'enforcers of rules', and this makes them 'the enemy' for students by leading both teachers and students to identify with an 'us and them' mentality that causes conflict. High school students have had to contend with a lot of pressure, much of it brought on by the expectations of many adults, including all those in their primary school hierarchy, as well as their parents. When I subsequently interviewed some high school students, their answers and comments helped to confirm this insight:

In my running, 'cause I like to run in athletics, when I sprint I can let all my anger out.

I like physical things not sitting in a classroom all day.

A lot of people get in trouble cause of their hair ... if you have streaks they send you home ... they tell you off for wearing two [sets of] earrings, and the headband is only allowed to be white or green or black, like only one colour, I got told off because it was white and black so one of the teachers told me to take it off.

... if the kids had more respect for other people, some of the kids. If some of them left or got taught a lesson so that they changed the way they act ... you worry about what they think, so you don't think you can do anything or say anything that's a bit different.

Many high school students carry a lot of anger and frustration that they have no outlet for, and have stored up over their years of schooling. While they are told that they have to go to school to learn for their own good and their future success, every day they face unimportant issues like having to abide by the rules of correct uniform wearing and having to keep their physicality in check – sit, stand, eat, and even go to the toilet when they're told, all rules that stem from traditional schooling dating from the Industrial Age. In the meantime they don't get any closer to their dreams, which they could've instead been supporting by nurturing their natural talents and potentials. Those things that they're passionate about, and could be taking the time to become really good at by developing them in every possible way, all of those things which could be making them thrive, are instead hidden from their immediate sight, as they've had to lock them away (or sometimes even squash them) so as to conform to expectations. James Ladwig and Jennifer Gore point out that:

The inconsistencies of requiring students to sit, by compulsion not choice, in classrooms in which they have little input or control, while we attempt to teach them to think for themselves and to participate in decision-making are clearly evident.[42]

Often kids are creative in certain areas but it doesn't fit into what we would expect as normal behaviour in a classroom, so this [creativity] may not be able to be expressed. That makes nurturing creativity hard to address in a classroom, especially in the context of 25 to 30 kids (educator).

As a result of this, and though they're not necessarily conscious of it, high school students feel frustrated, cheated, angry, empty ... and they feel like lashing out, they subconsciously want to make somebody pay for all their misery and they mostly do this by 'acting out' with their parents and/or teachers. The drug taking and drinking (surprisingly prevalent even in thirteen to fourteen-year-olds, as I discovered when teaching) could be seen as a very unfortunate symptom of despair of the reality that these young people are facing – a result of how they're being treated. As Marshall notes:

The fragmented and cultural story that sustains the current map and landscape of learning and schooling is slowly eroding the intellectual, emotional, and spiritual health of our children and the health of our global society. ... Despite our best intentions, the fragmented landscape of schooling inhibits the creative and courageous engagement with life that our children are yearning for.[43]

Children are born with a desire to live, to learn and to thrive; it's this 'creative and courageous engagement with life' they yearn for that Marshall speaks of, and yet at every turn our society prevents them from being able to fulfil this deep and vital desire. Just as I experienced in my own schooling, even those who are succeeding in education (as in getting good marks) are likely to be feeling resentful at what they're kept doing, as well as what this is keeping them from doing. *It's that we don't trust our children, or the teachers don't ... keep them busy, don't let them get into mischief ... at home they should be allowed to reflect on what they've done over the day ... and approach that with care and creativity* (parent about homework).

So what can a teacher do when faced with the enormity of a class (up to 35 or sometimes even more) of individual angry and needy teenagers? It's all so immediate, and gut-wrenchingly raw that it's very easy to become overwhelmed. When facing the extreme difficulty of wanting to find the right thing to do, even though as teachers we're taught to plan for and control students' behaviour, one's first reaction, when faced with anger that seems aimed at you, might be to defend yourself.

With the Year 9 class I mentioned above, because of my sudden realisation that the anger was not actually intended at me, I didn't defend myself, I paused and allowed their emotions to be. In retrospect I realised that in doing so I was in effect reflecting back to them their own selves; rather than trying to fix anything I was simply showing that I was willing to accept them as they were. However, I didn't keep holding this space – this 'suspension of assumptions' as Bohm calls it, which can get us to notice how thinking works, and from there if it is held long enough can lead to dialogue and connection between people.[44] Not being experienced, or in the least prepared for this, I somehow felt lost, and to 'fix' that I chose to go the way I had been trained, I chose to fulfil the expectations of my employers and started to 'teach'. In other words, the growing feeling of guilt that I wasn't fulfilling my role as teacher broke my suspension. Instead of allowing this emotion of guilt to simply be (which over a little time would've dissolved), in judging myself guilty I tried to bring the class back to some kind of content learning, and with that our tenuous first connections to dialogue collapsed like a tower of cards, and frustration ran high among all.

Although I can see it all quite clearly now, unfortunately I wasn't aware that any of this was actually happening at the time. The educational institution, which had placed me in the situation I had experienced, did not provide me with any kind of structure of support. Having impressed upon me the responsibility that I had to fulfil the role I was meant to fulfil – to impart specific content within a specific time – this institution was in fact the main reason behind the pressure that led me to forsake the particular opportunity I had for dialogue. *A lot of teachers I reckon these days get up and teach what they've got to teach and that's it, it's not as personalised for the kids ... if it was more personalised between teachers and students, rather than just teaching what you've got to teach out of a book ... smaller classes would probably be better ... knowing a bit about a student, not just being Mr so and so or Mrs so and so, I think that's really important* (parent).

Rather than being supported to provide the nurturing necessary for students to blossom, teachers are pressured into conforming to a standardised system. This system is one that grades and assesses students and aims to control their behaviour, instead of being willing to understand the students so as to foster their learning, and help them come to terms with understanding themselves in the context of their specific situation, within the world they inhabit. *I find creativity very scary because I can't assess it ... I have to be able to assess what I am doing ... because I have a timeline [a time when 'things' need to be done by]* (teacher).

Because of our interconnectedness, our living life within a web of relationships, when something is not supportive of whatever can nurture us, it will then more often than not actually end up hindering or even harming us. I have found that the way through a challenge will present itself more readily if I am totally present and simply aware of what *is*, without judging it, and without being eager to jump ahead with ready-made 'formulae' for solving anything. That is to say, through experience, both my own and of many others who have shared their stories with me (including those I've read), I have found that a challenge cannot be negotiated in the best possible way by any kind of book learning, planned approach, or training. The most successful way that I have faced and overcome all sorts of challenges, is through experience and practice, as well as by being as present to them as much as I possibly could so that my understanding of them might both deepen and widen.

The current way of teaching and teacher training in Australia, and probably in most of the Western world (with the exception of Finland), which is to focus on content and on a 'behaviour management' type of discipline, completely misses the opportunity of providing that which both children and teachers need. Marshall puts this quite clearly:

> It is time to let go of our false ideas about school system change and move from believing we can control change to delighting in the idea that we cannot. Our work as leaders is not to prescribe, but to evoke and liberate – to create generative conditions for deep learning ... that embody the creative processes of life and learning and invite our children to astonish us.[45]

They [adults] could ask for new ideas from children for making the environment better for everyone, like even for global warming – ways to solve that, 'cause sometimes kids can be geniuses too (student).

Releasing our belief in control requires trust and time, and again this is where dialogue can help, as through dialogue it is possible to acquire trust. A 'participatory consciousness'[46], as Bohm calls it, slowly pervades among those intent in dialogue as they become aware that they don't have to defend anything, and so they relax their mental boundaries and start to truly listen to each other. Entering into dialogue, and being in dialogue, not only enables us to connect to the concert of voices that we're constantly interacting with throughout life, but by allowing us insight into group consciousness it can also provide us with a deep consciousness of our own self – who we are and what our part is in the wholeness of life.

From this place of awareness, openness, and sharing, we may find that an impulse to 'celebrate' arises within us. So natural in young children, for whom life is a constant joyous celebration, especially if they feel loved and cared for, this spontaneous inclination may be rekindled in us when our creativity is nurtured. The next chapter, 'Celebrating Creativity' explores this, as well as many of the obstructions to our instinctive impulse for celebrating.

* * * * * * * * * * * * * * *

REVIEWING THE JOURNEY OF CHAPTER SIX

This chapter highlights the importance of becoming aware that as human beings we're embedded in a web of relationships. Despite the Western focus on independence and individualism, our society actually functions on interdependence. Because of this, consciously choosing to dialogue with the multiplicity of people we come into contact with would allow us to get closer and closer to being able to hear, and see, wholeness through our interconnectedness.

Furthermore, our interdependence does not just stop with human society but extends to all living things, in an intricate tapestry of interconnected ecosystems. By becoming more aware of this we would be able to see where we as individuals fit into the whole, as we are each of us unique, with a specific combination of gifts and potentials unrepeatable in any other living being. It is therefore not only in our own interest but also in the interest of the whole that our creativity be nurtured, so that we may become self-actualised and fulfilled. This would then allow us to improve our wellbeing at both individual and communal levels.

Rather than the focused reductive perspective (the *institutionalised perception*) that we've been taught to operate from, it is an open and egalitarian approach, or in other words an attitude of creativity, that could help us to achieve this awareness, and also self-fulfilment and wholeness. Through dialogue with others we could share our experiences and insights so that our individual awareness of wholeness may start to expand and our perspective begin to grow.

Chapter Seven:

CELEBRATING CREATIVITY

We become real when our inner work becomes work in the world; when our creativity, born of deep attention to both enchantment and nothingness, serves the cause of transformation, healing, and celebrating.[1]

– Matthew Fox

Waking up to a new moment of being, a snug feeling of excitement within, like having a precious parcel waiting to be unwrapped. I can no more control this seemingly unbidden and thrilling urge of living than I could stop the sun from rising. 'Creativity is the fragrance of individual freedom ... [and] of real health. When a person is really healthy and whole, creativity comes naturally ... the urge to create arises.'[2] One cannot just pretend to have an attitude of creativity; it's an essence that defines you. Similarly, once we have awakened to creativity it is impossible to go back to perceiving in a more restrictive way. Once we choose to approach living in a creative way, then this will keep on expanding and give rise to more creativity both in the self and in others – creativity is self-generating.

In this chapter I explore the state of mind that is engendered by the nurturing of creativity, and how this makes being creative very practical and liveable. I have found that 'walking my talk' comes easily, as creativity is applicable to any situation or project. This brings coherence, clarity and stability, from which arises an ever-widening spiral of transformation and self-realisation – an honouring of creativity, which is also a celebration of creativity. What's more, by living in this way it becomes easier to recognise what hinders creativity, and so it also becomes easier to avoid or overcome this. The process of awakening to creativity is not a solitary one (I have found this to be the case from the very beginning), so to acknowledge and honour others in this chapter I've included some of the thoughts and experiences that have been shared with me. As Lederach tells us, '[c]onversations with everyday people create connections to the environment and context'[3]. By seeking out and listening to the voices of 'ordinary' people, rather than only those of the researchers and authors (the 'experts'), we gain a more complete picture of what is actually present (real) and this reveals more of the wholeness of life.

The word 'celebrate' comes from the Latin *celebrare* and *celeber* meaning 'frequented or honoured'. This reveals meanings like 'to support' and 'to stand by', 'to respect' and 'to value', all of them connected to 'nurture'. In the *Oxford English Dictionary*, nurture is defined as 'encourage the development of' and 'cherish'. Looked at in this way, the nurturing, honouring, and encouraging of creativity is tantamount to celebrating creativity, and indeed this reflects my experience. As I've explained in previous chapters, trust and time are vital to the nurturing of creativity, for they both help to form and sustain a state of mind that is supportive of it. In practice I have found that, above all, this entails allowing the inherent wildness within me the necessary space it requires. Although it might not appear so at first sight, there's much of the whole of me that is wild.

Firstly my *beingness* – that profound sense of myself of which my consciousness is only a small part – is mostly wild. It could not be otherwise, for there is much of it that I have not yet explored. This includes my subconscious (or unconscious, as termed by Jung), which is obviously wild, not only because I don't know it but also primarily because by being beyond my control it has remained free. As Marie-Louise von Franz writes of Jung:

> [He] stressed that the only real adventure remaining for each individual is the exploration of his [sic] own unconscious. The ultimate goal of such a search is the forming of a harmonious and balanced relationship with the Self ... and because it is unique for each individual, it cannot be copied or stolen.[4]

There's yet another part of me that I acknowledge as being wild, and that is my body, as although it has somewhat been tamed by my mind, it is nonetheless essentially natural. Not only have our bodies come into being unaided by our consciousness - since quite simply our minds and our consciousness had nothing to do with our coming into existence – but our bodies also function by processes (like breathing, digestion, and growing) that are for the most part not dependent on our consciousness. O'Donohue reminds us that we are made of 'matter' that ultimately comes from the earth; we are made from the earth's 'clay':

> ... we belong beautifully to nature. The body knows this belonging and desires it. It does not exile us either spiritually or emotionally [nor does it exile our subconscious]. The human body is at home on the earth. It is probably a splinter in the mind that is the sore root of so much of our exile.[5]

So the *beingness*/body fusion that I see myself as is in fact mostly wild, and only partly civilised (as in tamed and controlled). Though the word 'wild' has been given many negative connotations, there are positive ones that can be connected to it, like, unrefined, unsophisticated, and natural, with these then leading to other meanings like, whole, childlike, innocent, ingenuous, candid, trusting, sincere, honest, spontaneous, genuine and open – all of them qualities that can enhance creativity and its nurturing. When I allow myself the freedom that my wild self needs, by consciously giving myself space, time, and trust, I am able to reach out to those wild parts of me on their own ground, and doing so makes it easier to establish an open dialogue. Through my behaviour I reflect the qualities inherent in my wild self, which means I am valuing and supporting the unknown within me. This fosters the forming of strong connections between the different parts of myself, and as a result I'm better able to see myself more and more as I am – whole.

It was sometime during the writing of my PhD thesis, that I firstly experienced just how important this open dialogue between the different parts of myself is to me. This was after my lower back had become very sore as a result of spending long periods of time sitting and writing. Maria Montessori, the founder of the Montessori Method of Education and the first woman in Italy to receive a medical degree, was already back in 1912 decrying the amount of time that children were made to sit at a desk at school:

> The vertebral column, biologically the most primitive, fundamental, and
> oldest part of the skeleton ... the most solid portion of the organism ...
> bends, and cannot resist, under the yoke of the school. ... Evidently the
> rational method of combating spinal curvature in the pupils, is to change
> the form of their work – so they shall no longer be obliged to remain for so
> many hours a day in a harmful position. It is a conquest of liberty which a
> school needs, not the mechanism of a bench.[6]

The outrage evident in this quote could be applied to a number of things other
than a school desk in our present days, since modern 'progress' often requires
us to keep our bodies still and/or repeating the same minimal movements.
Consequently many of us are fast making friends with physiotherapists or
chiropractors, given how frequently we flock to them to relieve us of pain. Yet
pain is the message from our bodies telling us that what we're doing is not good
for them, and rather than just seeking relief we would be wise to also pay more
attention to this so as to understand the message.

There have been times when I could barely sit without having my back spasm,
so that even driving was totally impossible. More recently when I've felt twinges
in my back I have made an effort to make myself available to listen more closely
to my body, as well as to really pay attention to my emotions. Inevitably, this has
reminded me that I've been neglecting myself by not making time for what I love
and need, and that I've been ignoring my stress rather than dealing with it. If at
this point I choose to pay more attention to myself, instead of berating myself for
my negligence, which only makes me feel guilty on top of stressed and sore, then
I find that I'm led to doing exactly what I need to do in order to reconnect to my
whole self, and this brings with it many insights.

Similarly to pain, forgetting to do what's good for me, or even thinking I have no
time for it and feeling stressed are also messages that there's something I need to
become aware of: something new is trying to come to light and I need to become
conscious of it. If I pay attention, eventually these 'feelings' about things that my
mind has been pondering on for a while (as yet only subconsciously) will present
as insights. It is only once my consciousness recognises them, that these insights

can be finally looked at, discussed, and perhaps even researched. Like Fox tells us (in the quote at the beginning of the chapter), what we are concerned with in life we become actively involved in; it seems reasonable then that as whole beings whatever we focus on would go beyond only dwelling in our minds, to being carried in our bodies as well as expressed by our emotions.

In many ways, the body mirrors that which the mind is experiencing, so that if the body is finding movement difficult and is in an almost 'frozen' state, then this means that the mind is also stuck. By listening to myself, I have learnt that in these situations (which don't always bring physical pain, as maybe pain is reserved for when I refuse to pay attention, so as to *really* get my interest) I need to become more aware, and be more present to myself. In other words I need to consciously take more notice of what's within me, so that by integrating it I can become more whole. This means that when I do start to pay more attention to myself I inevitably recognise that all the different parts of me are part of the whole of me. This experience brings an overwhelming feeling of familiarity and acceptance, akin to a 'homecoming' with feelings of welcome, and the dissolving of tension and anxiety. All this evokes such levels of joy and wellbeing that I am moved, and filled with gratefulness.

Moving towards wholeness brings healing; in fact, the origin of the term 'heal' is the Germanic word for 'whole', so that another way to understand the act of healing is as in making whole. Each time I am open by being patient and flexible with myself, or trusting and accepting of aspects of myself that are still unknown to me, I'm releasing the belief that these 'parts' are separate, and in doing so I heal any fragmentation within me that's been caused by a fragmented self-perception. This healing is a necessary ongoing process, as living in a hierarchical society that continues to make use of the *institutionalised perception* it is vital to constantly remind ourselves that we are in fact *whole*. Healing occurs each time I accept myself rather than try to change myself, each time I listen to my intuition and trust it, and each time I allow myself the time for inner dialogue rather than force myself to conform to the expectations of set roles. As I journey through processes that can reconnect the different parts of me, these help me to recognise how intertwined they already are, and this makes me more and more aware of my wholeness. In becoming more aware I'm allowing myself to transform in ways that nurture my creativity, so that in essence I'm also effortlessly and spontaneously celebrating creativity, which again brings feelings of unbidden joy.

Celebrating creativity is when you let go of everything that's been holding you back and you start dancing again to your own inner music – the music of your heart. This involves recognising and following your own unique rhythms. While children instinctively know how to celebrate, it sadly seems that many adults have long forgotten it. True celebration is unplanned, unlike societally set 'celebrations', which are imposed and often have an artificial feel about them. True celebration is a spontaneous and timely coming together of many facets of living into a synchronistic event (commonly bringing people together) that evokes joy and makes one feel deeply alive. *Make it as easy as possible for them to have a good experience; ... sometimes you just need to play, just have fun ...* (music teacher).

Celebration is a moment of truth, integrity and beauty where you reflect all that surrounds you, and what surrounds you reflects the inner you. Francesca Murphy writes: 'Part of what it means to be, is to be beautiful. Beauty is not superadded to things: it is one of the springs of their reality ... it is the interior geometry of things, making them perceptible as forms.'[7] It is the beauty and delight of seemingly simple things that can invite us to celebration. For me, this includes: picking ripe mulberries and tasting the sunlight in them through their warmth, catching the scent of boronia in the air – a delightful mix of spice and sweetness that is at the same time pleasing to my senses and imagination, hearing the unique gurgling song of magpies, or a well-loved tune playing on the sound-system of a car driving past, exchanging a fleeting smile with a stranger, a smile that despite its brevity is full of welcoming and understanding. In all these things, celebration is an opening of the heart that leads to recognising the presence of beauty and creativity in life, as well as a way to express the gratitude and rejoicing that arises from that recognition. O'Donohue tells us that:

> To recognize and celebrate beauty is to recognize the ultimate sacredness of experience, to glimpse the subtle embrace of belonging ... the beauty of every moment, of every thing. Beauty loves freedom ... Uncharted territories are always beckoning. Beauty is at home in this realm of the invisible, the unexpected and the unknown.[8]

Living life spontaneously, allowing colour to wash over the borders of the mind, means to consciously and willingly accept the invitation to participate in celebrating. Or to put it in another way, it means accepting the invitation to live fully and deeply, rather than just skate on the surface of life and be content with colouring in within the lines. This is not necessarily an easy invitation to accept, as we seem to be caught up in a 'thousand things' that imprison our attention and in doing so can keep us from receiving the message of that invitation. In this, more often than not there is fear involved – fear that saps the joy that would arise in us from living fully. When one has a closer look at what these 'thousand things' are, they turn out to be constructs, rules, dichotomies, and a belief in a world that is fragmented, which is inevitably accompanied by the emotions of fear and hopelessness. Interestingly, in the process of writing this chapter I found that many of these 'things' got in the way by demanding my attention, so that at times it became incredibly difficult for me to stay on task and keep the focus.

On some of the occasions when I have endeavoured to communicate my joy of being alive, the vital importance of maintaining a positive outlook, and the certainty that creativity and its nurturing are ways to transformation, I have been faced by people asking me, 'But what about the dark, or destructive side of creativity?' Rather than reply that this sort of question can only stem from a judgmental and dichotomous perspective – from the *institutionalised perception* that is ensconced within us, which I've been exposing throughout this book – I have taken the question to be deeper and to mean: is creativity the 'answer' to everything then, and is it always happy and wonderful?

The reply to this is: 'No, of course not.' Firstly, creativity is not an answer; if anything it is more of a question, it's an open and inquisitive way of looking at life, an attitude, a way of actually bringing our curiosity to life by putting it into action. This means that creativity is more of a process, and furthermore it's a holistic process that involves many 'parts' being brought together and connected through the process itself. Damasio explains this when he says (as already quoted in Chapter One), 'creative behaviour ... results from the interactions of the brain with physical, social and cultural environments.'[9] So, given that creativity is inclusive of 'us', it can only make us as happy or as positive as we feel, or are. Following the process of creativity is not easy; it needs time, trust, an ability to tolerate uncertainty, as well as a willingness to risk and to face fear and chaos, and all this before anything can crystallise into a form that can be recognised and worked with. So there is indeed much that can hinder this process. Based on all my research, however, as well as by simply looking at the state of the world, I know that we've barely had a taste of just how much joy and wholesome living can come from truly nurturing and honouring our creativity. It is the way we need to go, the path we need to take, to become all we can be and live as fully and as joyously as we can.

Fox highlights a prominent institutional belief that creativity is just an extra something that's not really necessary in our lives, and that it 'can be dropped like a sugary dessert from our diets.'[10] This belief comes from the mindset that is responsible for the reduction of art and creative classes from the curriculum when faced with budget cuts – something I saw happen over a number of years while I was on the school council and the financial committee of my daughter's primary school. In a parallel to this in higher education, the Australian Government announced on 18 June 2020 that it plans to more than double the cost of humanities degrees from 2021 – degrees in the arts, music, literature, and social sciences – so as to 'encourage' students into degrees based on science and technology, which are assumed to be more likely to lead to jobs.[11] What this money-counting outlook totally ignores is that 'the universe is intrinsically creative, always begetting, always birthing, always doing new things'[12], and to deny that and fail to flow along with it, because of budget or other concerns, is a severe case of 'tunnel vision'. Creativity is so much more than just the icing on the cake; it is in fact the whole cake, or more to the point – it is the whole delicious meal, and anything that would deny this is harmful to us.

All that impedes creativity also blocks true celebration. This hindering can be caused by any number of things, even if at face value they appear innocuous. These might be niggling bureaucratic details, like contractual requirements obliging academic university staff to submit time-sheets with set hours, for work that actually needs 'unlimited' thought time, openness and flexibility. It is also things like the rigidity of school timetables that cannot seem to be able to take the weather into account, so that outdoor physical education and sporting events might end up being scheduled to take place on rainy days or during the hottest hours of summer days, while during enticing spring days children are instead relegated to remain indoors, in classrooms lit by artificial lighting.

Young children embody the spirit of celebration, being ever ready to giggle, or to be caught up in reverie at the wonder of so many of the things we adults take for granted. *We learn in a fun environment, we take in more, I don't know why* (student). Yet from the time children are 'educated' by their parents and teachers, they are told to sit still and stop fidgeting, to be quiet and not ask so many questions. By being made to comply with school and classroom requirements, their attention is channelled into activities planned by adults, and those children who allow themselves to be distracted are disciplined by being shamed in front of their classmates. *They [students] have this ... unspoken [question] 'If I say something will you accept it, process it and give feedback without being judgmental?'* (teacher).

I see the socialisation and education of children, which altogether is a twelve to fourteen-year stint, as a campaign (even if not a conscious one) to turn a colourful bundle of wild creativity into a compliant 'grey' citizen who will fulfil the requirements of her/his roles according to the rank they are given in the social hierarchy. After this length of time, it's perhaps understandable that many adults find it difficult to remember how to truly celebrate; for celebrating involves being open to accepting, as well as allowing ourselves to be fully accepted, without hiding those parts that we've been taught are 'unacceptable'. By accepting, I simply mean recognising and acknowledging the things we see *as we see them*, without measuring them up against beliefs or expectations. One needs to be as open as possible to facilitate this sort of perception, this holistic perception, which as discussed throughout this book is very much part of an attitude of creativity.

I cried when each of my children started school, but they were not the joyful tears of a proud parent. I could feel an anxious knot between my heart and throat while I sobbed... I felt that I was letting down these precious little beings whose care and welfare I had been charged with. I did not *want* to cry, but in remembering so many of the sad, humiliating and frustrating times I had experienced in school, I took a long time to stop. I knew there had to be a better way, and turning my PhD thesis into a book is part of working towards this.

Having been on the journey of actively nurturing creativity for many years now, I have come to see that better ways could be found for many of the things we do as a society, but in order to facilitate their development many more of us need to consciously start nurturing our creativity. We also need to become clearly aware that we're constantly getting ourselves stuck when we operate from controlled, fragmented, and mechanised ways of being. To nurture and celebrate our creativity we need to let go of constructs that don't work for us, but to be able to do this we first need to see what these constructs (structures and tools, both physical and mental) are. By using our creativity we could fashion any constructs in ways that are appropriate for us, so that they could be of benefit and support without hurting us, the environment, or anything else. Yet to do this we need to trust our creativity, and this is especially difficult to do while so many of us continue to deny that we are creative.

Doidge tells us that as we grow to adulthood:

> ... the spontaneity, creativity, and unpredictability of childhood gives [sic] way to a routinized existence that repeats the same behaviour and turns us into rigid caricatures of ourselves. Anything that involves unvaried repetition – our careers, cultural activities, skills, and neuroses – can lead to rigidity. ... Because our neuroplasticity can give rise to both mental flexibility and mental rigidity, we tend to underestimate our own potential for flexibility, which most of us experience only in flashes.[13]

The rigidity of repetitive behaviour occurs most readily for those of us who in 'growing up' learn to abide by the (mostly invisible) structures that we have built, or adopted (though often virtually unconsciously), through an *institutionalised perception*. One of the results of this is that our creative growth is stunted. Indeed these very 'thought' structures prevent the ideas, light, colours, music, harmony, and beauty in the world from fully reaching us, as well as stopping our creativity from rising up within us to be shared with others. This routinised way of being also extends to the way we celebrate.

All our Western festive traditions seem to have been appropriated by consumerism, so that celebrating could be viewed as being one long shopping spree. Starting with Valentine's Day and ending with Christmas & New Year, these public holidays are interspersed with 'personal' birthdays, weddings, retirements, and so on. All of them occasions that require the purchasing of gifts, to be given and/or exchanged according to social conventions, as well as the 'appropriate merry making' as the season dictates. This can invariably result in frenzied preparations as we try to fit these social requirements into our already demanding schedules, and makes for gatherings of harried would-be revellers who may need more than a little alcohol to relax, and who are so determined to 'have a good time' that they turn celebrating into a chore, with a mental list of things they 'need' to do.

Many of us have become extremely accustomed to an innumerable amount of specific ways of doing things (habits, attitudes, plans) just to be able to navigate through life. Although routine can be useful, as Doidge points out too much of it can have quite a detrimental effect on us. Routine that's blindly followed can turn us into automatons: getting up at the same time each day, driving to and from work and picking up the children from school by following the same routes, shopping at the same stores, watching the same shows on television and listening to the same radio station, eating foods prepared in similar ways, and so on, throughout the weeks, months, and years. Though we might find this comforting, like a well-worn pair of slippers, it is also very limiting. Furthermore, we let our likes and dislikes define us (who we are) by believing that these won't change, and the less conscious we are of the patterns of our habits the more these become 'almost impossible to interrupt and redirect without special techniques.'[14]

With many of our behaviours, we often seem unaware of what we do or why we do them, with this being even more likely the case if our subconscious learned or developed the behaviour from a belief in our early childhood. Bruce Lipton tells us that '[y]oung children carefully observe their environment and download the worldly wisdom offered by parents directly into their subconscious memory. As a result, their parents' behaviour and beliefs become their own.'[15] Terms like 'download' and 'programming', are commonly used in relation to the subconscious, which processes information without our conscious awareness. Unbeknownst to us, our subconscious processes some 20 million stimuli per second (compared to the 40 stimuli per second that our conscious mind processes); it verifies this information with what is already stored, and accepts it together with what it perceives from the environment.[16]

As was discussed in Chapter Five, these habitual modes of behaviour, which can also be often connected to cultural behaviour, have an effect on how we are able to perceive. In *The Brain That Changes Itself,* Doidge refers to an experiment conducted with Japanese and American students that gives an example of what cultural habits of perception mean in practice. In the experiment the students were shown a number of scenes of different animations of fish swimming, and they were then asked to describe them. While the American students mostly focused their description on the main fish (the biggest, fastest, or brightest), the Japanese students described the other smaller fish and the surrounding environmental details more often than the Americans. When the Americans recognised specific objects they did so regardless of what background they were given, while instead the Japanese found it easier to recognise the objects in their original setting. These results, which are similar to those of many other comparable experiments, imply cultural differences of perception; the main one being that Easterners seem to see things more in context and in relation to each other, while Westerners have more of a tendency to see things separately to each other, and thus individually.[17]

Doidge states that '[e]verything we know about [the brain, and its] plasticity suggests that these different ways of perceiving, repeated hundreds of times a day, in massed practice, must lead to changes in neural networks responsible for sensing and perceiving.'[18] From this it's easy to deduce just how much of an effect going to school can have on children, especially in a classroom with a structured routine, where everything is repeated over and over. Doidge also notes that in 'totalitarian regimes ... much effort is made to indoctrinate the young from an early age'[19] and that:

> Human beings can be broken down and then develop, or at least "add on", neurocognitive structures, if their daily lives can be totally controlled, and they can be conditioned by reward and severe punishment and subjected to massed practice, where they are forced to repeat or mentally rehearse various ideological statements. In some cases, this process can actually lead them to "unlearn" their pre-existing mental structures ... [20]

Being about totalitarian regimes, this would not likely be seen as applicable to schools in our first world societies, so that we would commonly totally dismiss such a connection. It might, however, be worth taking a closer look. 'Totalitarian' actually means 'authoritarian', and schools are most certainly run according to a strict hierarchical system of authority where children have no power, or at least very little, with even the timing of their bodily needs (like toileting and eating) being usually completely controlled. What is 'severe punishment' for a young child? This will depend on the child, but I suspect that in many cases having their name written beneath 'the sad face' drawn on the board, or being told off by the teacher in front of the other children in the class, would be sufficient for the majority of young children to start to modify their behaviour to compliance, therefore beginning to alter and rigidify their neural patterning.

Interestingly, I had the occasion to discuss this very point with a group of people at a social gathering – how much of an impact might writing a child's name under 'the sad face' on a blackboard make on that child? Immediately after I'd finished speaking, a young man of twenty-seven confirmed that he'd had such an experience when he was around five; what's more, his mother together with another relative had also visited his classroom that day. He told us that he'd never forgotten this incident or his feelings about it, which had been extremely uncomfortable, and that the memory of it could still make him squirm within.

Sir Ken Robinson's claims align to all this:

> ...our current education system systematically drains the creativity out of our children ... Those students whose minds work differently – and we're talking about many students here; perhaps even the majority of them – can feel alienated from the whole culture of education. This is exactly why some of the most successful people you'll ever meet didn't do well at school. Education is the system that's supposed to develop our natural abilities and enable us to make our way in the world. Instead, it is stifling the individual talents and abilities of too many students and killing their motivation to learn.[21]

Many scholars have spoken out about this discrepancy, between what we 'expect' education to provide and what instead are its most likely outcomes. In considering these arguments, I have reflected about this *idea* that education is actually *meant to* foster our talents. Why do we assume this? It is commonly known that compulsory mass education began during the time of the Industrial Revolution (as mentioned in Chapter 6), and that it was a means to control the population and prepare people to be factory workers. Has education changed significantly since then? Do we have any 'evidence' that power in the world is now more equitably shared, and no longer monopolised as it was with the rise of capitalism at the time of the Industrial Revolution? From the antics of governments, extremely wealthy magnates, and big industry around the world, it would not seem so. In fact, the Industrial Revolution provided a pathway for corporations to establish themselves and they have since then proliferated, so that education is still seen as preparing students for work, as Berry confirms:

> Because the industrial-commercial corporation is so central to contemporary existence, our educational programs have become subservient to its control. High school and college students must prepare themselves for jobs within this industrial-commercial setting.[22]

This maintains the focus of education on control and power rather than on creativity. As I've already quoted in Chapter One, Plowman says that '[t]he need for power is in direct contradiction with the ability to be creative'[23]. This makes sense, since the power-hungry would want followers, needing them to uphold their power, while instead creativity thrives through collaboration and change. In support of this, Saul asserts that we (as in the race of humans) have not moved much further beyond the ideology of the sixteenth century:

> We are now more than four and a half centuries into an era which our obsession with progress and our servility to structure have caused us to name and rename a dozen times, as if this flashing of theoretically fundamental concepts indicated real movement.[24]

As part of this institutional structure that has (if anything) kept on increasing in size and influence since the sixteenth century, schools are recruited to be among the first preservers of the status quo. Even though they may not consciously be a willing party, schools do fulfil this role they are given despite all the 'surface' restructures they may undertake. Writing in 1998 about schools in Australia, Robert Hattam and colleagues state that:

> ...the logic of the market in concert with the government is infecting our public institutions and civil society ... [this] will result in unwanted outcomes for major sections of Australian society, particularly those who will be forced to rely on public institutions because they have no power in the market. Simply put, the majority will become increasingly marginal.[25]

This does not indicate much of a change from the days of the Industrial Revolution; furthermore, the reality of experience some twenty years on from when this quote was written shows it to be quite prophetic. Looking at education from a wider lens, Peter Abbs reminds us that it is a managerial perspective that is dictating how things are run. In agreement with Hattam and colleagues he asserts: '[i]n our schools and universities we have become pathologically obsessed with quantitative measurement rather than the qualitative flow of meaning, with a brute collective standardisation rather than more subtle modes of individuation.'[26] This obsession, which is nonetheless in line with 'controlling the masses', causes our educational institutions to be structured according to the logic of accounting firms that are very much aligned with the 'idea' of increasing productivity.

A managerial perspective is akin to the money-counting outlook I mentioned before, which, suffering from 'tunnel-vision' finds it difficult to be even aware of creativity, let alone allow any holistic type of approach or spontaneous celebrating – Heaven forbid! Any sort of celebration would have to be planned for and budgeted. Often it is precisely those who have ascribed to this sort of outlook who are given the power to run our schools and universities, or at least to prescribe how they are to be run.

One might expect that private schools might be different, as given their self-proclaimed focus on excellence they would be more likely to foster individuals' talents, but that is not necessarily the case. Private schools have traditionally been where the powerful and wealthy have sent their children to become leaders, yet there are now possibly more students frequenting private schools than ever before. Ladwig and Gore remind us that 'private schooling is inherently premised on notions of hierarchical provision of education rather than universal provision, on the idea that some students should receive a different (and by implication better) quality of schooling.'[27] It is therefore plausible that such a hierarchy would also operate within the schools, so that those chosen (or recognised) as being 'elites' would be the only ones encouraged to become leaders.

Parents I interviewed whose children attended private schools confirmed this by relaying to me that in their experience these schools promote 'elitism':

...a teacher's role is to enrich every child and not [just] the select group.

There is a real pervasive way that teachers see the 'elite' as opposed to the 'normal' or the 'base' group, and they've got to get that out of their systems ... they've got to understand that their role is to bring out the creative element in every student, not just the elite.

Apart from mainstream private schools, there are a few specialist schools that follow more holistic educational philosophies, these include the Montessori Method, the Reggio Emilia approach, and the Waldorf Steiner schools. The philosophies these schools are based on arose from of an awareness of what education was lacking (which reinforces the above discussion of the general role of schools as preservers of the 'status quo'), thus they all share similar aims of enabling self-directed learning and the development of each child's individual abilities. Though each claims a specific mission, and different schools following the same philosophy vary (for each philosophy a number of schools can be found world-wide), they are all meant to be child-centred and nurturing of creativity:

- According to the International Montessori Index website, the main message of the Montessori Method is to 'follow the child'. 'The child's choice, practical work, care of others and the environment, and above all the high levels of concentration reached when work is respected and not interrupted, reveal a human being that is superior not only academically, but emotionally and spiritually, a child who cares deeply about other people and the world, and who works to discover a unique and individual way to contribute.'[28]

- Focusing on early childhood (three to six-year-olds), the Reggio Emilia approach was established over forty years ago by the parents and community in the Italian town of Reggio Emilia. An excerpt from the travelling exhibition *The Hundred Languages of Children*, taken from the Reggio Children website, succinctly describes this approach: 'Children have a hundred languages, and they want to use them all. They learn very soon how difficult it is for this right to be recognized and above all respected. This is why children ask us to be their allies in resisting hostile pressures and defending spaces for creative freedom which, in the end, are also spaces of joy, trust, and solidarity.'[29]

- On the 'Steiner Schools in Australia' website, Hale and MacLean tell us:

'Steiner thought that schools should cater to the needs of the child rather than the demands of the government or economic forces, so he developed schools that encourage creativity and free-thinking. His teaching seeks to recognise the individuality of the child and through a balanced education, allows them to go into the world with confidence.'[30]

Though these styles of schools are widely known about, they remain, because of considerable cost, accessible to only a minority, which invariably makes them exclusive. Notwithstanding their ideal philosophies, this exclusivity can lead to other issues, like elitism, dichotomous thinking, and so on.

On the basis of all that we have explored so far regarding education, although many educational philosophies may have us convinced that education 'should' be about the development of talents and abilities, it appears that there is in fact little evidence to confirm this expectation. There may have been exceptions to this perhaps for short periods of time, with variations in different countries, when enlightened governments were in power. Although accepting this state of affairs seems quite demoralising, the removal of unrealistic expectation from our sights, in order to see what *is*, can help us to imagine an education that we would actually want – a way of truly enhancing our children's creative strengths.

Finland's education system (as looked at in depth in Chapter Four) shows us that this sort of education is possible. It is interesting to note, however, that Finland does not share the tradition of education as a means of control stemming from the Industrial Revolution. Instead, in Finland 'provisions were laid down in the 1919 Constitution on compulsory, free-of-charge basic education for all and on vocational training and academic educational institutions provided by public authorities.'[31] Being a relatively young institution without previous history, Finland's education system was founded on an understanding that education would be vital for the newly independent nation. As such, it claims to be inclusive and egalitarian, and based on trust rather than control. As they state on one of their websites, the '[u]nderlying values of basic education are human rights, equality, democracy.'[32] These are values that are also supportive of creativity.

With many schools unable or unwilling to provide the quality of education that parents would hope for, some parents end up opting for home schooling to ensure that their children are given a better chance to develop their potential. Accordingly, I included in my interviews a number of parents who had chosen to home school, and what they shared showed that they were very satisfied with their choice:

Creativity is really allowing the environment to occur, in which the person can actually develop their skills without negative influences.

Many parents who homeschool get together so as *to encourage one another in the areas that the children are good at ... it's really seeing the possibilities of not being confined by a box or a system, and that is so freeing.*

I don't know whether the [education] system is designed to be as flexible as that [that is to be able to nurture creativity] it comes down to the teachers as well, whether they're going to feel that's part of their role or if they've got enough on their plate as it is ... there isn't a high value placed upon teaching ... the lack of appreciation of what they do is so evident (this parent had a number of relatives who were teachers).

The children are self-taught and they have a real love of learning ... for each of my children I can see now an avenue where they can decide 'I'd like to do that, that's an area of interest I have' ... and I've learned from my own upbringing not to try and squeeze them into an area ... Money is not everything, it's really the ability to be free to express the gifts which may be innate in people rather than suppress them [which is important]. This last sentence reflects the celebration inherent in the fulfilment of our wholeness through learning, as well as in expressing ourselves by following what we are passionate about.

If, as has been shown in numerous ways throughout this book, it is indeed a natural inclination for children to desire to fulfil their inner potentials, then why, rather than supporting and nurturing them, do we as a society for the most part insist on blocking that? These children will be growing into the adults who will 'run the world'. Surely our mentality has now evolved beyond that which was prevalent in the Industrial Revolution in many European countries? Given the increasing worldwide challenges we're facing, how could it ever be a logical choice to stifle the development of possible solutions that might be achieved through the joint creativity of individuals?

Although I cannot answer these questions with any certainty, I believe that the majority of us do not purposely set out to inhibit our growth or hurt ourselves;

humans are kinder than that, as Kagan has specified of human nature (quoted and discussed in Chapter Four). I think what principally obstructs us is that we are fearful. Fear is in fact one of the main effects of the 'fighting' paradigm that our society exists in, which sees us constantly fight anything we don't want, like cancer, hunger, crime, and so on. The use of this fighting metaphor in our communication is especially effective in putting us in an immediate state of alert. By making us believe that we're in danger, it brings out our most visceral (and ancient) fear of death. We therefore see those things, ideas, or even people that we dislike as threats, which at the very least must be 'beaten', for us to be happy and successful, and ideally shouldn't even be allowed to exist in the world. This sort of mindset is not only applied to external matters but also to our own selves, as well as to our nearest and dearest, like our children. For in fact we are likewise ruled by the fear of not being perfect and/or of making mistakes, and we collude in preserving this state of affairs by being quick to judge ourselves and others on any supposed lack or flaw.

This thought pattern seems to have become such a protracted way of existence in our modern world that our fight or flight response – a physical reaction whereby hormones are released in our bloodstream when we experience fear, in a bid to save us by bolstering us to run away or defend ourselves – is only ever temporarily assuaged. The very act of thinking that we will be engaging in combat (even though in most cases this remains only in the mind) generates further fear, and this sets up the cycle all over again. This constant state of battling (struggling) and the belief that we are somehow 'under fire' never ends but is only ever punctuated with temporary periods of 'cease-fire'. This self-perpetuating fear/fighting cycle causes high levels of stress from which there is no relief, and this can result in chronic anxiety and/or depression.[33] In *The Biology of Belief*, Lipton likens this relentless primed state we're in to that experienced by an athlete in a 'get set' mode, who is about to start a race and awaiting for the 'go!' signal, which despite all our preparedness never comes:

> ...this protection mechanism was not designed to be continuously activated. ... We are constantly besieged by multitudes of unresolvable worries about our personal lives, our jobs, and our war-torn global community. ... our hyper-vigilant lifestyle is severely impacting the health of our bodies. Our daily stressors are constantly ... priming our bodies for action ... undermining

our quality of life ... frightening us into a chronic, soul-sapping protective mode.[34]

Feeling on edge, we are so terrified that the 'what ifs' hounding us will come true, that many of us put 'back stops' in place to protect ourselves, as well as to prevent us from facing our fears. Namely, we're afraid and very resistant to any suggestion to look at our fears and what they might mean, and whether they make any sense, especially given the possibility that this could talk us into relinquishing the huge defensive we've set up. In other words, we are unwittingly afraid of letting go of any of our fear (subconsciously our inbuilt protection), with this perhaps being our greatest fear. In an attempt to relieve some of our 'fear of letting go of fear', we very cleverly follow rigid paths and methods that we have set up to stop ourselves from having to confront our fears, hopefully forever.

We learn this pattern of avoidance and repression subconsciously as children, when we are prevented from expressing (even just talking about) those emotions most often termed as negative or toxic. Principally these are feelings of fear and anger, as well as other feelings like guilt, envy, jealousy, boredom, sadness, and so on. All of them can be kept in check when put under the ego's control, which doesn't allow them a voice in order to 'save face'. I have several times witnessed grown men and women regressing to childish behaviour of repression – like making loud incoherent noises (much like in a tantrum) in order to stop a discussion that might risk a fear-based prejudice being revealed; in the face of this it is obvious that this behaviour was acquired from childhood.

Goleman reminds us of something we have probably all experienced: 'emotions are contagious. We can "catch" strong emotions much as we do a rhinovirus – and so can come down with the emotional equivalent of a cold.'[35] Perhaps this is why parents might feel the need to prevent their children from expressing strong raw emotions, because it is very distressing for the parents when a child does that, and in the already stressful environment of modern living it is just too difficult to cope with. Additionally, parents may also feel responsible for how their children feel and behave, so consequently many zealously teach them what is acceptable behaviour and what is not. This brings up the parents' own subconscious programming, which can be passed on without the awareness of either the parents or the children.[36]

Yet feelings are feelings, the word 'feeling' itself suggesting that they need to be *felt*. While we might not yet know the full extent of their purpose, we might do well to avoid repressing them, especially as we know that stifling negative feelings seems to also inevitably prevent the positive ones from arising. In *The Wisdom of Forgiveness*, Victor Chan informs us that the practice of not revealing his emotions caused his 'ability to experience emotions [to] become impaired'[37], while instead he found that the Dalai Lama was 'totally at ease with displaying his emotions ... not [being] ashamed of his feelings; ... self-conscious or embarrassed about them ... [he] would laugh without restraint at something funny and then, within seconds, display the most serious concentration.'[38] Not allowing emotions to be expressed so that what one feels doesn't show, know as being 'inscrutable', has long been considered a form of protection against those who would take advantage of our vulnerability; yet it can severely curtail our ability to celebrate as it especially prevents us from feeling joy.

In allowing myself to express my emotions I have been able to catch sight of impulses that might otherwise have been blocked from my awareness. Any time I try to stop myself from feeling, for whatever reason, I have experienced an unpleasant fixation on the emotions I am trying to suppress. Then because I am paying too much attention to them they seem to grow out of proportion and overshadow my whole world. Instead, if I let myself fully feel whatever emotion arises, I can then see what is behind it, what gave rise to it. Any kind of new awareness is 'learning' and therefore this increases my consciousness, and I find that I am drawn to where an impulse originated from and that this often leads me to discover a specific belief connected to it. To be able to do this, however, I have to confront my emotions, meaning that I have to look at them and feel them – I have to accept them. That is not easy, especially when it comes to fear. Although fear can have a paralysing effect, it can also be mesmerising, with these two effects together being almost too much to resist, as countless box office successes from the scary to the horrific attest to.

An almost obsessive glamour seems to be attached to the idea of what is destructive. Think of the 'coolness' attributed to the 'hero' walking towards us and away from all sorts of explosions and destruction behind him, even those that he's been the cause of. At the same time, though we appear to have quite a lot of 'hang ups' about negative emotions, we somehow believe that allowing ourselves to feel them (let alone express them) shows us up as being less than civilised. In response to this we seek to control them, meaning that we're more likely to hide them away, repress and deny them rather than face them. The result of this is that they're relegated to our 'shadow' in our subconscious, where ironically we actually have less control over them, as Jung tells us:

> The shadow personifies everything that the subject refuses to acknowledge about himself [sic] and yet is always thrusting itself upon him [sic] directly or indirectly – for instance inferior traits of character and other incompatible tendencies ... [yet it] does not consist only of morally reprehensible tendencies, but also displays a number of good qualities, such as normal instincts, appropriate reaction, realistic insight, creative impulses ...[39]

Refusing to confront an emotion not only prevents us from discovering the impulse that might be behind it, but also gets us caught up in the emotional 'fall-out' (the connected baggage) from the subconscious. This can be so overwhelming that it stops us from feeling and exploring our positive emotions, which can then prevent us from nurturing and celebrating our creativity. Grave repercussions for mental health can come from this, adding to the (already discussed) mental health concerns that are ever increasing in current society. Conversely, when an emotion is faced and fully *felt*, it is then not unusual to find that it grows softer or even completely dissipates, making it easier to move past it. Like thoughts, emotions or feelings are ephemeral insubstantial things, but by obsessing about them – as in being fearful of them or focusing exclusively on them – we give them the energy to become 'solid' enough to get us stuck.

In Chapter Five, I shared that in my last year of high school I made myself fail a physics test to overcome the anxiety I had of not doing well enough at school. This is an example of facing a fear; although the prospect of what I proposed to myself terrified me, I chose to face it and I was able to do this relatively easily because I recognised the fear that was causing my anxiety. By not studying and failing I was basically testing a hypothesis – that nothing terrible would happen as a result of failing a test. Given that we live in a paradigm of constant fighting, many of our fears (maybe even most of them) are, however, much more cleverly disguised. Before beginning my PhD I had simply assumed that I would have to live with the niggling anxious feeling I often had about my health, especially that of my heart. Live with it that is, until it was proven 'right' and somehow killed me. Then sometime after I had written my thesis, and I had begun to put into practice my findings on creativity as well as those on time and trust, when it seemed that new insights arose in me every day, I made a connection that enabled me to uncover the reason for my fear regarding my health.

When I was just under three my younger sister by eleven months died (as I relayed in Chapter Two). According to the custom of the times of shielding children from grief, I was not told about her death, but no longer seeing her or having her around would naturally have led me to ask where she was. I did not remember what I was told exactly but I did (and still do) remember subsequently asking why she had died, to which the reply came that her heart had simply stopped beating. This was probably said so as not to go into an explanation of what adults might imagine would have been frightening details for a young child. What followed for me, however, were endless nights of falling asleep with my hand on my heart wondering if it would stop beating, and not wanting this to take me by surprise as my sister's disappearance had. As an adult now I might assume that it had been a sad and scary time for me, yet I remember that I had just wanted to be prepared, it was a very matter of fact reaction – young children are very practical as they live in the present. By having been excluded from participating in her funeral, and having been told that her heart had stopped beating instead of having her illness explained to me, I had internalised the fear of heart failure occurring 'out of the blue'. Facing this memory and allowing myself to feel all the emotions that came from it brought me to a full understanding, as it clearly showed me how my anxiety about my heart had originated.

As I keep walking along the path of transformation through creativity, insights about myself continue to reveal themselves. By *trusting* as fully as I can, and releasing myself to tears and laughter as I need, I find myself understanding and getting to know myself better and better. As trusting is what helps me to confront my more uncomfortable emotions, it has become for me the key to getting to know myself. Since realising that I did not trust myself much, I have hugely increased my self-trust; yet it seems I have barely dipped into the waters of what I can see is a very deep well of trust that's available to me, a trust as deep as my subconscious. Being an incredibly capable and fast processor of information (with most necessary bodily functions dependent on it) our subconscious is as trustworthy as life itself; to better enable ourselves to trust we need to improve the communication between it and our consciousness.

The discovery of ourselves by connecting to and exploring our subconscious, which then allows us to better fulfil our potentials through the process of growth, is what Jung called the 'process of individuation' (looked at in Chapter Five). This process is unique to each of us, and what's more, the pace at which it unfolds depends upon the sharing of information from the subconscious (termed unconscious by Jung), which reveals it to our conscious mind according to what we can cope with. In these conditions, choosing to trust really seems to be the best option, for while withholding ourselves from feeling emotions puts our mental health in danger, connecting to the subconscious willingly and with awareness allows for creative growth and self-knowledge, as Marie-Louise von Franz suggests:

> In order to understand the symbolic indications of the unconscious, one must be careful not to get outside oneself or "beside oneself", but to stay emotionally within oneself. ... Only if I remain an ordinary human being, conscious of my incompleteness, can I become receptive to the significant contents and processes of the unconscious.[40]

I have found that in times of need I have many answers within me, and to access them I have come to know that I can wait, trust, and allow myself to be guided by creativity by being open to any synchronicity or serendipity that will show itself. Still, this can be easier said than done, especially if I am 'fixed' on a strong emotion that is hindering my perception.

In *Social Intelligence*, Goleman explains how 'holding on to hatred and grudges has grave physiological consequence'[41], with studies showing that if people even think of anyone or anything they dislike, or that they feel has wronged them (with this even being the nebulous but frequently used 'they'), then their body is overrun by stress hormones, which raise their blood pressure and weaken the effectiveness of their immune system.[42] This has a tendency to happen more often than we might imagine, as we're inclined to become easily obsessed with what hurts us. On the other hand, it has also been found that forgiveness lowers stress hormones, blood pressure and heart rate, as well as lessening levels of depression and pain.[43] Given this alone, rather than revenge or holding on to anger, choosing to forgive would seem the most sensible choice to make. For although forgiveness doesn't condone what has happened, it nonetheless allows us to free ourselves from the grip of being overcome by what has hurt us.[44]

Obsessing or being overcome means focusing on something so strongly that we fixate, or in other words get stuck to the point that we are unable to move past it. It is almost as if we had 'hooked' this object with our focus – frozen, both it and us, at that particular point in time when we were hurt, when undoubtedly there were also many strong emotions present to further keep us stuck. By forgiving we are able to 'unhook' from what we've been focusing on, and in doing this the emotions become a little less frightening so that we can allow ourselves to *feel* them and move past them. This enables us to return to flowing with life rather than remaining 'frozen'. It also reconnects us with creativity, which can help us from getting stuck again by maintaining in us an open perspective.

Forgiveness is a concept that from time immemorial has been part of the wisdom of many different spiritual paths. Victor Chan tells us how the Dalai Lama links it to the 'theory of interdependence', which can be more easily understood through a holistic perspective. According to the Dalai Lama:

> The theory of interdependence allows us to develop a wider perspective ... With a wider mind, less attachment to destructive emotions like anger, therefore more forgiveness. In today's world, every nation heavily interdependent, interconnected. Under these circumstances, destroying your enemy – your neighbour – means destroying yourself in the long run. ... we're not talking about the complete removal of feelings like anger, attachment, or pride. Just reduction. Interdependence is important because it is not a mere concept; it can actually help reduce the suffering caused by these destructive emotions.[45]

From all these explanations on the effects of forgiveness it is easy to see that, in assisting us to 'let go', forgiveness is also conducive to the nurturing and celebrating of creativity. Similarly, because nurturing creativity fosters an open mind – a holistic perspective – it can in turn be seen as being clearly supportive of forgiveness. In supporting us to release emotions, forgiveness can help us to live deeply. Every time we live deeply and feel joyous we're essentially celebrating life and its creativity. In practice, this would also mean being able to listen to our own intuition on how to celebrate any occasion in life (any event we feel is special), rather than feel compelled to follow tradition for the sake of appearances.

Life is naturally creative, and being part of life we are called upon and invited to be co-creators. Traditions are human creations; in fact, it is worth considering that even the oldest and most revered customs were created by people. This then means that they could also be changed by people, maybe even by us. Although with many traditions it feels as if they're 'set in stone' and unchangeable, they could with tact, care, and creativity be adapted to suit new contexts and times, so that the implementation of new traditions might allow for more openness and creative expression. There is a quaint story told about the unquestioning following of a tradition – *it relates how a young, newly married, woman before roasting a turkey would always cut off one of its legs because that was how her grandmother had always done it, and she was certain that this was part of the reason the roasting turned out superb (her grandmother had passed away and her recipes were considered a family heirloom). Finally her husband, concerned that by doing this there would not be enough turkey for the Thanksgiving they would be hosting that year, asked her grandfather if he might tell him the reason for the mysterious removal of the turkey's leg. Amidst laughter, the reply was that it had been due to the grandmother only having access to a small oven, so she had used a pan that didn't have enough room for a whole turkey, and had had to resort to removing a leg.*

When we trust ourselves enough to be able to question anything that is being done (no matter who is doing it), if this does not seem appropriate or we can see connections that we feel would make other ways more suitable, then we are partaking fully in life. If we can see it, or have in some way become aware of it, then it is 'our business' too as we are all connected, and questioning the status quo with respect and thoughtfulness could even lead us to help overcome collective world challenges. This returns us to where this chapter began, to the *beingness* of the self and to celebrating creativity, with the exploration of the subconscious revealing the holistic creative nature of the 'Self' (the whole self, or psyche as Jung terms it). This is further explored in Chapter Eight, the last chapter, where all the main themes of this book are woven together to further reveal the 'whole' picture.

* * * * * * * * * * * * * * *

REVIEWING THE JOURNEY OF CHAPTER SEVEN

In the Introduction I relayed Atkinson's words that '[s]tory is a tool for making us whole ... a tool for self-discovery.'[46] When we delve within, with the purpose of writing 'the story' of ourselves, we help to make sense of life and we give meaning to it. In this chapter I connect to one of the central meanings of life – that of celebration. Through the journey of transformation that I am travelling by being alive and consciously partaking of life, I have come to the realisation that living fully is in fact a celebration. It is a celebration of the process, discovery, and creativity of living, and this chapter explores the state of mind of what it actually feels like to have an 'attitude of creativity'.

Importantly, this chapter also looks at some of that which hinders an attitude of creativity from being nurtured and thus celebrated. It therefore investigates how the so-called 'toxic' emotions can get us stuck and prevent us from flowing along with life and creativity, and how this is often made worse by repressing them. It especially looks at the experience of fear as something that can cause ongoing societal stress, and also discusses how forgiveness can help us to release many 'negative' emotions as well as other obsessions we may be 'stuck' on.

Chapter Eight:

THE BIG PICTURE

Creativity is a state of mind in which all of our intelligences are working together. It involves seeing, thinking and innovating.[1]

– Bill Lucas

There is a Chinese proverb that says, 'If we don't change our direction we're likely to end up where we're headed'. We live in a world that is politically divided into nation-states where small groups of 'technocrats' and 'elites' hold power in ever-increasing amounts (as is the custom in a hierarchy), and through an intricate system of institutions control the majority of the population who allow themselves (for a myriad of reasons, including fear and a belief of a lack of time) to be controlled by conforming and complying, and who are in this way 'forced' to live in ways that they wouldn't otherwise choose.[2] This has so far led (with many other things stemming from these) to social isolation, alienation, poverty, war with the potential for destruction on a global scale due to the copious arsenals of arms and technologies held by many countries, pollution and destruction of our natural environment through the use of fossil fuels and other toxic concoctions, all in the name of progress, and the direction we're headed in seems to be pointing to more of the same.[3]

Despite this, creativity is still very present and indeed leads those who allow themselves to recognise it and flow with it to live fulfilling lives. Yet, as I have shown, it is severely hampered by the current state of where we are at; imagine where it could take us if we consciously made more room for it and nurtured it.

It might be argued that things could be worse, and indeed they could be; the horrors that we seem to be able to imagine, as shown on so many of the movies that are meant to 'entertain' us, do eclipse reality. But that's just it, they're fiction, and perhaps the reason that some of them are so dire is that we are actually trying to convince ourselves that things are not so bad. However, they could also be much, much better; for while we're mesmerized by the fear associated with catastrophic future scenarios in fictional alternate realities, *we nonetheless allow 'business-as-usual' to continue in ways that are hurting us now*, as in hurting our health and wellbeing, our relationships and our environment, as well as hurting the creatures that cohabit the earth with us.

Perhaps not enough of us are convinced that we need to change the direction we're heading in. In *Requiem for a Species*, Clive Hamilton points out that there's much ongoing argument in regard to global warming and the measures that climate scientists are suggesting we take, with some people thinking they are too drastic; as a result of this, environmentalists have even been accused of deliberately arousing public fear.[4] I find it interesting that 'climate change' is the specific wording that has been chosen for this issue that is so greatly debated; it is, after all, a phrase that is easy to politicise, with much room for argument and denial.

In the meantime, pollution and its effects cannot be denied – like the smog in China, which in many cities drastically reduces visibility and has people (including tourists) wearing masks, with children being kept indoors for protection a regular occurrence. A comprehensive study at the Harvard T.H. Chan School of Public Health, published in September of 2015, revealed that 3.3 million (3,300,000) deaths each year worldwide are attributable to air pollution, and that this number could double by the year 2050 if there is no change to our rate of emissions.[5] Although this makes a rather urgent case for change, it surprisingly hasn't received much news airtime at all, and doesn't seem to be part of conversations regarding climate change, notwithstanding the obvious connection.

This silence is even more bizarre when we consider that total deaths from the COVID-19 pandemic to date (7 July 2020), so over six months, have been reported as being approximately 538,000[6], comparatively less than a third of the above rate, and yet the Western world has been essentially panic-stricken. This terror is directly connected to the singular emphasis on pandemic deaths reported by the media. While there are limitations to what we seem to be able to do to halt the course of a virus, it appears (astoundingly) that hardly anything at all is being done, or planned, about significantly reducing air pollution, even though some of the highest concentration of deaths from COVID-19 have occurred in areas of the world with the highest air pollution, a fact that has been verified in a recent study by the Harvard T.H. Chan School of Public Health[7].

Seeing where our current direction has brought us so far, it is clear that if we don't consciously set out to change it, we can expect it to lead us to a much worse reality, with Dante's 'Hell' coming to mind as an image. Dante Alighieri, the fourteenth century Italian visionary poet who wrote the *Divine Comedy* – a mythical journey through Hell, Purgatory and Heaven – describes Hell as a place that's barren and desolate, devoid of plant life and filled with all types of pollution. In *The Comedy of Survival: Literary Ecology and a Play Ethic,* Joseph Meeker sees this description as a 'premonition of twentieth-century problems'[8]. He further points out that Dante could've depicted Hell by abiding to the symbolism of the times, which saw nature, rather than anything man-made, as being dangerous and evil, however:

> Dante's decision to describe Hell as an environment polluted by people and excluding all wild or natural forms is a deliberate innovation that he executes with care and consistency. It is necessary to his idea that humans are responsible creators of the world in which they must live.[9]

The website 'The World Counts', which was started and is maintained in Copenhagen, Denmark, by providing 'an overview of many of the critical global challenges we face'[10] confirms just how correct Dante's prophetic writing was. The makers of this website also state:

> We know that this site shows many negative trends. This is to illustrate that something has to change. And we believe that change is possible. In fact, it's possible to change pretty much every single one of the negative trends. We already have the tools to do it. It's just a question of getting started for real – and things are already happening.[11]

So, no matter where we are and where we're heading, we could and we still *can* choose to change our direction and head for different, more creative and more pleasing vistas in healthier environments; but to accomplish such a change we need to keep the 'big picture' in our sights. Interestingly, those who populate Dante's Hell 'are people who have focused their attention on some fragment of the world ... [and therefore] have lost the capacity for seeing themselves in the context of a larger perspective.'[12] This mirrors the overwhelming preferred (or often imposed) trend of our hierarchical society to focus on the details of fragments, while disregarding holistic perspectives.

Perhaps this sort of perception was useful for a while, in order for us to see the whole bit by bit, because of course the whole is *immense*; but we're now way beyond the point where this has persisted for too long. What particularly astonishes me is how this almost random focusing on certain 'bits' is constantly ongoing, side by side with what appears to be a deliberate avoidance of looking at the 'big picture' – as if not wanting to even accidentally catch sight of it. It reminds me of the way people can be masterful at ignoring and quickly walking past people asking for alms on the street, or others who would approach them. It is this sort of attitude that allows fragments (even tiny ones) to be perpetrated for the whole, while the whole is instead mostly ignored.

The predisposition we have (for which we've been trained a long time) of accepting this perspective is why appearances are taken to be immensely important, like for example an energy company widely publicising that it had 'saved 7.9 million tonnes of CO_2 in total since 2002 ... [without however specifying that it] ... adds about 1.7 million tonnes of CO_2 to the atmosphere daily.'[13] Or in other words, that '[e]very 30 hours ... [it] wipes out the emissions savings that thousands of its customers voluntarily made via the company's offset programs over the past decade.'[14] By looking at the bigger picture connected to examples similar to this, William McDonough and Michael Braungart (respectively an architect and a chemist) point out that the 'eco-efficiency' that's widely pushed in slogans like 'reduce, reuse, recycle' actually serves to retain the same sort of outlook that was the initial cause of what it is now presumably trying to change.[15] They argue that eco-efficiency is not ultimately likely to arrive at any kind of resolution that is liveable, but can only succeed in preserving our mindset of consumption:

... merely slowing it down with moral proscriptions and punitive measures.

It presents little more than an illusion of change. Relying on eco-efficiency to save the environment will in fact achieve the opposite; it will let industry finish off everything, quietly, persistently, and completely.[16]

Rather than upholding the idea of a 'sustainability' that measures how well we're doing by reducing activity and limiting our exploitation of the environment, while this is nonetheless still based on exploitation as designed by human beings who believe themselves unable to do any better than that, they propose a completely new approach – that of 'eco-effectiveness'.[17] The main difference between eco-effectiveness and eco-efficiency is the creativity that comes into its conceptualising; in other words, eco-effectiveness is a creative approach.

By creatively re-thinking our designs to everything, in their book *Cradle to Cradle: Remaking the Way We Make Things*, McDonough and Braungart indicate that the structures we live and work in could actually be designed to produce energy instead of just using less energy. What's more, the products we make could, at the end of their 'life', become food for animals or plants, or raw materials for new products rather than waste, with this approach allowing us to live in harmony with nature so that we could experience an abundant life of contentment and innovation.[18] A practical example of this kind of thinking that I've experienced is placing food scraps into a compost bin and a worm farm. This removes the need to throw spoilt food and scraps away (with all the associated guilt), and instead very easily turns it into compost and worm castings, both valuable ingredients for improving the soil in our gardens, which thereby also aid the growth of trees, plants and vegetables. *With creativity you're expanding your imagination and you make up whatever* [you need] *according to your imagination* (student).

By leading us to make connections between things that might seem disconnected, connections that were always there anyway but just needed to be seen, creativity can help us to develop new ways of thinking, living and being in the full context of the bigger picture. To be able to do this it is essential that we step away from our intrinsic habit of focusing exclusively on 'fragments'. With many of these fragments being taken out of context, with sections of them expanded or shrunk out of proportion, and 'protective' borders or boundaries placed around them, this all blocks a holistic perspective too efficiently. As Bohm indicates, a reductionist perspective endorses a way of thinking which breaks 'things up into bits, as if they were independent. It's not merely making divisions, but it is breaking things up which are not really separate'[19].

Even though we might not be aware of it, this way of perceiving and living causes stress (often also associated with anxiety and/or depression), for we need meaning in our lives. To make sense of fragments, we need to look at them in context. It is quite a different matter to see and explore fragments in the context of a big picture perspective; in this way, it can be seen quite clearly that they're interconnected, and the detailed information we learn about them can then also add meaning to the whole. As most of us care about our wellbeing, as well as that of our fellow humans and our world as a whole, if we saw and understood things holistically we would probably make rather different choices when hearing and seeing advertisements, or come to different conclusions when watching the news or other stories presented by the media, as most of these are all delivered as fragments.

In *A Whole New Mind,* Daniel Pink quotes Martin Seligman who says that meaning is a 'form of happiness that is ineluctably pursued by humans ... knowing what your highest strengths are and deploying them in the service of something larger than you are.'[20] This has Pink anticipating that '[m]eaning will move to the center of our lives and our consciousness'[21], and that this is set to become a widespread phenomena before we know it. Having experienced what he describes in my own life, I can relate to his expectation. By nurturing my creativity I have become aware of much more than I ever thought possible, and this has led me to recognise a deeper meaning in my life that has also been instrumental in my choosing to be an advocate for the nurturing of creativity.

I believe that Pink has picked up on a strong underlying societal consciousness shift that we're ripe for and is currently beginning to occur – that of realising the importance of the big picture, which he says is becoming more and more obvious, from business to health, from work to caring for the environment.[22] Yet despite this, holistic perspectives are still being resisted, and the reductive approach is still being pushed, as Pink writes 'we've been in the thrall of reductionist, binary thinking ... [and] there remains a strong tilt toward[s it] ...'[23] Tellingly, this is mostly the case where the hierarchical value system has greatest control; namely in formal structures and institutions, like for example in the education system and in government offices. It is in institutions, in these 'corridors of power', that governs a staid climate of standard methodologies and conformity, and it is this systemic attitude that is the biggest hurdle to a holistic perspective being widely accepted and implemented. *Creativity is a case of vision, having wide vision, as well as be enabled to examine the full possibilities* (educator).

Writing in 1992, Saul stated that:

> This is an age of conformity. It is difficult to find another period of such absolute conformism in the history of Western civilization. The citizens are so completely locked inside their boxes of expertise that they are effectively excluded from open public debate.[24]

Since he wrote this, if anything, we have gone further into conformity: *We have expectations of what we should be able to do ... that's prescribed to us by society ... that's why we look at people who are a little bit different, people who dress a bit differently ... and think 'Oh they're a bit weird', but they're not really they're just showing their creative sides, they're just daring to show how true they are to themselves* (parent and teacher). This level of conformity has both ensued from, and reinforced, the reductive thinking resulting from an *institutionalised perception* that has also given rise to standardisation and specialisation, both of which are symptoms of conformity.

Pink tells us that it is the left hemisphere of our brain that is known to handle analysis, the content of language and sequential reasoning, while the right hemisphere's main tasks include interpreting emotions and nonverbal facial expressions, pattern recognition and holistic reasoning.[25] I would add that these are only 'probably' the tasks of each hemisphere rather than 'definitely' so. I say this because brain function is very complex, and we are constantly making new discoveries of just how intricately the two hemispheres can work together, or even take over each other's 'tasks' through neuroplasticity.

In *The Brain that Changes Itself,* Doidge recounts how a woman with only half a brain – the right side, as the left hemisphere had failed to develop before she was born – was able to lead quite a normal life 'because her right hemisphere took over for her left, and such essential mental functions as speech and language moved to her right.'[26] This ability of the human brain to adapt and change and make the best possible use of whatever is available is a perfect example of creativity, which again demonstrates that creativity is a process, as well as an attitude, that leads to certain ways of being and doing that are holistic and so also affect us physically (as discussed in Chapter 1).

In typical dichotomous thinking, Western society has placed greater value on what Pink calls 'L-Directed thinking' (thinking stemming from the left hemisphere) than on 'R-Directed thinking' (thinking stemming from the right hemisphere), which tends to be regarded as somehow less important.[27] Furthermore, the supremacy of 'left-brain thinking' spread right across the world as a consequence of Western society self-appointing to be at the helm of the globe – directing the course of life via its aggressive attitudes of dominion in its conquest of nation-states through war and colonisation, as well as in its competitive economic dealings, as historian Thomas Berry tells us:

> After the fifteenth century ... European nations, especially England, saw themselves as saviors of the peoples of the earth in terms of their civilizing mission. This led to the colonial enterprise, the control of the peoples and lands and resources of the entire planet by the nation-states of the European world.[28]

In the same way that 'history is written by the victors', so too do the victors get to impose their perspective on those they have conquered. Hence analytical, sequential, reductive thinking has since then been the dominant and rising type of thinking; this is the thinking embodied by computer programmers, focused on in schools, and valued by the toughest of organisations.[29] On the other hand, the 'right-brain' holistic, contextual, innovative thinking that is demonstrated by artists and carers is given short shrift by all but those already accepting of holistic thinking.[30] This categorising completely lacks the understanding that in fact creativity utilises both hemispheres of the brain, including both holistic and analytical ways of reasoning – seeing the big picture as well as the details, while enabling us to switch between them at will.

Interestingly, according to psychologist Simon Baron-Cohen, men are generally more in tune with the left side of the brain and better at analysing systems; women instead have a greater tendency to be better at empathising and have greater connection between the hemispheres, with this also being the case with language, which for men is mostly left-brain directed.[31] Importantly though, Baron-Cohen emphasises that this is only a generalisation, and that in most cases men and women are equally capable of both systematising and empathising.[32] Still, this generalised difference in men's and women's way of thinking might assist in further explaining the dominance of left-brain directed thinking in society, especially given that patriarchy's rule has mostly placed men in positions of power. Although this dominance occurred before we knew much about the brain, it is now actually quite irrational that it should continue. As Chris McManus' quote from *Right Hand Left Hand* (repeated in *A Whole New Mind*) reiterates (below), having discovered that we have the ability to both systematise and empathise it is obvious that we need to use both of them equally:

> However tempting it is to talk of right and left hemispheres in isolation, they are actually two half-brains, designed to work together as a smooth, single, integrated whole in one entire, complete brain. The left hemisphere knows how to handle logic and the right hemisphere knows about the world. Put the two together and one gets a powerful thinking machine. Use either on its own and the result can be bizarre or absurd.[33]

This absurdity is indeed apparent when one looks at the direction that we (as a society) are heading in, where a dichotomous judgmental point of view that chooses particular fragments to the exclusion of the whole is still being championed, or at least is allowed to be the most vocal and 'mainstream' perspective. As Meeker tells us, Dante indicates that 'misery' comes from 'mistaking or distorting one's vision so that only a fragment of reality can be seen, and then taking that fragment for the whole.'[34] This mistaking of a fragment for the whole stems from an *institutionalised perception*.

First explained in Chapter One and referred to throughout this book, '*institutionalised perception*' is the phrase I use to mean a way of perceiving that accepts, and by extension internalises, the hierarchical viewpoint of our patriarchal society. The parameters of this way of seeing, together with the fragmentation needed to perpetuate them, are so endemic in society that they lead many to automatically operate from them regardless of whether they agree with the value system that endorses them. This is the value system that champions binary reductive thinking and that would keep masculine attributes from feminine ones, and left-brain from right-brain, by setting false 'opposites' against each other. Given that the language we use has developed in accordance to these parameters, this renders any attempt to expose fallacies by using the same language that perpetrates them both difficult and frustrating. As Bohm points out: 'The subject-verb-object structure of [most] modern languages implies that all action arises in a separate subject, and acts either on a separate object, or else reflexively on itself.' [35]

As has been pointed out throughout this book (and particularly in Chapters Two and Three), patriarchy has built our society on the 'values of conquest and dominion'.[36] These values make use of the fighting paradigm/metaphor (examined in Chapters Two, Four, Five, Six and Seven) based on the promotion of a competitive mindset that backs 'winners' and marginalises 'losers', and this is supported by the fragmenting structure of language. In other words, language perpetuates the value system of that which has structured it, and this is understandable.

As Koestler specifies, 'prejudices and impurities which have become incorporated into the verbal concepts of a given 'universe of discourse' cannot be undone by any amount of discourse within the frame of reference of that universe.'[37] Hence adhering to set methodologies and argument within a limited perspective is unlikely to enable any change from the status quo. This is usually the type of arguing that mostly occurs in public debate, but in order to usher in change, a much wider perspective needs to be considered, one that is dialogic rather than argumentative, especially since:

> ... verbal thinking is the most articulate, the most complex, and the most vulnerable to infectious diseases. It is liable to absorb whispered suggestions, and to incorporate them as hidden persuaders into the code. Language can become a screen which stands between the thinker and reality. This is the reason why true creativity often starts where language ends.[38]

In being open to creativity we connect to a way of being that transcends language because it doesn't rely on language to impart meaning; in utilising a holistic way of reasoning which includes analysis (when this is required) we are enabled to see both the big picture and the details. One of the parents I interviewed provided me with a perfect example of what it means to be open to creativity and nurture it. Being also an educator, this person related to me the experience of being part of a group of people who put together a drama production in a secondary school. Many schools put on drama productions, but this particular project stood out as being quite unique. It ran over two years and involved 50 to 60 students from diverse backgrounds, two drama teachers, an art teacher, a music teacher and a number of teachers from other departments in the school; it was moreover community oriented.

In the first year, a professional writer and director were hired to work with the community and the students to create the script and direct the performance; a choreographer and a musical director were also brought in. Then in the second year it was redeveloped, and the production toured Perth, performing at a festival and other various public venues. It also toured in the bush (the less populated Australian countryside), and ran workshops as an adjunct to the performance. The production ended up being '*absolutely brilliant*' and sparked some extraordinary learning experiences, as a considerable number of cultural exchanges took place. From how it was explained to me by this parent and educator, it was the extra dimension of really nurturing creativity as a community group that made it exceptional:

... there were kids among that group for whom it is no exaggeration to say that it changed their lives, it was a transformational experience. It actually put them on a different path, quite dramatically because of the opportunities it provided - the change in their self-belief, the change in their world view, even the change in their confidence in the people around them, [like] the teachers that they dealt with and the change in their relationship; actually relationships are probably the most important thing of all. It also set those kids onto pathways for further education. ... It was quite extraordinary ... If you try to share that with people who haven't experienced that ... it can be very difficult to try and get those ideas to grow. If you try and talk to people about that sort of approach to doing things they find it bewildering, they can't get their heads around the possibilities, all they can think of is all the problems of how are you going to find the time, how are you going to get the money ... and out of fear or doubt ... people often won't go for it ... and you do have to take some risks and you do have to be in an environment where you are allowed to do that ... Experience also tells me that in many schools that would be very hard to do, you would not be given permission to do this sort of thing.

The above quote sums up, within a specific experience, much of what this book promotes – the need for trust, time, risk-taking, having a holistic perspective, and above all, the desperate need we have to be open to our own creativity and to nurturing it. The alternative to this is to remain confined within an *institutionalised perception*, which is restrictive even for those at the top of the hierarchy – those who are seen as the elites and winners that a system like patriarchy is meant to favour. With the ideal of 'winning' (which requires conformity) being valued above all else, even the elites are prevented from the fulfilment of nurturing their creativity and of getting to know themselves. Instead, they receive the winner's spoils – all the 'luxury' and 'toys' that money can buy, but as the saying goes that is 'cold comfort' if the payoff is that their creativity is to remain bereft of its true expression. By colouring in within the lines and conforming to the role of 'winner' they continue to be reductive and predictable, and may never get to experience the flavour of their uniqueness or the reality of a life fully lived.

The experience related above, of the school performance, makes it clearly evident that although we can do much of our own nurturing, being interdependent we also need to nurture each other's creativity. As mentioned before, it's when people are not competing for positions that they are able to see their differences as ways of complementing each other, and this lets their creativity bloom. Conversely, competition can cause us to feel stressed and anxious; Julia Cameron, author of *The Artist's Way*, describes the following scenario:

> You pick up a magazine – or even your alumni news – and somebody, *somebody you know*, has gone further, faster, toward your dream. Instead of saying, "That proves it can be done," your fear will say, "He or she will succeed *instead* of me."... Competition lies at the root of much creative blockage...The desire to *be better than* can choke off the simple desire to *be*... It leads us away from our own voices and choices and into a defensive game that centers outside of ourselves... It asks us to define our own creativity in terms of someone else's.[39]

As I pointed out in Chapter One, young children have to be taught to be competitive because it is not natural to them; as they are socialised they are removed from their own games, those they invent as endless meanderings in creativity, and are instead introduced to games with rigid rules that end when just one team or person wins. From then on a competitive way of life is presented to them at every opportunity, especially at school where almost everything they do results in them being assigned a 'grade' or a 'rank'. *I think that a pressured environment doesn't let you be as creative as you otherwise would* (student). Though competition is touted by our patriarchal society as being a healthy way to bring out the best we can offer to both others, and ourselves, Saul reveals that, in fact, competition usually has quite the opposite effect:

> In a world devoted to measuring the best, most of us aren't even in the competition ... we eliminate ourselves from the competition in order to avoid giving other people the power to eliminate us. Not only does a society obsessed by competition not draw people out, it actually encourages them to hide what talents they have, by convincing them that they are insufficient.[40]

Convinced that we are not good enough to be one of the best, since being 'one of the best' is all that we are allowed to be in this age of conformism, many of us choose to keep our unique creativity under wraps instead of exploring it, and this can also be because most of us have no desire to be subjected to the pressures of 'stardom' that winning can bring (regardless of what field this is in). Nonetheless, there are those who seem to thrive on competition and highly pressured jobs, but it's been shown that many of these people often have narcissistic tendencies.

In *Why Is It Always About You?* Sandy Hotchkiss tells us that narcissistic disorders are everywhere. Children who have been deeply hurt through shame can grow up into adults who are terrified of being shown up as not being good enough, and/ or having their carefully hidden feelings of worthlessness unmasked.[41] Envious of anyone who appears to have more than they have, they are insatiable and always want more. Hotchkiss points out that '[n]arcissism is not just tolerated in our day and age, it is glorified. Many of our leaders and the public figures we admire flaunt their narcissistic proclivities ...'[42] This is hardly surprising given the competitive climate we live in.

Juxtaposing some of the typical behaviour traits of the narcissistic personality disorder – lack of empathy, egocentricity, obsessive focus, need for obvious adulation – to the behaviour implicitly encouraged by the values of patriarchy – an aggressive competitive approach in business, an authoritative controlling approach in governance and public institutions, together with militaristic references that reinforce a 'fighting' mentality – it is clear to see that there is a close match. It then becomes easily understandable why this sort of backdrop and influence to our daily life would give rise to individuals behaving in such ways. One could go as far as stating: 'Here are those who have learnt their lessons exceptionally well!' As in learnt all that they were taught by the internalised *institutionalised perception*. After all, as the saying goes, 'we reap what we sow'. This also connects back to those characters populating Dante's Hell, those who are unable to see themselves within the larger context.

From the 'state of play' in our society it can look as if the only 'acceptable' choices we have are those of conforming to predictable, almost mechanical behaviour, or indulging in developing a personality disorder so as to have an edge to 'winning'. Yet even 'winners' can be readily discarded; what is valued is the *role* of winner rather than the unique individual who is in that position – in a society that upholds conformity and competition above all else, the flesh and blood real person is merely a placeholder of no intrinsic value. The hubris lent by narcissism only serves to make the winner more disposable. We do, however, have at least another choice, and that is the choice of nurturing our creativity, which can then help us to develop a holistic perspective that enables the 'individuation of the self', as advocated by Jung – that deep growth and blossoming into our unique 'Selves'.

Since beginning to research creativity in 2006, I have found that an *institutionalised perception* that sees the world as being mechanistic and fragmented, where each fragment has been given a specific hierarchical 'value' with a judgement attached to it, is finally being called into question more widely. As I've discussed, particularly in Chapters Two and Three, people from a myriad of backgrounds are making interdisciplinary connections and recognising the central importance of relationships and lived experience. This includes most of the authors I've quoted and many of the people I interviewed, as well as many more whose work I've read or whom I've spoken with (including so-called 'ordinary' people).

This to me indicates our readiness and, in many cases, even our passionate need to embrace a more holistic perspective. By allowing and nurturing the expression of creativity, a more holistic perception starts to become apparent and this enables us to more clearly see our place within the whole – the place where we belong. This contextualising of ourselves can provide us with the meaning that we need and desire, which can help us to see a way through to fulfilment. In saying this, I share Marshall's belief:

> I believe we are in the midst of a silent yet discernable transformation of consciousness. Our cultural mind is slowly shifting from fragmentation and reductionism, expressed in excessive competition, unbridled acquisition, winning, short-term thinking, and isolated self-interest to integration and interdependence – collaboration, shared purpose, and global sustainability.[43]

In our search for meaning we are finally beginning to become more aware, on a wider scale, that we need a more holistic type of perception to gain the meaning we crave. Consequently this is starting to look more appealing. It is perhaps not surprising, with all the changes and challenges we're facing, that some of us are finally choosing to unshackle ourselves from the chains of conformism: *Creativity is their ability to do their own thing* (educator).

This book tells the story of my journey of transformation; it's a representation in words of a personal change in attitude – a conscious opening to looking from an attitude of creativity, through to the nurturing of creativity. This process of transformation that has begun within me, and will continue to unfold as I grow and change, not only enables me to perceive things more openly, but it also makes me conscious of having a wider perspective, a clearer vision. At the same time I am aware that I'm only able to clearly perceive *some* of the whole picture before me; there is still much of it that I cannot quite see, or totally make out, as I've not experienced it before – there is an almost hazy quality to this, similarly to as if I were viewing something under water. What I can perceive is metaphorically the tip of the iceberg, so that although I can't see the submerged part, I'm nonetheless aware of it and therefore also open to it.

Among many other things, this transformation had instilled in me a deep awareness that it is only by choosing to awaken out of the hypnotic hold we've been under, and really see the direction that we're heading in, that we can actually change that direction. To do this, we need to look past the *institutionalised perception* that is keeping our perspectives confined. Furthermore, this is something that we each have to do for ourselves regardless of the many methods prescribed for us to follow in order to 'succeed' at any number of specific things, with some people wanting to control and direct others, while countless others allow (or even require) themselves to be directed and controlled. Though prescriptive ways boast 'ultimate' answers, I have found that it's not answers that are needed, since answers cannot be universal. What we need is the openness of questions asked from a holistic perception.

As Saul says, '[in] a civilization which seeks automatically to divide through answers ... our desperate need is to unify the individual through questions.'[44] 'Ready-made' answers are divisive because they limit what can be accepted and looked at; by being *definite* they set up boundaries and are exclusive. Questions, on the other hand, have us staying within the process of dialoguing, as we discover our own and each other's creativity and keep pace with the transformations of our perspectives. When we are open to our creativity our perspectives are necessarily dynamic, given that we move through life and each of us has a unique perspective, since nobody can ever 'be' in exactly the same place as anybody else. The need for meaning that Pink and Seligman speak of is something that each of us needs, and what's more, each of us needs an individual unique meaning that is true for the unique reality we each inhabit. In other words, the meaning we long for has to be a 'perfect fit in motion' and, for all the reasons I've given so far, I believe that nurturing our creativity is as sure a way of achieving this as possible.

In this book I have looked at several issues that concern our current society – education, mental illness, rate of suicide, pollution, and so on – I have included these because they are issues that one way or another affect us all, and also because they are all issues that have stemmed from an internalised *institutionalised perception*. This way of perceiving the world and everything in it that we come into contact with, including ourselves, has had most of us living a reductive life of conformity – of 'colouring in within the lines' – that can only lead us to an ominous and catastrophic future if we continue with it. As I am a representative of my time and environment, it's reasonable to take my transformation as a sign of what other individuals, who likewise are also representative of this time, might be experiencing. As previously mentioned, I've come across many who believe that we are finally starting to realise that we can indeed move towards a more holistic direction, and their belief is probably (at least in part) due to their own transformations and growth.

Among those enticing us to open our perspectives, are previously mentioned architect William McDonough and chemist Michael Braungart, who question the reductive approach of a mentality of scarcity in which humans have to be 'punished' by some awful future catastrophe because of all the mistakes they've made. To counter this outlook they have chosen to focus on creative alternatives that reflect the realities they can imagine, as they write in their book:

> How can we support and perpetuate the rights of all living things to share in a world of abundance? How can we love the children of all species – not just our own – for all time? Imagine what a world of prosperity and health in the future will look like, and begin designing for it right now. What would it mean to become, once again native to this place, the Earth – the home of *all* our relations? This is going to take us all, and it is going to take forever. But then, that's the point.[45]

What McDonough and Braungart suggest is also a perfect example of appreciative inquiry (explored in Chapter Three), where instead of looking at things from a problem-based perspective we can choose to look at them in a more positive, holistic, and creative way. Another who values and promotes such a holistic approach is the Dalai Lama, who says, 'look at humanity as a whole. Today's reality: whole world almost like one body. One thing happens some distant place, the repercussions reach your own place. Destruction of your neighbour as enemy is essentially destruction of yourself. Our future depends on global well-being.'[46]

In *Harmony: A New Way of Looking at Our World*, the Prince of Wales with Tony Juniper and Ian Skelly also promote a holistic perspective:

> ... the closer we dance to the rhythms and patterns that lie within us, the closer we get to acting in what is the right way; closer to the good in life, to what is true and what is beautiful – rather than swirling around without an anchor, lost 'out there' in the wilderness of a view shaped solely by four hundred years of emphasis on mechanistic thinking and the output of our industrialized processes. ... this will mean somehow replacing our obsession with pursuing unlimited growth and competition with a quest for well-being and cooperation.[47]

If we take the time to really look around us, we will see that we are surrounded by a whole reality, both in the world that we inhabit and in each other, that is richer and more rewarding than anything we could imagine. Understanding this deeply and embracing a holistic perspective so that we can see it more clearly would enable us to live more fully in a participative way; it would help us to nurture creativity and celebrate it. What this means in practical terms is being able to utilise our creativity to navigate the challenging changes that seem to be occurring so fast all around us. It also means being able to recognise our deep connection to nature, to each other, to the world and all its creatures, and it means making use of that understanding to establish sustainable environments that honour and celebrate the connections we can envision, which are also the ones that can best take us into the future. This would be a future where we have consciously changed the current direction we've been heading in, a future that is holistic and creative, where we can all thrive.

If we are open and trusting enough to allow the transformation that can inevitably be generated from the nurturing of creativity (the creativity available to each of us), and if we are open and trusting enough to let it envelop us and support us, so it can truly transform every particle and every space within us, then we would have no cause to ever feel alienated again, for we would be conscious participants in a universal awakening to creativity. This awakening is already underway, and even though patriarchy and the *institutionalised perception* are still at large, this doesn't need to concern us; we only need to be aware of them and how they have affected us, so that we may more readily forgive ourselves for not having been true to ourselves. Apart from that, we'll not even see them as obstacles when we side-step them by focusing on the beauty within us that calls to us, and by allowing our perspective to continue to widen so it can support us in nurturing our creativity. An event in a fairy tale by Hans Christian Andersen works well as a metaphor to explain this:

Once upon a time, ... there was a truly beautiful girl who had elicited the jealousy of a wicked queen, her stepmother. The queen had sent her away when she was a child, and now she was fifteen her father the king had wished for her to return to the palace. The girl had returned and was preparing herself to meet her father the king. With the pretext of getting a bath ready for her, the queen (who was also a witch) brought in three toads to put a spell on her. Kissing the first toad she told it to get on the girl's head so that she might become stupid, then kissing the second toad she told it to get on the girl's forehead so that she might become ugly, finally she kissed the third toad telling it to go on the girl's heart so that she might become evil. Quickly she put them all into the clear bath water, which turned green, and then she called to the girl to come in and get into the bath. The toads did as they had been told and went on the girl's head, forehead and heart, but she hardly noticed them as she was too kind, innocent and trusting for the spell to have any effect on her, in fact it worked in reverse. When she got out of the bath, the toads had become three poppies, if the witch had not kissed them they would have become fragrant roses.[48]

By trusting in her own self and not 'buying into' or 'fighting' the evil plans of her stepmother, the girl had become impervious to her powers. In this case, the power of the girl's kindness and innocence corresponds to the power of the creativity that's innate in us all. Creativity is much more than a purely intellectual ability, and in order to be able to connect to it fully our intellect needs to take a step back, as it were. This mostly involves a 'toning down' of left-brain directed thinking, which (as explained earlier) is the sort of thinking that's been leading the way for quite some time now. This doesn't mean dumbing ourselves down, but merely turning down the volume a little of this super-focused left-brain directed thinking that's not been allowing us to perceive anything else. As Aronie suggests, we need to 'get out of our own way', and restore a more balanced way of being, where our multifaceted selves – our emotional, physical and spiritual sides – are no longer ignored, or at best seen as the poor relations to the intellect, but are allowed to take their rightful place of equal importance through a more holistic way of being.

I was overjoyed when I came across *The Open-Focus Brain*, as what Les Fehmi and Jim Robbin reveal in their book very much supports what I've been advocating. From their research findings, they tell us that most of us ordinarily pay attention to everything in our lives and our environment in a narrow and rigid way, where we focus on chosen things to the exclusion of everything else.[49] After discovering (almost by chance) a simple way to counter narrow focus, Les Fehmi spent over thirty years verifying its incredible usefulness by holding workshops to help people to train their attention in order to transform it from a narrow focus to an open focus attention. By being more open and gaining the ability to release the narrow focus we have been taught by the *institutionalised perception*, which we've internalised, we can reach the understanding we need to fully live our human legacy, which indeed as Fehmi and Robbin suggest is 'to live creatively, spontaneously, and flexibly.'[50]

Creativity is also best nurtured within a connected community (as discussed in chapters One, Five and Six). Richard Florida reminds us of this in *The Rise of the Creative Class*: '[W]e must harness all of our intelligence, our energy and most importantly our awareness. The task of building a truly creative society is not a game of solitaire. This game, we play as a team.'[51] Yet rather than a 'team', which in our society would inevitably be expected to play against other teams, I envision this more as a return to the endless creative games we played as young children, where all of us can be fulfilled and, as Bohm indicates (already quoted in Chapter One), our 'interest in what is being done is wholehearted and total.'[52] With this sort of holistic state of mind, creativity could be applied to any of the individual issues we face in our lives, as well as to those that we are faced with in the world.

An example of one of our many modern societal concerns is that of healthy ageing; I became aware of this when I undertook some research work with older people and social isolation. Healthy ageing is particularly relevant to Western societies given that developed countries are primarily becoming ageing societies. From educators and psychologists to aged care providers, from neuroscientists and geriatricians to community workers, all have noted the increased health and wellbeing, including mental health and agility, of those who partake in creative activities. Additionally, social inclusion is another of the benefits resulting from the nurturing of creativity. Indeed, as Fontana and Slack indicate, creative pursuits of all types are ideal conduits for bringing people together, and they can successfully bridge the gap between generations by restoring meaningful communication: 'Creativity, in a real sense, serves as the voice of the community, articulating harmonies and tensions, and helping to make us comprehensible to each other.'[53]

When people mix for the purpose of creative endeavours (such as in the high school drama production described earlier) they experience an atmosphere that is both enjoyable and safe, which invariably helps them relax their mental boundaries. This allows them to consider the diverse perspectives that are brought to the group through the participation of people of different ages, various backgrounds, diverse cultures, and so on, and can then further lead them to open up to a spirit of playful curiosity about each other. As participants explore the possibilities of integrating various aspects of differing points of view that they may never have previously considered but which nonetheless they find themselves drawn to, this can result in many of them attaining more open and fuller perspectives. Lucas confirms that people in touch with their creativity 'question the assumptions they are given ... see the world differently, are happy to experiment, to take risks and to make mistakes. They make unique connections often unseen by others.'[54] Just being willing to be open enables the nurturing of creativity to have a more lasting transformative impact on them, which in turn makes them ideal facilitators and catalysts for the nurturing of creativity in others.

In telling the story that began during my PhD journey, this book is about the nurturing of creativity in a unique 'self' – myself; it relates the experience of my journey of transformation through a holistic perspective. As Bohm states, experience is also knowledge, since the two are intrinsically linked:

> ... it is useful to emphasize that experience and knowledge are one process, rather than to think that our knowledge is *about* some sort of separate experience. We can refer to this one process as experience-knowledge (the hyphen indicating that these are two inseparable aspects of one whole movement).[55]

As quoted in the Introduction, Atkinson tells us that '[o]ur stories illustrate our inherent connectedness with others. ... In the life story of each person is a reflection of another's life story.'[56] Thus if we can accept and 'see' what has been said by so many for so long – that we are each of us unique – then we will realise that everybody's life, each individual life, has a unique contribution to make to the whole of life. Simply by being, by living, one flows along the movement that Bohm calls the process of 'experience-knowledge'. Even if one never has a chance to *formally* share this knowledge and experience, as in by writing it or somehow relating it, because we are 'living it' our inherent interconnectedness will ensure it has an effect on others, and so it will nonetheless make a contribution to the whole.

The effect that our experience-knowledge can have on others is exemplified in Frank Capra's 1946 film, *It's a Wonderful Life*, which is about the uniqueness and importance of even just one life. Based on the short story *The Greatest Gift* by Philip Van Dorn Stern, the movie follows the life of a man who never seems to be able to achieve his dreams. Finally, through some unfairness and bad luck he finds himself one Christmas Eve seriously contemplating suicide; his guardian angel saves him and then asks God to grant him his wish of 'never having been born'. The man, who didn't think his life was very important, is then able to see all that has been made possible because of him, which includes: his brother's life (who would otherwise have drowned), the wellbeing of many working class people who through him were able to get fair loans to buy homes, his wife who without him would never have married, his four children, his mother and uncle, and so on. In this way he realises what a wonderful gift his life is, and not just for him but also for many others.

If one accepts that one's life is unique then it makes sense that it is important to know oneself and also be true to oneself. Being true to oneself might however be compromised if one is persuaded to strive to copy the content of someone else's life, or even to live up to an abstract ideal held up as a role model. Marie-Louise von Franz gives us a common example of this enticement to copy role models, through religious doctrine:

> Time and again in all countries people have tried to copy in "outer" or ritualistic behaviour the original religious experience of their great religious teachers – Christ or Buddha or some other master – ... [yet] To follow in the steps of a great spiritual leader does not mean that one should copy and act out the pattern of the individuation process made by his [sic] life. It means that we should try with a sincerity and devotion equal to his [sic] to live our own lives.[57]

We are constantly encouraged, both as children and adults, to copy role models and ideals, as these are 'held up' and prescribed for us in different circumstances, including at school, work, in public life, and so on, with rewards offered for meeting certain criteria in living these 'ideal' roles. Because of the predominance of the left-directed way of thinking (which *is* a literal way of thinking) we are therefore more likely to take this literally, and so we might strive to achieve a role, like for example those for careers that we are 'sold' as being ideal – doctors, lawyers, CEOs – and yet neglect to nurture our own creativity. This also encourages literal ways of prescribing, and abiding to, methodologies and policies throughout modern life, particularly in institutions. Children at school are consistently shown exactly how to do something. A multitude of books are about 'how to ...' in regard to almost every imaginable subject, and this includes spiritual matters and self-development, where even in the New Age specific ways of doing something, or achieving growth and development are 'spelt out' and valued, complete with gurus and masters to be followed exactly.

These prescriptive ways of being and doing inevitably fragment the self; by emphasising ways 'to be' they also specify ways 'not to be', and so they leave little room for the unfolding of the self's creativity. I have written this book from a holistic perspective that doesn't pretend to be objective, but recognises the self's subjectivity and speaks from it, since the only place I could ever speak from is myself. Being in this way unique, though open, this book seeks to: share experience-knowledge from as many voices as I could gather, advocate for a holistic perspective and the nurturing of creativity, and inspire to live as fully as possible one's own life, through the fulfilment that the nurturing of creativity can bring.

Afterword:

BEING AND BECOMING ... REVISITED

To see a world in a grain of sand,

And a heaven in a wild flower.

Hold infinity in the palm of your hand,

And eternity in an hour.[1]

– William Blake

The above quote sums up the whole essence of this book by eloquently and succinctly stating the transformative outlook, or state of mind, that someone in touch with their creativity is capable of. This isn't just pretty 'poetry' – the above words barely touch the page they're written on, as in being read they expand and transmute into images, sensations and feelings. Touching and filling the deepest core of the self, they simultaneously continue to expand past the self, linking the visible with the invisible, present with past and future, and the self to all those who have, or will have, read, heard or written these words, or can understand and dwell with the sensations that the meaning of these words evoke. This experience lasts but a few seconds of 'real' time, yet is capable of staying with one forever, with just a glimpse revealing a full feeling of wholeness. To gain this however, we need a holistic perspective.

That this quality of writing is even possible makes me rejoice, as it means that language can be used to enhance our awareness of wholeness. Despite all that's been said about it reinforcing the status quo, writing can nonetheless cross boundaries and heal fragmentation. Although in writing thoughts are 'captured', so in a sense they're frozen and prevented from transforming, if they are put in a creative format (as in the example of Blake's verse) words can release a dawning of meaning for a reader. This is due to the writing being approached with an attitude of creativity, as it is this holistic perspective of creativity that liberates the meaning. Verily, any human endeavour approached in the same way will be imbued with magic and life, in the sense that it will then be an expression of the creativity of the one who created it, while at the same time it will also encapsulate a whole new world capable of engendering creativity in others; this will be easily apparent, and all the more so to those with a holistic perspective.

Presented in this book is the story of my quest for creativity through my PhD journey and beyond. This has been formed by words that have come from a combination of my thoughts on what I've discovered through research, questioning and talking with people, combined with much that I have experienced. Thoughts are only 'snapshots' of moments from the dynamic process of thinking, which is an ongoing part of being alive and therefore of any experience. Just as thoughts easily arise, so do they also readily dissolve back into that dynamic process, to then arise again as new and transformed thoughts. This is to be expected because we are constantly moving, changing, growing, and transforming, with this perhaps happening all the faster (or at least with more complexity) in a 'self' who is open to creativity. Nurturing our creativity allows us to continue on the path of self-discovery we began as young children; it teaches us about ourselves deeply, as well as about ourselves in context to the 'whole', and leads us on a journey of ongoing transformation through creativity.

Many years ago, I did some trekking in the Alps of Italy and Austria – it was exhilarating! Being on a narrow path which meanders all over the mountains is very humbling and uplifting at the same time. The view is constantly changing as the path skirts steep slopes, climbs through passes and descends into valleys. The colours, scents, and all that your senses pick up around you is constantly transforming at but a touch from the different weather conditions that succeed each other in kaleidoscopic wonder, so that at times it seems that all the seasons make their appearance within just a few hours. Yet while taking in the views, sounds, and the feel of the weather, I also had to pay attention to where I was on the path. In other words, I needed to be present in the 'here and now' of the journey. Apart from aiming to spend the night at a particular mountain hut, I couldn't really plan for the journey ahead past where I could see the path, as I didn't know what lay around the bend. At the same time I needed to be aware of how I was feeling in order to take care of myself – it made more sense to wait and rest, instead of forcing myself to climb steep slopes in inclement weather that could make the footing very treacherous and put me in danger of tripping and falling.

To do all this I had to be open to taking in whatever my senses could garner from my surroundings, while at the same time also remain connected to my inner self – my *beingness*. Time and trust were my constant companions; I trusted my senses, my abilities to make decisions and my skills, I also trusted my environment enough to be open to it and learn from it. I listened to myself and flowed with time, rather than put myself under pressure by measuring it and setting myself time limits. In a sense I forgot time: since I was always within it, there was nothing I needed to remember about it anyway.

What I learnt while trekking could be applied to almost any situation in my life. This is through the process that Bohm refers to as 'experience-knowledge' (discussed in Chapter Eight), with experience and knowledge being intrinsically connected. Above all, trekking taught me that I knew how to get to know myself better and be true to myself in whatever situation I was in, and that I knew how to make use of a holistic perspective to do this. Yet it was only while on my PhD journey, when I again experienced this process of 'experience-knowledge' – this process of transformation – that I realised I was already familiar with it; re-experiencing it was a perfect way to be reminded of it, and also enabled me to access it and further expand on it.

As explained in the Introduction, it was interacting with and nurturing my creativity that helped me to realise that as an adult I had lost touch with my inner 'knowing' and with my sense of self – my *beingness*. Thus the principal and most lasting transformation of my journey of creative nurture has been reconnecting to my *beingness*. In addition, this has allowed me to return to looking at things from an open perspective, empowering me to continue to nurture my creativity, to trust and to flow with time.

Viewing life in this way – from an open (holistic) perspective – has deepened my understanding of both my inner and outer worlds, and brought me to recognise the many links between them. It has also led me to increasingly accept my emotions, and in doing so I have developed an almost curious-like detachment from outcomes. Although I still picture and feel how I would like things to end up, in being aware that my perspective is always somewhat limited I have released the need to have them turn out in a particular way for me to be satisfied, that is I'm not confined by plans or expectations. The future I imagine for myself is becoming more and more open-ended; by trusting time and my sense of timing to be connected to the best possible outcome, I am also finally coming to more fully accept myself.

Though this has been for me an incredible journey of transformation – starting with the writing of my thesis, followed by years of walking my talk, and then continuing through the writing of this book – this transformative new way of seeing is still unfolding. What this means is that at any time, as a result of my perspective opening a little more, something I thought I knew well might look completely new and need to be rediscovered. An example of this is how I view the things we make – the books we write, the clothes we wear, the tools we use, and all the things in our homes, cities, and so on. I see that in making them we cannot help but impart on them some of what we're experiencing, so that these objects (or things) are in fact signs and expressions of how we view and live life. With this understanding, I am certain that it is essential for us to express ourselves freely in making them. Thus we need to devise them through creativity, instead of by any methodological or prescribed approach (often controlled by monetary bottom line thinking) that would sap meaning from them by fragmenting them.

The more we can allow whatever we make to be expressed creatively, rather than prescriptively, the more we will infuse our creations with meaning that can help us to see the whole (life) even more clearly. At the same time, however, regardless of how creative or superlative any of these things we make might be, they can only ever be 'snapshots' of particular moments we're in – reflections of what we were experiencing at the time we made them, which mirror our process of growth. Seeing them in this way brings the knowing that they can never be 'finished', so that they could be recurrently changed and adapted to make room for the new and help us to continue to creatively unfold. Ultimately, to allow ourselves to usher in creative growth in a timely manner, we might even need to let some of our creations go completely. Like the beautiful sand mandalas that Tibetan Buddhist monks create, which are swept up and released to the wind, or into flowing waters, soon after they're completed.

Epilogue:

THE STORY CONTINUES...

Life is everywhere!

It is manifest in thriving gardens, from the trees and bushes cascading with fragrant blossoms to the vigorous climbers twining themselves around trellises and over arches, from the lush native plants to the carpet of moss-like ground cover interspersed with tiny flowers.

It is palpable in the gentle breathing of children in their beds, now stretching and turning, eyelids fluttering in their slumber.

It is heightened in the warmth of friendship – understanding running between all kinds of people amidst the carefree, joyous laughter.

The senses glory in the richness of life when spying rainbows and beholding sunsets, when touching dewdrops and smelling damp earth in a summer shower, when hearing waves crashing on the beach on a hot day and feeling the breeze caressing the skin.

In dreams at night, life is replayed, re-lived, and breathed in trustingly while consciousness is released. Then upon waking it is felt rushing in, filling one with the bliss of being.

All this and more ... she takes in while her gaze glides over creation. In places the sparkling outline of the ancient loom of starlight can still be made out through the webs of life it supports. She smiles, the depth and delight of it spreading throughout the universe, as she moves on through and into the future...

Acknowledgements

It isn't just the raising of a child that involves a village, for I have a veritable village to thank for all the support, help and encouragement that has enabled me to send this book out into the world.

Firstly, thank you to Jennipher McDonald for telling me (back in 2005) all about Ken Robinson's keynote presentation at the National Arts and Education Symposium – Backing our Creativity, that was held in Melbourne in 2005; that was the very beginning.

I am hugely grateful to Trish Harris for the enthusiastic offer to read my editing; that was the pivotal moment where I took the definitive step to turn my thesis into a book. Many others were then part of the process of reading and discussing the gradually transforming manuscript, and I thank them all for providing valuable feedback and constant reassurance that kept me going. From among them, my mother, Marialuisa, and my neighbour Glennys were especially instrumental in making my writing more accessible to a wider readership – grazie mille!

There are a few more I want to particularly mention for their invaluable support: Peter Murnane, whose insightful comments were like the missing pieces of the puzzle in my understanding on how to make my writing clearer; Alex Main, who has been a consistent source of advice throughout my journey, from the writing of my PhD thesis to its transformation into this book; Elizabeth R. Stein (AKA Wendy Donellan) who provided inspiration for the cover with one of her original works; Marianne Quinton and Libby Baker who have been my artistic guides; Serene Maisey for her brilliant photographic flair; and finally Carol Hoggart for her calming influence and editing advice.

There's a saying that 'when the student is ready the teacher will appear', however, another one says that 'we teach what we most need to learn' as it's through the teaching and sharing with others that we can really integrate and live our insights and learning. I'm hugely thankful to all the students I've tutored and mentored (as well as to students I have yet to meet): you're the ones who continually inspire me to stay open to learning and wonder.

Ultimately, it was the love and support of my family and friends that first enabled the writing of my thesis, and then made this book possible. Spending time with someone who has a book 'under their skin' is not necessarily easy, as there is often a tendency to ignore those closest and dearest to be with the unfolding book instead, or to turn conversations to the impending writing. For this I thank my husband and daughters for their patience as well as all the other wonderful people in my life who, together with those I've already mentioned, make up my 'village' (you all know who you are).

From this 'village' I want to single out Nicole Gruel for her wise and timely suggestion to contact That Guy's House. I couldn't be happier than having you publish my book – you are truly innovators for the future of publishing – and I want to thank everyone involved in setting it up, starting with Sean Patrick, as well as the whole wonderful team who helped me get my book ready.

Another from my 'village' who deserves an enormous Thank You is my sister, Henrietta Quinlan, for all the amazing help with the proofreading of my final manuscript.

A grateful extra thank you to my father for making me witness to his endless creative endeavours, and to my mother for showing me, through her tireless example, how curiosity constantly feeds creativity by keeping the mind young and eager to continue learning and exploring right to the very end of life.

Finally, the biggest thanks goes, for the gift of Creativity, to that indelible and loving Mystery of Life that would have us all become all that we can be, that we may fulfil the awesome Wholeness we were born with.

Appendix

The full text of the Appeal by Federico Mayor:

"There is a lack of mediation and creativity everywhere, especially in schools. The arts are missing from our lives and we are giving way to violence". This is what the famous violinist and conductor Lord Yehudi Menuhin saw around him at the close of this century, after having devoted his life to music and the quest for a better world.

Today we are clearly and strongly aware of the important influence of the creative spirit in shaping the human personality, bringing out the full potential of children and adolescents and maintaining their emotional balance - all factors which foster harmonious behaviour.

At a time when family and social structures are changing, with often adverse effects on children and adolescents, the school of the twenty-first century must be able to anticipate the new needs by according a special place to the teaching of artistic values and subjects in order to encourage creativity, which is a distinctive attribute of the human species. Creativity is our hope.

A more balanced kind of education is now needed, with scientific, technical and sports disciplines, the human sciences and art education placed on an equal footing at the different stages of schooling, during which children and adolescents must be able to accede to a learning process that is beneficial, more broadly, to their intellectual and emotional balance. In that respect play activities, as a vital form of creativity, are one of the factors that deserve to be encouraged in the teaching of the arts.

Arts teaching should stimulate the body as well as the mind. By setting the senses in motion, it creates a memory which sharpens the sensitivity of the child and makes him or her more receptive to other forms of knowledge, notably scientific knowledge. Furthermore, it develops individuals' creative faculty and directs their aggressiveness towards the symbolic objects of their choice.

The time has come to give all school-going children the benefit of such teaching.

The Constitution of UNESCO provides that since "the wide diffusion of culture, and the education of humanity for justice and liberty and peace are indispensable to the dignity of man", all nations are duty-bound to ensure, in a spirit of mutual assistance, that this task is effectively fulfilled.

Accordingly, on behalf of the United Nations Educational, Scientific and Cultural Organization, I solemnly call upon the Member States of UNESCO to take appropriate administrative, financial and legal measures to ensure that the teaching of the arts - which covers disciplines such as poetry, the visual arts, music, drama, dance and film - is compulsory throughout the school cycle, i.e. from nursery school up until the last year of secondary school. To that end, encouragement must be given to the participation of artists, musicians, poets, playwrights, producers, film directors, actors and dancers in workshops held within school establishments to stimulate creativity and creative work.

I invite school arts teachers to co-operate with artists called in to work in their schools so that arts education can play its educational role - which is to stimulate children's and adolescents' creativity - to the full.

I invite teachers of all disciplines to pool their efforts and work towards breaking down the barriers between the teaching of scientific, technical, general, literary and artistic subjects. This interdisciplinary approach is fundamental to enabling young people to understand the universal nature of the world.

I invite artistic and cultural institutions such as theatres, opera houses and concert halls, cinemas, literary and poetry centres, museums, cultural centres and libraries to open their doors to pupils from the schools in their neighbourhood, district or city, running special activities for them and opening their facilities to them so that they can exhibit their own work as well.

I invite producers of artistic and musical material and equipment, and civil society, especially sponsoring firms, to take part in this effort by providing financial backing for artistic creation projects for children and adolescents.

I call upon the written press and audiovisual media to run art, music, drama and poetry programmes designed for children and young people, and to open their columns and programmes to outstanding examples of practice developed in the school environment.

I invite art, music, theatre, film and poetry festivals, and also contemporary art fairs and book fairs, to create a section for children and adolescents.

Lastly, I invite parents, members of the international community and international, regional and national non-governmental organisations specialising in the promotion of arts education to do their utmost to publicise this Appeal as widely as possible.

Notes

Introduction

1. David Abram, 1997, *The Spell of the Sensuous*, p. 49.

2. Robert Nash, 2004, *Liberating Scholarly Writing: The Power of Personal Narrative*, p. 59.

3. Ibid, p. 29.

4. Marie-Louise von Franz, 1978, 'The Process of Individuation', in *Man and his Symbols*, pp. 161-162.

5. Daniel Goleman, 2006, *Social Intelligence: The New Science of Human Relationships*, p. 151.

6. Marie–Louise von Franz, 'The Process of Individuation', in *Man and his Symbols*, 1978, p. 220.

7. Ibid, p. 221.

8. Midnight Davies, Creative Spirits Website, Aboriginal culture - Spirituality - What is the 'Dreamtime' or the 'Dreaming'? Viewed from https://www.creativespirits.info/aboriginalculture/spirituality/what-is-the-dreamtime-or-the-dreaming

9. Ken Robinson, 2005, 'Keynote presentation', in *proceedings of the Backing our creativity symposium*, viewed from http://www.australiacouncil.gov.au/research/education_and_the_arts/reports_and_publications/backing_our_creativity_symposium_final_report

10. Nancy Aronie, 1998, *Writing from the Heart: Tapping the Power of your Inner Voice*, p. 178.

11. David Abram, 1997, *The Spell of the Sensuous*, p. 46.

12. Liz Stanley, 1992, *The Auto/biographical I: The Theory and Practice of Feminist*

Auto/biography, p. 246.

13.   Robert Atkinson, 1995, *The Gift of Stories*, pp. 3-4.

Chapter One

1.   Nancy Aronie, 1998, *Writing from the Heart: Tapping the Power of your Inner Voice*, p. 151.

2.   Ken Robinson, 2001, *Out of Our Minds: Learning to Be Creative*, p. 118.

3.   Lee Nichol, 2004, in the Foreword of *On Dialogue*, p. 116.

4.   David Bohm, 2004, *On Creativity*, p. 1.

5.   Arthur J. Cropley, 2003, *Creativity in Education and Learning: A Guide for Teachers and Educators*, p. 124.

6.   These are just a few of the authors who have mentioned 'the creative age' – Seltzer & Bentley, 1999; Earls, 2002; Florida, 2004.

7.   Norman Doidge, 2008, *The Brain That Changes Itself*, p. 276.

8.   David Henry Feldman, Mihaly Csikszentmihalyi and Howard Gardner, 1994, *Changing the World: A Framework for the Study of Creativity*, p. 2.

9.   David Bohm, 1980, *Wholeness and the Implicate Order*, pp. 15-16.

10.   Ibid, p. 17.

11.   Arthur Koestler, 1975, *The Act of Creation*, p. 176.

12.   David Bohm, 2004, *On Creativity*, p. 48.

13.   Arthur J. Cropley, 2003, *Creativity in Education and Learning: A Guide for Teachers and Educators*, p.1.

14.   Norman Doidge, 2008, *The Brain That Changes Itself*, p. xv.

15.   Ibid, p. 214.

16.   Dayton, 2007, 'A Case of Mind over Matter', *The Australian (Review)*, 21 July, p. 6.

17.   Evian Gordon, 2009, Brain Revolution Project, viewed from http://brainrevolution.org/contactus.html

18.   Ken Robinson, 2001, *Out of Our Minds: Learning to Be Creative*, p. 11.

19.   Antonio Damasio, 2001, 'Some notes on brain, imagination and creativity', in *The Origins of Creativity*, pp. 59-60.

20.   Jack Cohen and Ian Steward, 2000, *The Collapse of Chaos*, p. 169.

21.   John Ralston Saul, 1993, *Voltaire's Bastards: The Dictatorship of Reason in the West*, pp. 38-76.

22. Ibid, pp. 38-39.

23. David Bohm, 2004, *On Creativity*, pp. 22-23.

24. Bill Lucas, 2001, 'Creative Teaching, Teaching Creativity and Creative Learning', in *Creativity in Education*, p. 42.

25. David Bohm, 1980, *Wholeness and the Implicate Order*, p. 6.

26. John Paul Lederach, 2005, *The Moral Imagination: The Art and Soul of Building Peace*, pp. 22-38.

27. Viewed from http://www.unesco.org/education/ecp/art_edu.htm. The full text of the appeal can be read in the appendix.

28. Mark Earls, 2002, *Welcome to the Creative Age: Bananas, Business, and the Death of Marketing*, p. 17.

29. Christine Swanton, 2003, *Virtue Ethics: A Pluralistic View*, p. 161.

30. Ibid.

31. Awakin.org - Waking up to wisdom in stillness and community, *House of 1000 Mirrors*, viewed from https://www.awakin.org/read/view.php?tid=95 (though not the original place this was first discovered).

32. John Paul Lederach, 2005, *The Moral Imagination: The Art and Soul of Building Peace*, pp. 163-173.

33. Ibid, p. 174.

34. Mark Earls, 2002, *Welcome to the Creative Age: Bananas, Business, and the Death of Marketing*, p. 23.

35. Ibid, pp. 21-23.

36. Robert Fisher, 2004, 'What is Creativity?', in *Unlocking Creativity: Teaching Across the Curriculum*, p. 13.

37. Norman Doidge, 2008, *The Brain That Changes Itself*, p. 173 (original emphasis).

38. Arthur J. Cropley, 2003, *Creativity in Education and Learning: A Guide for Teachers and Educators*, p. 67.

39. Ibid, p. 150.

40. Robert Fisher, 2004, *Unlocking Creativity: Teaching Across the Curriculum*, p. 1.

41. Karl H. Pfenninger, 2001, *The Origins of Creativity*, p. 91.

42. Mihaly Csikszentmihalyi, 1996, *Creativity: Flow and the Psychology of Discovery and Invention*.

43. David Fontana and Ingrid Slack, 2007, *Teaching Meditation to Children*, p. 81.

44. Ibid, p. 82.

45. David Bohm, 2004, *On Creativity*, p. 20.

46. Ibid.

47. Ken Robinson, 2005, 'Keynote presentation', in *proceedings of the Backing our creativity symposium*, p. 11.

48. Mark Earls, 2002, *Welcome to the Creative Age: Bananas, Business, and the Death of Marketing*, p. 257.

49. Ian Plowman, 2007, *Options*, 20, p. 18.

50. Ibid.

51. Daniel Goleman, 2006, *Social Intelligence: The New Science of Human Relationships*, p. 125.

52. Ibid, p. 124.

53. Carl Robinson, 2009, 'Narcissistic Executives – A pre-emptive approach for dealing with them', viewed from http://www.leadershipconsulting.com/narcissistic-executives.htm

54. Sohrab Vossoughi, 2012, 'Today's Best Companies are Horizontally Integrated', *Harvard Business Review*, 14 December, viewed from https://hbr.org/2012/12/todays-best-companies-are-hori

55. Ibid.

56. Ibid.

57. David Bohm, 2004, *On Creativity*, p. 21.

58. David Henry Feldman et al, 1994, *Changing the World: A Framework for the Study of Creativity*, p. 2

59. John Ralston Saul, 1993, *Voltaire's Bastards: The Dictatorship of Reason in the West*, pp. 38-76.

60. David Bohm, 2004, *On Creativity* p. 21.

Chapter Two

1. John O'Donohue, 2004, *Anam Cara: A Book of Celtic Wisdom*, p. xv.

2. Thomas Berry, 1988, 'Patriarchy: A New Interpretation of History', in *The Dream of the Earth*, p. 145.

3. Ibid, p. 159.

4. Ibid, p. 153.

5. Mary Daly, 1998, *Quintessence ... Realizing the Archaic Future: A Radical Elemental Feminist Manifesto*, p. 234.

6. Adriana Cavarero, 2000, *Relating Narratives: Storytelling and Selfhood*, p. 53.

7. Dale Spender, 1980, *Man Made Language*, p. 4.

8. Chris Hayes, 2010, 'The Twilight of the Elites', *Time*, vol. 175, no. 11, p. 38.

9. Sara Anderson and Sam Pizzigati, 2018, *How Taxpayers Subsidize Giant Corporate Pay Gaps*, p. 3.

10. Marie-Louise von Franz, 1978, 'The Process of Individuation', in *Man and His Symbols*, pp. 162-163.

11. David Abram, 1997, *The Spell of the Sensuous*, p. 45.

12. Helene Cixous, 1981, 'Sorties', trans. A. Liddle, in *New French Feminisms*, p. 91.

13. David Bohm, D. 1980, *Wholeness and the Implicate Order*, p. 1.

14. Lisa Schlein, 2017, February 23, 'WHO: Depression Largest Cause of Disability', VOA (Voice of America) News Website.

15. Albert-László Barabási, 2003, *Linked: How Everything is Connected to Everything Else and What it Means for Business, Science, and Everyday Life*, p. 6.

16. Alan Watts, 1989, *The Book On the Taboo Against Knowing Who You Are*, pp. 10-11.

17. David Bohm, 2004, *On Creativity*, p. 76.

18. Daniel Pink, 2005, *A Whole New Mind*, p. 106.

19. Mads Soegaard, 2010, *Gestalt principles of form perception*, viewed from http://www.interaction-design.org/encyclopedia/gestalt_principles_of_form_perception.html

20. Ludwig Wittgenstein, 1968, *Philosophical Investigations*, 32ᶜ

21. Stephanie Pace Marshall, 2006, *The Power to Transform: Leadership That Brings Learning and Schooling to Life*, p. 38.

22. David Abram, 1997, *The Spell of the Sensuous*, p. 56.

23. Ajahn Brahm, 2008, *Opening the Door of Your Heart*, p. 156.

24. Ibid.

25. David Abram, 1997, *The Spell of the Sensuous*, p. 46.

26. Jack Cohen and Ian Stewart, 2000, *The Collapse of Chaos*, p. 169.

27. M. Mitchell Waldrop, 1992, *Complexity: The Emerging Science at the Edge of Order and Chaos*, p. 293.

28. Nicolis and Prigogine, 1989, *Exploring Complexity: An Introduction*, p. 218.

29. John Ralston Saul, 1993, *Voltaire's Bastards: The Dictatorship of Reason in the West*, p. 35.

30. Adriana Cavarero, 2000, *Relating Narratives: Storytelling and Selfhood*, pp. 57-58.

31. Australian War memorial website, 2016, 'The Anzac Day Tradition'.

32. Rachel B. Vogelstein and Alexandra Bro, May 22, 2020, 'Women's Power Index', on Council on Foreign Relations website, viewed from https://www.cfr.

org/article/womens-power-index

33. YouTube, December 2016, *Ex-Soldier Speaks Truth: "The Real Enemy is here at Home the Rich"*, viewed from https://www.youtube.com/watch?v=b1eQPhqm93k

34. Veterans for Peace website, 2020, Who we are, viewed from https://www.veteransforpeace.org/who-we-are

35. Thomas Berry, 1988, 'Patriarchy: A New Interpretation of History', in *The Dream of the Earth*, p. 153.

36. Adriana Cavarero, 2000, *Relating Narratives: Storytelling and Selfhood*, p. 8.

37. Carl Jung, 1977, *Memories, Dreams, Reflections*, p. 417.

38. Harville Hendrix, 1988, *Getting the Love You Want*, p. 50.

39. Ibid.

40. Kenway & Willis, 1996, 'The post-school options of post-modern girls' in *Schools in Context: Unit Guide and Reader 2003*, p. 62.

Chapter Three

1. Barbara Sher & Annie Gottlieb 1979, *Wishcraft: How to Get What You Really Want*, p.145.

2. Adriana Cavarero, 2000, *Relating Narratives: Storytelling and Selfhood*, p. 33.

3. James Philip Zappen, 2000, 'Mikhail Bakhtin (1895-1975)', in *Twentieth-Century Rhetorics and Rhetoricians: Critical Studies and Sources*, pp. 7-20.

4. Robert Nash, 2004, *Liberating Scholarly Writing: The Power of Personal Narrative*, pp. 24-26.

5. Roland Barthes, 1977, 'The Death of the Author', in *Image Music Text*, pp. 142-148.

6. Ken Robinson, 2001, *Out of Our Minds: Learning to Be Creative*, p. 117.

7. Robert Nash, 2004, *Liberating Scholarly Writing: The Power of Personal Narrative*, p. 69.

8. Nancy Aronie, 1998, *Writing from the Heart: Tapping the Power of Your Inner Voice*, p. 179.

9. Jane Tompkins, 1996, *A Life in School: What the Teacher Learned*, p. 3.

10. Daniel Goleman, 1999, *Working with Emotional Intelligence*, p. 102.

11. Margaret Boden, 2001, 'Creativity and Knowledge', in *Creativity in Education*, p. 98.

12. Robert Nash, 2004, *Liberating Scholarly Writing: The Power of Personal Narrative*, p. 48.

13. James Philip Zappen, 2000, 'Mikhail Bakhtin (1895-1975)', in *Twentieth-Century Rhetorics and Rhetoricians: Critical Studies and Sources*, pp. 7-20.

14. John Paul Lederach, 2005, *The Moral Imagination: The Art and Soul of Building Peace*, p. 76.

15. James D. Ludema et al., 2001, 'Appreciative Inquiry: the Power of the Unconditional Positive Question', in *Handbook of Action Research: Participative Inquiry and Practice*, p. 189.

16. Daniel Goleman, 1999, *Working with Emotional Intelligence*, p. 102.

17. Reason and Bradbury, 2001, *Handbook of Action Research*, p. xxiv.

18. David Bohm, 2004, *On Dialogue*, p. 71.

19. Ibid, p. 73.

20. Ibid.

21. James D. Ludema et al., 2001, 'Appreciative Inquiry: the Power of the Unconditional Positive Question', in *Handbook of Action Research: Participative Inquiry and Practice*, pp. 189-191.

22. Ibid, p. 192.

23. Ibid, p. 191.

24. Ibid.

25. Ibid, p. 192.

26. Ibid.

27. Ibid.

28. Ibid.

29. David Bohm, 2004, *On Dialogue*, p. 109.

30. Ludema et al., 2001, 'Appreciative Inquiry: the Power of the Unconditional Positive Question', in *Handbook of Action Research: Participative Inquiry and Practice*, p. 192.

31. Patricia Maguire, 2001, 'Uneven Ground: Feminisms and Action Research', in *Handbook of Action Research: Participative Inquiry and Practice*, pp. 59-64.

32. Robert Nash, 2004, *Liberating Scholarly Writing: The Power of Personal Narrative*, p. 155

33. John Ralston Saul, 1993, *Voltaire's Bastards: The Dictatorship of Reason in the West*, p. 49.

34. Ibid.

35. Patricia Maguire, 2001, 'Uneven Ground: Feminisms and Action Research', in *Handbook of Action Research: Participative Inquiry and Practice*, p. 61.

36. James D. Ludema et al., 2001, 'Appreciative Inquiry: the Power of the Unconditional Positive Question', in *Handbook of Action Research: Participative Inquiry and Practice*, p. 198.

37. Ken Robinson with Lou Aronica, 2009, *The Element*, pp. 258-259.

38. Ibid, p. 257.

39. David Abram, 1997, *The Spell of the Sensuous*, p. 56.

40. Stephanie Pace Marshall, 2006, *The Power to Transform: Leadership That Brings Learning and Schooling to Life*, p. 48.

41. Adriana Cavarero, 2000, *Relating Narratives: Storytelling and Selfhood*, p. 33.

42. Ibid, p. 3.

43. Ibid, p. 51.

44. Thomas Berry, 1988, 'Patriarchy: A New Interpretation of History', in *The Dream of the Earth*, p. 143.

45. Adriana Cavarero, 2000, *Relating Narratives: Storytelling and Selfhood*, p. 122.

46. Ralph Alan Dale, 2002, *Tao Te Ching: A New Translation and Commentary*, p. 172.

47. Adriana Cavarero, 2000, *Relating Narratives: Storytelling and Selfhood*, pp. 121 – 123.

48. Ibid, p. 123.

49. David Bohm, 2004, *On Dialogue*, p. 87.

50. James D. Ludema et al., 2001, 'Appreciative Inquiry: the Power of the Unconditional Positive Question', in *Handbook of Action Research: Participative Inquiry and Practice*, p. 192.

Chapter Four

1. Lao Tzu Quotes Website, 2001.

2. Sherry Ruth Anderson and Patricia Hopkins, 1992, *The Feminine Face of God: The Unfolding of the Sacred in Women*, p. 56.

3. Robert Nash, 2004, *Liberating Scholarly Writing: The Power of Personal Narrative*, p. 18.

4. James D. Ludema et al., 2001, 'Appreciative Inquiry: the Power of the Unconditional Positive Question', in *Handbook of Action Research: Participative Inquiry and Practice*, p. 191.

5. Marek Kohn, 2008, *Trust: Self-Interest and the Common Good*, p. 9.

6. Ludwig Wittgenstein, 1968, *Philosophical Investigations*, 32^e.

7. Robert Nash, 2004, *Liberating Scholarly Writing: The Power of Personal Narrative*, p.

150.

8. Arthur J. Cropley, 2003, *Creativity in Education and Learning: A Guide for Teachers and Educators*, p. 150.

9. Roger Fowler, 1986, *Linguistic Criticism*, p. 40.

10. Ibid.

11. John Paul Lederach, 2005, *The Moral Imagination: The Art and Soul of Building Peace*, p. 39.

12. Marek Kohn, 2008, *Trust: Self-Interest and the Common Good*, p. 8.

13. Ibid, p. 133.

14. Nancy Aronie, 1998, *Writing from the Heart: Tapping the Power of Your Inner Voice*, p. 208.

15. Marek Kohn, 2008, *Trust: Self-Interest and the Common Good*, pp. 123-124.

16. Roger Fowler, 1986, *Linguistic Criticism*, p. 29.

17. Robert Hattam et al., 1998, 'Schooling for a fair go: (re)making the social fabric', in *Schooling for a Fair Go*, p. 231.

18. Daniel Goleman, 2006, *Social Intelligence: The New Science of Human Relationships*, p. 62.

19. Ibid, p. 214.

20. Ibid, p. 227.

21. Business Spectator online, 4 June 2010, viewed from http://www.businessspectator.com.au/bs.nsf/Article/Palmer-calls-for-Gillard-to-dump-RSPT-6Q7D6?OpenDocument&src=tnb

22. Ibid.

23. Ibid.

24. Hiroko Tabuchi, 2012, 'Inquiry Declares Fukushima Crisis a Man-Made Disaster', *The New York Times*.

25. Marek Kohn, 2008, *Trust: Self-Interest and the Common Good*, p. 131.

26. David Abram, 1997, *The Spell of the Sensuous*, p. 202.

27. Ibid. p. 208.

28. John Paul Lederach, 2005, *The Moral Imagination: The Art and Soul of Building Peace*, p. 19.

29. David Bohm, 2004, *On Dialogue*, p. 87.

30. OECD Programme for International Student Assessment (PISA) website, viewed from http://www.pisa.oecd.org/pages/0,3417,en_32252351_32235731_1_1_1_1_1,00.html

31. Ibid.

32. Korpela, 2004, 'The Finnish school – a source of skills and well-being', Virtual Finland, p. 3.

33. Ibid.

34. Tim Walker, December 2016, viewed from https://finland.fi/life-society/the-simple-strength-of-finnish-education/

35. Tim Walker, 'How to Bring Finnish-Style Teaching and Learning to Your Classroom', April 2017, viewed from http://neatoday.org/2017/04/18/teach-like-finland/

36. Coughlan, 2004, 'Education key to economic survival', BBC News website, p. 1.

37. Korpela, 2004, 'Free Schooling for all: The Finnish school system supports lifelong learning', Virtual Finland, p. 2.

38. Ken Robinson with Lou Aronica, 2009, *The Element*, pp. 20-21.

Chapter Five

1. Kabir Quotes Website, 2006.

2. Marie–Louise von Franz, 1978, 'The Process of Individuation', in *Man and His Symbols*, p. 167.

3. Ken Robinson, 2001, *Out of Our Minds: Learning to Be Creative*, p. 6.

4. Ibid, p. 8.

5. Stephanie Pace Marshall, 2006, *The Power to Transform: Leadership That Brings Learning and Schooling to Life*, p. 86.

6. Peter McLaren, 2001, 'Critical Pedagogy and the Curriculum', in *Understanding Teaching*, p. 38.

7. Ibid.

8. Robert Nash, 2004, *Liberating Scholarly Writing: The Power of Personal Narrative*, p. 99.

9. Ibid, p. 100.

10. Matthew Fox, 1995, *The Reinvention of Work: A New Vision of Livelihood for Our Time*, p. 118.

11. John Paul Lederach, 2005, *The Moral Imagination: The Art and Soul of Building Peace*, p. 172.

12. Stephanie Pace Marshall, 2006, *The Power to Transform: Leadership That Brings Learning and Schooling to Life*, p. 16.

13. David Bohm, 1980, *Wholeness and the Implicate Order*, p. 31.

14. James D. Ludema et al., 2001, 'Appreciative Inquiry: the Power of the Unconditional Positive Question', in *Handbook of Action Research: Participative Inquiry and Practice*, p. 192.

15. Marie–Louise von Franz, 1978, 'The Process of Individuation', in *Man and His Symbols*, pp. 163-167.

16. Ibid, p. 167.

17. Ibid.

18. Oriah Mountain Dreamer, 2005, *What we ache for: Creativity and the Unfolding of Your Soul*, p. 7.

19. Ken Robinson, 2001, *Out of Our Minds: Learning to Be Creative*, pp. 11-12.

20. Janet Goodrich, 1985, *Natural Vision Improvement*, p. 1.

21. Ibid, p. 6.

22. Ibid, pp. 1-13.

23. Ibid, pp. 135-181.

24. Francoise Gilot, 2001, 'A painter's perspective', *The Origins of Creativity*, p. 171.

25. Janet Goodrich, 1985, *Natural Vision Improvement*, p. xiv.

26. Although the quote is from a previous version of the *Extraordinary Mind Project* website (in 2008), this can still be accessed at http://www.extraordinarymind. com.au/

27. Marie-Louise von Franz, 1978, 'The Process of Individuation', in *Man and His Symbols*, p. 226.

28. David Abram, 1997, *The Spell of the Sensuous*, p. 47.

29. Marion Milner, 1971, *On Not Being Able to Paint*, pp. 146-147.

30. David Bohm, 1980, *Wholeness and the Implicate Order*, p. 9.

31. Marion Milner, 1971, *On Not Being Able to Paint*, pp. 145-147.

32. John O'Donohue, 2004, *Anam Cara: A Book of Celtic Wisdom*, pp. 63-64.

33. Natalie Southgate, 2018, *Chakradance: Move Your Chakras, Change Your Life*, p. xiii.

34. Marie-Louise von Franz, 1978, 'The Process of Individuation', in *Man and His Symbols*, p. 169.

35. Carl Jung, 1977, *Memories, Dreams, Reflections*, pp. 221-222.

36. Peggy Phelan, 1997, *Mourning Sex: Performing Public Memories*, p. 54.

37. Ken Robinson, 2001, *Out of Our Minds: Learning to Be Creative*, p. 14.

Chapter Six

1. Stephanie Pace Marshall, 2006, *The Power to Transform: Leadership That Brings Learning and Schooling to Life,* p. 114.

2. James D. Ludema et al., 2001, 'Appreciative Inquiry: the Power of the Unconditional Positive Question', in *Handbook of Action Research: Participative Inquiry and Practice,* pp. 191-192.

3. John Heron and Peter Reason, 2001, 'The Practice of Co-operative Inquiry: Research 'with' rather than 'on' People', in *Handbook of Action Research: Participative Inquiry and Practice,* p. 179.

4. Ibid.

5. Stephanie Pace Marshall, 2006, *The Power to Transform: Leadership That Brings Learning and Schooling to Life,* p. 26.

6. Mark Earls, 2002, *Welcome to the Creative Age: Bananas, Business, and the Death of Marketing,* pp. 88-89.

7. Robert Jay Lifton, 1993, *The Protean Self: Human Resilience in an Age of Fragmentation.*

8. Stephanie Pace Marshall, 2006, *The Power to Transform: Leadership That Brings Learning and Schooling to Life,* pp. 180-181.

9. David Bohm, 2004, *On Dialogue,* p. 59.

10. Nancy Aronie, 1998, *Writing from the Heart: Tapping the Power of Your Inner Voice,* p. 209.

11. Marie-Louise von Franz, 1978, 'The Process of Individuation', in *Man and His Symbols,* p. 167.

12. John Paul Lederach, 2005, *The Moral Imagination: The Art and Soul of Building Peace,* p. 75.

13. Ibid, p. 76.

14. Ken Robinson with Lou Aronica, 2009, *The Element,* pp. 138-139.

15. David Bohm, 2004, *On Dialogue,* p. 7.

16. Mikhail Bakhtin, 1984, Problems of Dostoevsky's Poetics, ed. and trans. C. Emerson, repeated in Mikhail Bakhtin (1895-1975), p. 287.

17. James Philip Zappen, 2000, 'Mikhail Bakhtin (1895-1975)', in *Twentieth-Century Rhetorics and Rhetoricians: Critical Studies and Sources,* pp. 7-20.

18. Ken Robinson with Lou Aronica, 2009, *The Element,* p. 255.

19. World Health Organisation, 2002, pp. 5-6.

20. Ibid.

21. GetUp Mental Health campaign email.

22. David Fontana and Ingrid Slack, 2007, *Teaching Meditation to Children*, p. 81.

23. John Paul Lederach, 2005, *The Moral Imagination: The Art and Soul of Building Peace*, p. 118.

24. Ibid.

25. Barbara Sher with Annie Gottlieb, 1979, *Wishcraft: How to Get What You Really Want*, p. 82.

26. Ken Robinson with Lou Aronica, 2009, *The Element*, p. 21.

27. Mihaly Csikszentmihalyi, 1996, *Creativity: Flow and the Psychology of Discovery and Invention*.

28. Barbara Sher with Annie Gottlieb, 1979, *Wishcraft: How to Get What You Really Want*, p. 84.

29. Twyla Tharp, 2003, *The Creative Habit: Learn It and Use It for Life*, p. 55.

30. Barbara Sher with Annie Gottlieb, 1979, *Wishcraft: How to Get What You Really Want*, p. 90.

31. Ken Robinson with Lou Aronica, 2009, *The Element*, p. 50.

32. Barry York, 12 November 2015, 'Royal Commissions: what are they and how do they work', The Museum of Australian Democracy online, viewed from https://www.moadoph.gov.au/blog/royal-commissions-what-are-they-and-how-do-they-work/#

33. Paulo Friere, 1982, 'Creating alternative research methods. Learning to do it by doing it', in *Creating Knowledge: A Monopoly*, pp. 29-37.

34. John Paul Lederach, 2005, *The Moral Imagination: The Art and Soul of Building Peace*, p. 122.

35. David Bohm, 2004, *On Dialogue*, p. 101.

36. Brian Schultz, 2008, *Spectacular Things Happen Along the Way: Lessons from an Urban Classroom*, pp. 152-153.

37. John Paul Lederach, 2005, *The Moral Imagination: The Art and Soul of Building Peace*, p. 123.

38. Leslie Safran, 2001, 'Creativity as 'Mindful' Learning: A Case from Learner-Led Home-Based Education', in *Creativity in Education*, p. 81.

39. Ken Robinson, 2001, *Out of Our Minds: Learning to Be Creative*, p. 11.

40. James Ladwig and Jennifer Gore, 1998, 'Nurturing democracy in schools', in *Schooling for a Fair Go*, p. 19.

41. Ibid.

42. Ibid, p. 18.

43. Stephanie Pace Marshall, 2006, *The Power to Transform: Leadership That Brings Learning and Schooling to Life*, p. 194.

44. David Bohm, 2004, *On Dialogue*, pp. 22-24.

45. Stephanie Pace Marshall, 2006, *The Power to Transform: Leadership That Brings Learning and Schooling to Life*, pp. 167-168.

46. David Bohm, 2004, *On Dialogue*, p. 30.

Chapter Seven

1. Matthew Fox, 1995, *The Reinvention of Work: A New Vision of Livelihood for Our Time*, p. 114.

2. Osho, 1999, *Creativity: Unleashing the Forces Within*, pp. xi-1.

3. John Paul Lederach, 2005, *The Moral Imagination: The Art and Soul of Building Peace*, p. 122.

4. Marie-Louise von Franz, 1978, 'The Process of Individuation', in *Man and His Symbols*, pp. 231, 228.

5. John O'Donohue, 2004, *Anam Cara: A Book of Celtic Wisdom*, p. 95.

6. Maria Montessori, 2005, *The Montessori Method*, pp. 18-19.

7. Francesca Murphy, 1995, *Christ the Form of Beauty*, p. 48.

8. John O'Donohue, 2003, *Divine Beauty: The Invisible Embrace*, p. 51.

9. Antonio Damasio, 2001, 'Some notes on brain, imagination and creativity', in *The Origins of Creativity*, pp. 59-60.

10. Matthew Fox, 1995, *The Reinvention of Work: A New Vision of Livelihood for Our Time*, p. 116.

11. SBS News online, 19 June 2020, 'Uni fees to be slashed for in-demand courses, but cost of arts degrees set to soar', viewed from https://www.sbs.com.au/news/uni-fees-to-be-slashed-for-in-demand-courses-but-cost-of-arts-degrees-set-to-soar

12. Matthew Fox, 1995, *The Reinvention of Work: A New Vision of Livelihood for Our Time*, p. 116.

13. Norman Doidge, 2008, *The Brain That Changes Itself*, p. 244.

14. Ibid.

15. Bruce Lipton, 2009, *The Biology of Belief: Unleashing the Power of Consciousness, Matter and Miracles*, p. 133.

16. Ibid, pp. 125-140.

17. Norman Doidge, 2008, *The Brain That Changes Itself,* p. 302.

18. Ibid.

19. Ibid, p. 305.

20. Ibid, p. 306.

21. Ken Robinson with Lou Aronica, 2009, p. 16.

22. Thomas Berry, 1988, 'Patriarchy: A New Interpretation of History', in *The Dream of the Earth*, p. 156.

23. Ian Plowman, 2007, *Options*, 20, p. 18.

24. John Ralston Saul, 1993, *Voltaire's Bastards: The Dictatorship of Reason in the West,* pp. 13-14.

25. Robert Hattam et al., 1998, 'Schooling for a fair go: (re)making the social fabric', in *Schooling for a Fair Go*, pp. 3-4.

26. Peter Abbs, 2003, *Against the Flow: Education, the Arts and Postmodern Culture,* p. 2.

27. James Ladwig and Jennifer Gore, 1998, 'Nurturing democracy in schools', in *Schooling for a Fair Go*, p. 18.

28. Montessori, the International Montessori Index, 'The Montessori Method', 2009.

29. Reggio Children, *The Hundred Languages of Children*, 2008

30. Hale and MacLean, 2004, Steiner Schools in Australia Website.

31. Korpela, 2004, 'Free Schooling for all: The Finnish school system supports lifelong learning', Virtual Finland, p. 1.

32. Louekoski, 2007, 'New National Core Curricula', p. 1.

33. Bruce Lipton, 2009, *The Biology of Belief: Unleashing the Power of Consciousness, Matter and Miracles,* pp. 118-120.

34. Ibid, pp. 120-123.

35. Daniel Goleman, 2006, *Social Intelligence: The New Science of Human Relationships,* p. 13.

36. Bruce Lipton, 2009, *The Biology of Belief: Unleashing the Power of Consciousness, Matter and Miracles.*

37. Victor Chan, 2004, p. 35.

38. Ibid, pp. 36-37.

39. Carl Jung, 1977, *Memories, Dreams, Reflections*, p. 417.

40. Marie-Louise von Franz, 1978, 'The Process of Individuation', in *Man and His Symbols*, p. 236.

41. Daniel Goleman, 2006, *Social Intelligence: The New Science of Human Relationships,*

p. 308.

42. Ibid.

43. Ibid.

44. Ibid.

45. Dalai Lama and Victor Chan, 2004, *The Wisdom of Forgiveness*, pp. 117-118.

46. Robert Atkinson, 1995, *The Gift of Stories*, p. 3.

Chapter Eight

1. Bill Lucas, 2001, 'Creative Teaching, Teaching Creativity and Creative Learning', in *Creativity in Education*, p. 38.

2. Saul, 1993; Bohm, 2004; Berry, 1988.

3. Hamilton, 2010; Bohm, 2004

4. Clive Hamilton, 2010, *Requiem for a Species*, p. 6.

5. Lelieveld et al, 2015, 'The contribution of outdoor air pollution sources to premature mortality on a global scale', *Nature*, 525, 17 September, pp. 367-371.

6. These figures were given on the internet when I looked up deaths by COVID-19 and were listed as ultimately coming from: 'government health ministries, The New York Times, and other authoritative sources.' (https://support.google.com/websearch/answer/9814707?p=cvd19_statistics&hl=en-AU&visit_id=637297284484175457-795569774&rd=1), viewed from https://en.wikipedia.org/wiki/COVID-19_pandemic, and referenced as *"COVID-19 Dashboard by the Center for Systems Science and Engineering (CSSE) at Johns Hopkins University (JHU)". ArcGIS. Johns Hopkins University.* Retrieved 7 July 2020.

7. Amanda King, 13 April 2020, 'Linking Air Pollution to Higher Coronavirus Death Rates', Department of Biostatistics, Harvard T.H. Chan School of Public Health, viewed from https://www.hsph.harvard.edu/biostatistics/2020/04/linking-air-pollution-to-higher-coronavirus-death-rates/

8. Joseph Meeker, 1997, *The Comedy of Survival: Literary Ecology and a Play Ethic*, p. 91.

9. Ibid, p. 94.

10. The World Counts, 2020, TheWorldCounts, 2020, viewed from https://www.theworldcounts.com/about

11. The World Counts, 2020, viewed from https://www.theworldcounts.com/about/keep_the_optimism, viewed 27 July 2020

12. Joseph Meeker, 1997, *The Comedy of Survival: Literary Ecology and a Play Ethic*, pp. 92-93.

13. Pearse, 2010, 'Greenwash', *The Monthly,* Issue 59, p. 15.

14. Ibid.

15. William McDonough and Michael Braungart, 2002, *Cradle to Cradle,* pp. 53-63.

16. Ibid, p. 62.

17. Ibid, p. 45.

18. Ibid, pp. 68-91.

19. David Bohm, 2004, *On Dialogue,* p. 56.

20. Daniel Pink, 2005, *A Whole New Mind,* p. 217.

21. Ibid, p. 218.

22. Ibid, pp. 136-141.

23. Ibid, p. 27.

24. John Ralston Saul, 1993, *Voltaire's Bastards: The Dictatorship of Reason in the West,* p. 497.

25. Daniel Pink, 2005, *A Whole New Mind,* p. 14.

26. Norman Doidge, 2008, *The Brain That Changes Itself,* p. 260.

27. Daniel Pink, 2005, *A Whole New Mind,* pp. 26-27.

28. Thomas Berry, 1988, 'Patriarchy: A New Interpretation of History', in *The Dream of the Earth,* p. 153.

29. Daniel Pink, 2005, *A Whole New Mind,* p. 26.

30. Ibid.

31. Simon Baron-Cohen, 2004, *The Essential Difference,* pp. 1-13.

32. Ibid.

33. Chris McManus, 2002, *Right Hand, Left Hand: The Origins of Asymmetry in Brains, Bodies, Atoms and Cultures,* repeated in Daniel Pink, 2005, *A Whole New Mind,* pp. 25-26.

34. Joseph Meeker, 1997, *The Comedy of Survival: Literary Ecology and a Play Ethic,* p. 88.

35. David Bohm, 1980, *Wholeness and the Implicate Order,* p. xii.

36. Thomas Berry, 1988, 'Patriarchy: A New Interpretation of History', in *The Dream of the Earth,* p. 153.

37. Arthur Koestler, 1975, *The Act of Creation,* p. 177.

38. Ibid.

39. Julia Cameron, 1995, *The Artist's Way: A Course in Discovering and Recovering your Creative Self,* pp. 172-173.

40. John Ralston Saul, 1993, *Voltaire's Bastards: The Dictatorship of Reason in the West*, p. 507.

41. Sandy Hotchkiss, 2003, *Why Is It Always About You?* pp. xiii-xix.

42. Ibid, p. xv.

43. Stephanie Pace Marshall, 2006, *The Power to Transform: Leadership That Brings Learning and Schooling to Life*, p. 179.

44. John Ralston Saul, 1993, *Voltaire's Bastards: The Dictatorship of Reason in the West*, p. 585.

45. William McDonough & Michael Braungart, 2002, *Cradle to Cradle: Remaking the Way We Make Things*, p. 186.

46. Dalai Lama and Victor Chan, 2004, *The Wisdom of Forgiveness*, p. 7.

47. HRH Prince of Wales, Tony Juniper, and Ian Skelly, 2010, *Harmony: A New Way of looking at Our World*, pp. 322-324.

48. Hans Christian Andersen, 1838, 'The Wild Swans', in 2015, *Andersen's Fairy Tales and Stories: Fairy Tales, Folktales Collections*, ebook, viewed from https://books.google.com.au/ books?id=yROeCgAAQBAJ&printsec=frontcover&source=gbs_ge_ summary_r&cad=0#v=onepage&q&f=false

49. Les Fehmi and Jim Robbins, *The Open-Focus Brain: Harnessing the Power of Attention to Heal Mind and Body*, 2007.

50. Ibid, p. 174.

51. Richard Florida, 2004, *The Rise of the Creative Class and How It's Transforming Work, Leisure, Community and Everyday Life*, p. 326.

52. David Bohm, 2004, *On Creativity*, p. 21.

53. David Fontana and Ingrid Slack, 2007, *Teaching Meditation to Children*, p. 82.

54. Bill Lucas, 2001, 'Creative Teaching, Teaching Creativity and Creative Learning', in *Creativity in Education*, p. 38.

55. David Bohm, 1980, *Wholeness and the Implicate Order*, p. 6

56. Robert Atkinson, 1995, *The Gift of Stories*, pp. 3-4.

57. Marie-Louise von Franz, 1978, 'The Process of Individuation', in *Man and His Symbols*, p. 236.

Conclusion

1. William Blake from Auguries of Innocence.

Bibliography

Abbs, P. 2003, *Against the Flow: Education, the Arts and Postmodern Culture*, Routledge Falmer, London.

Abram, D. 1997, *The Spell of the Sensuous*, Vintage Books, New York and Toronto.

Anderson, S. & Pizzigati, S. 2018, *How Taxpayers Subsidize Giant Corporate Pay Gaps*, Institute for Policy Studies, Washington DC, viewed 24 May 2020, <https://ips-dc.org/wp-content/uploads/2018/09/EE18-FINAL.pdf>.

Anderson, S.R. & Hopkins, P. 1992, *The Feminine Face of God: The Unfolding of the Sacred in Women*, Bantam Books, New York, Toronto, London, Sydney and Auckland.

Aronie, N.S. 1998, *Writing From the Heart: Tapping the Power of Your Inner Voice*, Hyperion, New York.

Atkinson, R. 1995, *The Gift of Stories*, Bergin & Garvey, Westport.

Australian Government 2001, Australia's Culture Portal, *Anzac Day*, viewed 16 March 2010, <http://www.cultureandrecreation.gov.au/articles/anzac/>.

Australian War Memorial 2010, The Anzac Day Tradition, Canberra, viewed 16 March 2010, <http://www.awm.gov.au/commemoration/anzac/anzac_tradition.asp>.

Australian War Memorial 2016, The Anzac Day Tradition, Canberra, viewed 22 September 2016, <http://www.awm.gov.au/commemoration/anzac/anzac-tradition/>.

Bakhtin, M. 1984, Problems of Dostoevsky's Poetics, ed. and trans. C. Emerson, repeated in Mikhail Bakhtin (1895-1975) (Online), viewed 9 August 2002, <http://www.rpi.edu/-zappenj/Bibliographies/bakhtin.htm>.

Barabási, A-L. 2003, *Linked: How Everything is Connected to Everything Else and What it Means for Business, Science, and Everyday Life,* Plume, New York.

Baron-Cohen, S. 2004, *The Essential Difference,* Penguin Books, London.

Barron, F. 1995, *No Rootless Flower: an Ecology of Creativity,* Hampton Press, Cresskill.

Barthes, R. 1977, 'The Death of the Author', in *Image Music Text,* trans. S. Heath, Hill and Wang, New York.

Berry, T. 1988, 'Patriarchy: A New Interpretation of History', in *The Dream of the Earth,* Sierra Club Books, San Francisco.

Berry, T. 1988, *The Dream of the Earth,* Sierra Club Books, San Francisco.

Blake, W. 1994, 'Auguries of Innocence', in *Seven Centuries of Poetry in English,* ed. J. Leonard, Oxford University Press, Oxford, Auckland, New York and Melbourne.

Boden, M.A. 2001, 'Creativity and Knowledge', in *Creativity in Education,* eds. A. Craft, B. Jeffrey and M. Leibling, Continuum, London and New York.

Bohm, D. 1980, *Wholeness and the Implicate Order,* Routledge & Kegan Paul Ltd, London and Boston.

Bohm, D. 2004, *On Creativity,* Routledge, London and New York.

Bohm, D. 2004, *On Dialogue,* Routledge, London and New York.

Bradley, L. 2010, 'The Butterfly Effect', in Chaos and Fractals online, viewed 14 August 2010, <http://www.stsci.edu/~lbradley/seminar/butterfly.html>.

Brahm, A. 2008, *Opening the Door of Your Heart,* Hachette Australia, Sydney.

Business Spectator, viewed 4 June 2010, <http://www.businessspectator.com.au/bs.nsf/Article/Palmer-calls-for-Gillard-to-dump-RSPT-6Q7D6?OpenDocument&src=tnb>.

Cameron, J. 1995, *The Artist's Way: A Course in Discovering and Recovering Your Creative Self,* Pan Books, Basingstoke and Oxford.

Cavarero, A. 2000, *Relating Narratives: Storytelling and Selfhood,* trans. P.A. Kottman,

Routledge, London and New York.

Cixous, H. 1981, 'Sorties', trans. A. Liddle, in *New French Feminisms*, eds. E. Marks & de I. Courtivron, The Harvester Press, Brighton.

Cohen, J. & Stewart, I. 2000, *The Collapse of Chaos*, Penguin Books, London.

Coughlan, S. 2004, 'Education key to economic survival', BBC News, London, viewed 7 September 2007, <http://newsvote.bbc.co.uk/mpapps/pagetools/print/news.bbc.co.uk/2/hi/uk_news/education>.

Cropley, A.J. 2003, *Creativity in Education and Learning: a Guide for Teachers and Educators*, Kogan Page, London.

Csikszentmihalyi, M. 1996, *Creativity: Flow and the Psychology of Discovery and Invention*, Harper Collins, New York.

Dalai Lama & Chan, V. 2004, *The Wisdom of Forgiveness*, Hodder, Sydney.

Dale, R.A. 2002, *Tao Te Ching: A New Translation and Commentary*, Watkins Publishing, London.

Daly, M. 1998, *Quintessence ... Realizing the Archaic Future: A Radical Elemental Feminist Manifesto*, Beacon Press, Boston.

Damasio, A.R. 2001, 'Some notes on brain, imagination and creativity', in *The Origins of Creativity*, eds. K.H. Pfenninger & V.R. Shubik, Oxford University Press, Oxford and New York.

Darling-Hammond, L. 2010, *The Flat World and Education*, Teachers College Press, New York and London.

Dayton L. 2007, 'A Case of Mind over Matter', *The Australian (Review)*, 21 July, p. 6.

Doidge, N. 2008, *The Brain That Changes Itself*, Scribe, Melbourne.

Earls, M. 2002, *Welcome to the Creative Age: Bananas, Business, and the Death of Marketing*, John Wiley & Sons, Chichester.

Feldman, D.H., Csikszentmihalyi, M. & Gardner, H. 1994, *Changing the World: A*

Framework for the Study of Creativity, Praeger, Westport.

Fisher, R. 2004, 'What is Creativity?', in *Unlocking Creativity: Teaching Across the Curriculum*, eds. R. Fisher & M. Williams, David Fulton, London.

Florida, R. 2004, *The Rise of the Creative Class and How It's Transforming Work, Leisure, Community and Everyday Life*, Basic Books, New York.

Fontana, D. & Slack, I. 2007, *Teaching Meditation to Children*, Watkins Publishing, London.

Fowler, R. 1986, *Linguistic Criticism*, Oxford University Press, Oxford and New York.

Fox, M. 1995, *The Reinvention of Work: A New Vision of Livelihood for Our Time*, Harper Collins, New York.

Franz, M-L. von, 1978, 'The Process of Individuation', in *Man and His Symbols*, ed. C. Jung, Picador, Basingstoke and London.

Freire, P. 1982, 'Creating alternative research methods. Learning to do it by doing it', in *Creating Knowledge: A Monopoly*, eds. B. Hall, A. Gillette & R. Tandon, Society for Participatory Research in Asia, New Delhi.

Gilot, F. 2001, 'A painter's perspective', *The Origins of Creativity*, eds. K.H. Pfenninger & V.R. Shubik, Oxford University Press, Oxford and New York.

Goleman, D. 1999, *Working with Emotional Intelligence*, Bloomsbury, London, Berlin and New York.

Goleman, D. 2006, *Social Intelligence: The New Science of Human Relationships*, Bantam Books, New York.

Goodrich, J. 1985, *Natural Vision Improvement*, Viking O'Neil, Melbourne.

Gordon, E. 2009, Brain Revolution Project, viewed 9 October 2010, <http://brainrevolution.org/contactus.html>.

Hale, B. & MacLean, K. 2004, Steiner Schools in Australia, 2004, viewed 25 November 2010, < http://www.steiner-australia.org/other/overview.html>.

Hamilton, C. 2010, *Requiem for a Species: Why We Resist the Truth about Climate Change*, Allen and Unwin, Sydney.

Harding, S. 1987, 'The instability of the analytical categories of feminist theory', in *Sex and Scientific Inquiry*, eds. S. Harding & J.E. O'Barr, University of Chicago Press, Chicago.

Hattam, R., Smyth, J. & Lawson, M. 1998, 'Schooling for a fair go: (re)making the social fabric', in *Schooling for a Fair Go*, eds. R. Hattam, J. Smyth & M. Lawson, The Federation Press, Sydney.

Hayes, C. 2010, 'The Twilight of the Elites', *Time*, vol. 175, no. 11, pp. 38-39.

Heaton, J. & Groves, J. 1994, *Wittgenstein for Beginners*, Icon Books, Cambridge.

Hendrix, H. 1988, *Getting the Love You Want*, Schwartz & Wilkinson, Melbourne.

Heron, J. & Reason, P. 2001, 'The Practice of Co-operative Inquiry: Research 'with' rather than 'on' People', in in *Handbook of Action Research: Participative Inquiry and Practice*, eds. P. Reason & H. Bradbury, SAGE, London and Thousand Oaks.

Hocking, B., Haskell, J. & Linds, W. (eds), 2001, *Unfolding Bodymind: Exploring Possibility Through Education*, Foundation for Educational Renewal, Brandon.

Hodgkin, R.A. 1976, *Born Curious: New Perspectives in Educational Theory*, John Wiley & Sons, London, New York, Sydney and Toronto.

Hotchkiss, S. 2003, *Why Is It Always About You?*, Free Press, New York, London, Toronto, Sydney and Singapore.

HRH The Prince of Wales, Juniper, T. & Skelly, I. 2010, *Harmony: A New Way of Looking at Our World*, Harper Collins, New York.

Hyde, L. 2007, *The Gift: How the Creative Spirit Transforms the World*, Canongate, Edinburgh, New York and Melbourne.

It's a Wonderful Life (film) 1946, screenplay F. Goodrich, A. Hackett, J. Swerling` & F. Capra, dir. F. Capra, produced by F. Capra, Liberty Films, United States.

Jung, C.G. 1977, *Memories, Dreams, Reflections*, Collins Fount Paperbacks, Glasgow.

Jung, C.G. 1978, 'Approaching the Unconscious', in *Man and His Symbols*, ed. C. Jung, Picador, Basingstoke and London.

Kabir Quotes, 2006, viewed 21 March 2007, <http://www.goodreads.com/author/quotes/96714.Kabir>.

Kaufman, G.D. 2004, *In the Beginning – Creativity*, Fortress Press, Minneapolis.

Kaufman, J.C. & Baer, J. (eds.), 2005, *Creativity Across Domains: Faces of the Muse*, L. Erlbaum Associates, Mahwah, N.J.

Keyes, R. 2003, *The Courage to Write: How Writers Transcend Fear*, H. Holt, New York.

Kenway, J. & Willis, S. 1996, 'The post-school options of post-modern girls', in Critical visions: Rewriting the future of work, schooling and gender, DEET, Canberra, pp 116-121, Rpt in *E231 Schools in Context: Unit Guide and Reader 2003*, Murdoch University, Murdoch.

Knierim, T. 1999, *The Tao Te Ching*, viewed 22 November 2010, <http://www.thebigview.com/download/tao-te-ching-illustrated.pdf>.

Koestler, A. 1975, *The Act of Creation*, Pan Books Ltd, London.

Kohn, M. 2008, *Trust: Self-Interest and the Common Good*, Oxford University Press, Oxford and New York.

Korpela, S. 2004, 'The Finnish school – a source of skills and well-being', Virtual Finland, Helsinki, viewed 7 September 2007, <http://www.finland.fi/netcomm/news/showarticle.asp?intNWSAID=30625>.

Korpela, S. 2004, 'Free Schooling for all: The Finnish school system supports lifelong learning', Virtual Finland, Helsinki, viewed 7 September 2007, <http://www.finland.fi/netcomm/news/showarticle.asp?intNWSAID=41557>.

Ladwig, J. & Gore, J. 1998, 'Nurturing democracy in schools', in *Schooling for a Fair Go*, eds. R. Hattam, J. Smyth & M. Lawson, The Federation Press, Sydney.

Lao Tzu Quotes (2001), viewed 13 April 2006, <http://www.brainyquote.com/quotes/authors/l/lao_tzu.html>.

Lederach, J.P. 2005, *The Moral Imagination: The Art and Soul of Building Peace*, Oxford University Press, New York.

Lelieveld, J., Evans, J. S., Fnais, M., Giannadaki, D., Pozzer, A. 2015, 'The contribution of outdoor air pollution sources to premature mortality on a global scale', *Nature*, 525, 17 September, doi:10.1038/nature15371.

Lifton, R.J. 1993, *The Protean Self: Human Resilience in an Age of Fragmentation*, Basic Books, New York.

Lipton, B.H. 2009, *The Biology of Belief: Unleashing the Power of Consciousness, Matter and Miracles*, Hay House, Carlsbad, California, New York, London, Sydney, Johannesburg, Vancouver, Hong Kong & New Delhi.

Lorie, P. 1989, *Wonder Child: Rediscovering the Magical World of Innocence and Joy Within Ourselves and Our Children*, Simon & Schuster, New York, London, Toronto, Sydney and Tokyo.

Louekoski, H. 2007, 'New National Core Curricula', The Finnish National Board of Education, Helsinki, viewed 7 September 2007, <http://www.oph.fi/english/DoPrint.asp?printStep=createPage&path=447;18918;65218/>.

Lucas, B. 2001, 'Creative Teaching, Teaching Creativity and Creative Learning', in *Creativity in Education*, eds. A. Craft, B. Jeffrey & M. Leibling, Continuum, London and New York.

Ludema, D.J., Cooperrider, D.L. & Barrett, F.J. 2001, 'Appreciative Inquiry: the Power of the Unconditional Positive Question', in *Handbook of Action Research: Participative Inquiry and Practice*, eds. P. Reason & H. Bradbury, SAGE, London and Thousand Oaks.

McDonough, W. & Braungart, M. 2002, *Cradle to Cradle: Remaking the Way We Make Things*, North Point Press, New York.

McLaren, P. 2001, 'Critical Pedagogy and the Curriculum', in *Understanding Teaching*, ed. E. Hatton, Harcourt, Sydney, Fort Worth, London, San Diego and Toronto.

Maguire, P. 2001, 'Uneven Ground: Feminisms and Action Research', in

Handbook of Action Research: Participative Inquiry and Practice, eds. P. Reason & H. Bradbury, SAGE, London and Thousand Oaks.

Manne, A. 2006, 'What about me? The new narcissism', *The Monthly,* Issue 13, pp. 30-40.

Marshall, S.P. 2006, *The Power to Transform: Leadership That Brings Learning and Schooling to Life,* Jossey-Bass, San Francisco.

Meeker, J. 1997, *The Comedy of Survival: Literary Ecology and a Play Ethic,* The University of Arizona Press, Tucson.

Midnight Davies, 'Aboriginal culture - Spirituality - What is the 'Dreamtime' or the 'Dreaming'?', www.CreativeSpirits.info, viewed 25 April 2017, <https://www.creativespirits.info/aboriginalculture/spirituality/what-is-the-dreamtime-or-the-dreaming#ixzz4fEk4xO00>

Milner, M. 1971, *On Not Being Able to Paint,* Heinemann Educational Books, London.

Moriarty, R. 2010, *Listening to Country: A Journey to the Heart of What It Means to Belong,* Allen & Unwin, Crows Nest.

Montessori, M. & Hunt, J. 2005, *The Montessori Method,* Kessinger Publishing, Whitefish Montana.

Montessori, the International Montessori Index, 'The Montessori Method', 2009, Loyola College Maryland, viewed 25 November, 2010, < http://www.montessori.edu/>.

Murphy, F.A. 1995, *Christ the Form of Beauty,* T & T Clark, Edinburgh.

Nash, R.J. 2004, *Liberating Scholarly Writing: The Power of Personal Narrative,* Teachers College Press, New York.

Nathanson, S. 1994, 'The Classical Ideal', in *The Idea of Rationality,* Open Court, Chicago.

Neumann, E. 1994, *The Fear of the Feminine and Other Essays on Feminine Psychology,* Princeton University Press, Princeton.

Nichol, L. 2004, *On Dialogue*, Routledge, London and New York.

Nicolis, G. & Prigogine, I. 1989, *Exploring Complexity: An Introduction*, W.H. Freeman, New York.

OECD Programme for International Student Assessment (PISA), viewed 11 June 2010, <http://www.pisa.oecd.org/pages/0,3417,en_32252351_32235731_1_1_1_1_1,00.html>

O'Donohue, J. 2004, *Anam Cara: A Book of Celtic Wisdom*, Harper Perennial, New York.

O'Donohue, J. 2003, *Divine Beauty: The Invisible Embrace*, Bantam Press, London, New York, Toronto, Sydney and Auckland.

Oriah Mountain Dreamer, 2005, *What We Ache For: Creativity and the Unfolding of Your Soul*, HarperCollins, New York.

Osho 1999, *Creativity: Unleashing the Forces Within*, St. Martin's Griffin, New York.

Pearse, G. 2010, 'Greenwash', *The Monthly*, Issue 59, pp. 14-16.

Pfenninger, K.H. 2001, *The Origins of Creativity*, eds. K.H. Pfenninger & V.R. Shubik, Oxford University Press, Oxford and New York.

Phelan, P. 1997, *Mourning Sex: Performing Public Memories*, Routledge, London and New York.

Pink, D.H. 2005, *A Whole New Mind*, Riverhead Books, New York.

Pinker, S. 1997, *How the Mind Works*, W.W. Norton, New York and London.

Reason, P & Bradbury, H. 2001, 'Preface', in *Handbook of Action Research: Participative Inquiry and Practice*, eds. P. Reason & H. Bradbury, SAGE, London and Thousand Oaks.

Reggio Children, *The Hundred Languages of Children*, 2008, viewed 25 November 2010, < http://zerosei.comune.re.it/inter/reggiochildren.htm>.

Robinson, C. 2009, 'Narcissistic Executives - A pre-emptive approach for dealing with them', Advanced Leadership Consulting, Seattle, viewed 12

December 2010, <http://www.leadershipconsulting.com/narcissistic-executives.htm>.

Robinson, K. 2001, *Out of Our Minds: Learning to Be Creative*, Capstone Publishing, Oxford.

Robinson, K. 2005, 'Keynote presentation', in *proceedings of the Backing our creativity symposium*, Melbourne, 12-14 September 2005, Australia Council for the Arts (Online), viewed 16 August 2007, <http://www.australiacouncil.gov.au/research/education_and_the_arts/reports_and_publications/backing_our_creativity_symposium_final_report>.

Robinson, K. & Aronica, L. 2009, *The Element*, Penguin Books, London.

Safran, L. 2001, 'Creativity as 'Mindful' Learning: A Case from Learner-Led Home-Based Education', in *Creativity in Education*, eds. A. Craft, B. Jeffrey & M. Leibling, Continuum, London and New York.

Saul, J.R. 1993, *Voltaire's Bastards: The Dictatorship of Reason in the West*, Vintage Books, New York.

Schlein, L. 23 February 2017, 5:00 PM Lisa 'WHO: Depression Largest Cause of Disability Worldwide', VOA News Website, viewed 21 March 2017, <http://www.voanews.com/a/who-depression-statistics/3737024.html>

Schmid, T. (ed.), 2005, *Promoting Health through Creativity: for Professionals in Health, Arts and Education*, Whurr, London.

Schueler, G. J. 1996, 'An investigation into the relationship between the chaos theory of predictability and the phenomenon of synchronicity as defined in Jungian psychology', Minn, Ph.D. Dissertation. MN: The Graduate School of America.

Schultz, B. 2008, *Spectacular Things Happen Along the Way: Lessons from an Urban Classroom*, Teachers College Press. New York.

Sher, B. & Gottlieb, A. 1979, *Wishcraft: How to Get What You Really Want*, Ballantine Books, New York.

Sher, B. 1994, *I Could Do Anything If I Only Knew What It Was*, Hodder &

Stoughton, London.

Seltzer, K. & Bentley, T. 1999, *The Creative Age: Knowledge and Skills for the New Economy*, Demos, London.

Soegaard, M. 2010, *Gestalt principles of form perception*, viewed 2 September 2010, <http://www.interaction-design.org/encyclopedia/gestalt_principles_of_form_perception.html>.

Southgate, N. 2018, *Chakradance: Move Your Chakras, Change Your Life*, p. xiii.

Spender, D. 1980, *Man Made Language*, Routledge & Kegan Paul, London, Boston and Henley.

Stanfield, B.R. for The Canadian Institute of Cultural Affairs, 2002, *The Workshop Book: from Individual Creativity to Group Action*, eds R. Seagren & B. Griffin, New Society Publishers, Gabriola Island.

Stanley, L. 1992, *The Auto/biographical I: The Theory and Practice of Feminist Auto/biography*, Manchester University Press, Manchester and New York.

Swanton, C. 2003, *Virtue Ethics: a Pluralistic View*, Oxford University Press, Oxford and New York.

Tabuchi, H., 2012, 'Inquiry Declares Fukushima Crisis a Man-Made Disaster', *The New York Times*, viewed 20 August 2017, <http://www.nytimes.com/2012/07/06/world/asia/fukushima-nuclear-crisis-a-man-made-disaster-report-says.html>.

Tharp, T. 2003, *The Creative Habit: Learn It and Use It for Life*, Simon & Schuster, New York.

Tompkins, J.P. 1996, *A Life in School: What the Teacher Learned*, Addison Wesley, New York.

Waldrop, M. M. 1992, *Complexity: The Emerging Science at the Edge of Order and Chaos*, Simon & Schuster, New York.

Walker, T. December 2016, viewed 3 September 2017, < https://finland.fi/life-society/the-simple-strength-of-finnish-education/>

Walker, T. April 2017, 'How to Bring Finnish-Style Teaching and Learning to Your Classroom', National Education Association, viewed 22 June 2020, <http://neatoday.org/2017/04/18/teach-like-finland/>

Watson, D. 2004, *Watson's Dictionary of Weasel Words, Contemporary Clichés, Cant & Management Jargon*, Random House, Sydney, New York, Toronto, London, Auckland and Johannesburg.

Watts, A. 1989, *The Book On the Taboo Against Knowing Who You Are*, Vintage Books, New York.

Wawrytko, S. 1981, *The Undercurrent of Feminine Philosophy in Eastern and Western Thought*, University Press of America, Washington D.C.

Wittgenstein, L. 1968, *Philosophical Investigations*, trans. G.E.M. Anscombe, Basil Blackwell, Oxford.

World Health Organisation, 2002, *World Report on Violence and Health*, World Health Organisation, Geneva, viewed 22 July 2010, <http://whqlibdoc.who.int/hq/2002/a77019.pdf>.

Zappen, J.P. 2000, 'Mikhail Bakhtin (1895-1975)', in *Twentieth-Century Rhetorics and Rhetoricians: Critical Studies and Sources*, ed. M. G. Moran and M. Ballif, Greenwood Press, Westport, Connecticut, Repeated Online, viewed 4 January 2010, <http://www.rpi.edu/~zappenj/Publications/Texts/bakhtin.html>.

Index

CPSIA information can be obtained
at www.ICGtesting.com
Printed in the USA
LVHW050143080221
678682LV00011B/664

9 781913 479640